T0328954

PENSION AND WIDOWS'
AND ORPHANS' FUNDS

This volume forms part of a series of text-books published under the authority of the Institute of Actuaries and the Faculty of Actuaries and is designed to meet the needs of students preparing for the actuarial examinations.

PENSION AND WIDOWS' AND ORPHANS' FUNDS

BY

R. J. W. CRABBE, F.I.A.

AND

C. A. POYSER, M.A., F.I.A.

CAMBRIDGE

Published for the Institute of Actuaries and the
Faculty of Actuaries

AT THE UNIVERSITY PRESS

1953

CAMBRIDGE UNIVERSITY PRESS
Cambridge, New York, Melbourne, Madrid, Cape Town,
Singapore, São Paulo, Delhi, Mexico City

Cambridge University Press
The Edinburgh Building, Cambridge CB2 8RU, UK

Published in the United States of America by Cambridge University Press, New York

www.cambridge.org
Information on this title: www.cambridge.org/9781107621749

First published 1953
First paperback edition 2013

A catalogue record for this publication is available from the British Library

ISBN 978-1-107-62174-9 Paperback

CONTENTS

FOREWORD

The present volume has been prepared as a textbook on Pension and Widows' and Orphans' Schemes for the examinations of the Institute of Actuaries and the Faculty of Actuaries.

The field now covered is one in which practical experience is an essential part of the actuary's equipment. Nevertheless, as all practice should be soundly based, the theoretical development of the subject has been given in some detail; in addition some indication of the practical application of the theory has been included so as to assist the student in making the difficult transition from theory to practice.

As this is a subject of which students usually have little, if any, practical knowledge it has been decided to confine the first few chapters to matters which should provide a general background and the 'feel' of the subject and only in later chapters are formulae introduced. The formulae required in Pension and Widows' and Orphans' Fund work, although more complicated than those normally used in life office work, are nevertheless in essence quite simple, being derived directly by manipulation of commutation functions. The student will already be familiar with some of the simpler formulae as these have been dealt with in *Life and other Contingencies* by P. F. Hooker and L. H. Longley-Cook, but in order to make the present volume complete in itself and to avoid cross-reference most of the basic formulae required have been developed *ab initio*.

The book has been written in the light of the position as it existed in the early 1950's and in particular the income tax position at that time. As pointed out in Chapter 18 taxation has such important repercussions that any changes which may be introduced, e.g. as a result of the enquiry now being undertaken by the Millard-Tucker Committee, may well influence the structure of Pension and Widows' and Orphans' Schemes. Again, owing to the high incidence of taxation in recent years the provision of pensions and of widows' and orphans' benefits has become a matter of increasing importance and the whole subject is, in a sense, in a state of flux.

Whilst this book was in the hands of the printers the Income Tax Act 1952 became law. In order to assist students, a comparative table of corresponding sections in the new Act and in earlier legislation affecting Pension and Widows' and Orphans' Schemes has been given as Appendix III.

This book is intended to cover the fundamental principles of the subject and their straightforward application as regards privately established schemes. We do not make any claim to have broken any fresh ground, nor to have superseded the classic writers who originally developed the subject, and to whom clearly we are heavily in debt. Acknowledgements are also due to Mr D. A. Porteous who kindly gave his consent to the unrestricted use of extracts from his own book *Pension and Widows' and Orphans' Funds*.

We also wish to place on record our thanks and our indebtedness to Mr F. A. A. Menzler and Mr J. M. Ross for their numerous and helpful suggestions in the preparation of this volume.

R. J. W. C.
C. A. P.

April, 1952

CHAPTER I

INTRODUCTORY

1.1. Historical development

The first approach to the subject of Pensions and Widows' and Orphans' Funds frequently involves some difficulty. The bewildering variety of schemes which have to be considered and the relative complexity of the benefits and contributions payable tend to obscure the essential nature of the problems to be solved. It must always be borne in mind, however, that each case can be dealt with by the application of a limited number of straightforward principles, even though its detailed treatment may involve complications demanding a considerable degree of trained judgement. Before proceeding to consider the treatment of existing funds, it will be helpful to discuss briefly the historical development of Pensions and Widows' and Orphans' Funds.

Although the initiation of widows' schemes for the benefit of certain special groups occurred at a very early date (the Scottish Ministers' Fund is about 200 years old), the provision of pension or retirement benefits for their staffs by individual employers came much later. There was originally no set scheme of pension benefits, but, as employers came to realize their responsibilities for the welfare of ageing employees, the practice grew up of granting *ad hoc* pensions in individual cases of hardship. In many cases the grant of such pensions became a recognized practice without the creation of any formal scheme.

Next came the formulation of definite schemes of benefits without any very definite arrangements being made for meeting the cost. Even though the employee made contributions towards his pension under such an arrangement, he might well be left entirely dependent upon the financial stability of his employer for the eventual payment of the pension. It is not difficult to see that, in the case of a young and vigorous company which develops rapidly, a burden of liability may be built up which, whilst it may be very many years in maturing, may ultimately fall with crippling effect upon the company's finances. As employers began to appreciate the dangers involved in failure to make provision in advance for the burden of prospective retirements, the modern practice developed of setting up specific funds to meet pensions as they emerged, the necessary contributions being usually met jointly by employer and employee.

1.2. Nature of benefits

It will be seen from this outline that the form of the benefits granted under staff pension schemes is primarily concerned with meeting as closely as possible the needs of both employer and employee rather than with simplifying the financial provision therefor. The nature of the contract is dictated by the needs of the client with less regard to the requirements of financial stability and actuarial convenience than is the case in life assurance.

The actuary dealing with pension funds has not the comparatively straightforward task of fitting a limited number of rigid financial contracts to the requirements of the employer. His function is rather that of rationalizing the great variety of existing schemes, and of advising whether suggested schemes which have been designed to meet the particular circumstances of an employer are reasonably practicable and theoretically sound. If he comes to the conclusion that a particular proposal should be rejected, he must be ready to explain his reasons in language which is understandable not only by the employer but also by employees, to whom actuarial work will always remain something of an esoteric mystery.

It follows that, although every effort must be made to achieve the maximum financial stability, this is not always the primary consideration. A very high proportion of schemes provide pensions which are in some way related to the future level of salaries, and it is thus impossible to avoid the risk of a serious deficiency arising if the level of salaries should rise appreciably above that anticipated. The purpose of establishing a fund on actuarial principles is to enable proper and systematic financial provision to be made during the working lifetime of an employee for the pension benefit which he has been promised. The actuary should aim, by his advice and guidance, at the establishment of a fund in which the risk of financial instability is restricted to causes which flow from the function of 'management', viz. salary changes, varying retirement ages and the like.

1.3. Widows' and orphans' funds

As already indicated, the development of schemes for the provision of annuities or allowances to the widows and orphans of members of particular groups ante-dated the development of ordinary pension schemes for employees. Over the years, the principles on which they have operated have been manifold; many were financially unsound. Some schemes are still purely benevolent in character, dependent upon charitable contributions, but the majority of the funds which will now be met in practice are constituted on a reasonably sound basis in which contributions and benefits are, on the whole, properly related to one another. In some cases, however, schemes may also receive extraneous assistance in the form of legacies or grants.

The development of employer-assisted schemes for the benefit of the dependants of employees of a particular undertaking came much later, and only in recent years have employers generally begun to adopt the policy of providing such benefits for their staffs. For this reason, the form of benefits has not undergone the degree of evolution towards a standard basis that may be observed in the case of schemes providing retirement benefits. The greatest care, therefore, may be necessary in the establishment and guidance of widows' and orphans' funds to ensure sound and satisfactory development.

1.4. Assurance Company schemes

Various types of policy are issued by Life Assurance Companies for the purpose of providing pension, retirement and widows' and orphans' benefits. This class of business has increased very rapidly in recent years, and the total business in force has now reached large proportions. Great ingenuity has been exercised in meeting the requirements of employer and employee, but this method of providing for retirement and widows' benefits is still open to the criticism that it cannot achieve the flexibility of the privately administered fund. It is clearly impossible for Life Assurance Companies to accept the risks which arise from causes not susceptible of reasonable actuarial assessment. Hence, it has been necessary for them to design schemes which are immune from the risk of loss arising from 'management' decisions, with the result, for example, that the provision of pensions bearing a definite relation to salaries at date of retirement and of adequate 'ill-health' pensions is impracticable. This question will be dealt with in greater detail at a later stage.

CHAPTER 2

PENSION FUNDS: TYPES OF PENSION BENEFIT

2.1. Reasons for establishing a fund

It will be helpful at this stage to consider the motives which prompt both employer and employee to co-operate in the establishment of a formal fund for the provision of pensions.

To consider first the employee—the primary consideration is, of course, the sense of security which follows from the assurance of a pension for himself on retirement, whether through advancing age or ill-health, and of some form of protection for his widow and children in the event of his untimely death. These objects can, however, be achieved in large measure without the co-operation of an employer and the surrender of direct control over personal savings which is involved in the establishment of a joint contributory pension fund. In exchange for this surrender, however, the employee secures definite advantages. Quite apart from the employer's contribution towards the cost of pensions, his co-operation renders possible a flexibility and a close adaptation of benefits to the needs of members which cannot be achieved by any other means. If, in addition, the favourable treatment of contributions and interest for income-tax purposes is borne in mind, it will be clear that the establishment of a fund is very attractive to the employee.

The advantages to the employer are less tangible, but they are not less real. The existence of the fund tends to promote efficient service by inducing a more settled and contented frame of mind among the staff. Employees at the older ages, whose efficiency is diminishing, can be placed upon the retired list and replaced by energetic younger men without feelings of hardship being aroused, thus achieving the double object of improving the driving power of the business and giving more definite prospects of advancement to the more important and highly paid positions.

Where there is no fund in existence and an employee breaks

down or dies in service, appeals *ad misericordiam* will frequently be made by him or by his dependants. Further, when his powers fail after many years' service, the employer may feel a moral obligation to grant some form of retirement allowance. All these demands may be difficult to meet unless some provision or reserve is set aside for the purpose during the working lifetime of the employee. A pension fund which will achieve this purpose will thus afford valuable protection against a drain on profits which may result from heavy unfunded pension charges. Finally, the existence of a fund will encourage the older employees to retire upon reaching the usual retiring age by removing the bar which would be presented by the prospect of a violent drop in income.

2.2. Types of pension scheme

Reference has already been made to the adaptability which can be achieved in the provisions of a private pension scheme. One result of this is a very great variety in the types of benefit, etc., which have to be dealt with by the actuary who is dealing with schemes of this type. An analysis of the benefit provisions, however, usually shows that the majority are combinations of a limited number of basic types of (*a*) pension benefits; (*b*) retirement provisions; and (*c*) subsidiary benefits, i.e. payments on death, withdrawal, etc. The most important is, of course, the pension benefit, and the following paragraphs give a brief summary of the various forms it may assume.

2.3. Classification of pension benefits

A. Privately financed schemes, i.e. those schemes where the whole of the financial arrangements are retained in the hands of the employer or of trustees appointed for the purpose.

I. Pension benefit independent of salary (in general, 'salary' where appropriate should be understood to include 'wages').

    (*a*) A pension of a fixed amount, irrespective of the employee's salary or length of service.

    (*b*) A pension varying with the period of service but independent of salary, e.g. 1*s*. per week or £2. 10*s*. per annum for each year of service.

II. Pension benefit indirectly related to salary.

(a) 'Savings Bank' type of scheme: the employee (and the employer on his behalf) pays yearly contributions related to his salary. These are accumulated, and the sum to the credit of the employee's individual account at the date of retirement is applied to purchase a pension on a prescribed scale.

(b) 'Money Purchase' scheme: under this contributions are made of a similar character to those mentioned in the preceding paragraph. Each contribution is, however, applied immediately to secure a paid-up deferred pension determined according to a fixed scale or scales.

(c) 'Deferred Annuity' scheme: this is similar to a money purchase scheme, except that the pension is built up from a series of deferred annuities, each purchased by means of a level annual payment.

As already indicated, pensions falling within this group are usually related indirectly through the contributions to salary. However, this is not necessarily the case, as the contributions made for the purpose of securing pensions may not be fixed by reference to salary but may be quite independent thereof.

III. Pension benefit directly related to salary.

The majority of pension schemes established in recent years fall within this category, the pension being defined as either a fixed percentage of 'pensionable' salary, irrespective of length of service or, more commonly, a fraction (e.g. $\frac{1}{60}$th) of 'pensionable' salary for each year of service. Schemes of this type are normally classified according to the definition of 'pensionable' salary, viz.

(a) average salary schemes—based on the average annual salary received during the whole of the working lifetime;

(b) final salary schemes—based on the annual salary at the moment of retirement; and

(c) final average salary schemes—based on the average annual salary received during the last few years of the working lifetime.

Occasionally the pension is partly on basis (a) and partly on basis (c).

The annual salary on which the pension is based is usually the normal salary excluding any overtime or bonus payments and, in some cases, there is an upper limit to the total amount of salary which will rank for pension. Sometimes an upper limit is placed on the pension that may be payable. On the other hand, the provision of a minimum pension is not uncommon. There may also be a provision that only salary received in any one year in excess of a lower limit (e.g. £100) shall rank. Funds containing this provision have become more numerous in recent years, as the device has frequently been adopted as a method of adjusting the fund pension to allow for the pension receivable under the National Insurance Act, 1946.

B. Schemes financed through a Life Office.

A Life Office scheme is, of necessity, less flexible than the privately financed pension scheme, for such schemes are subject to the limitations

(a) that the amount of benefit shall be precisely determined at the time the premiums are paid and not subject to variation with subsequent changes in the level of salaries;

(b) that, although the circumstances of individual members should, as far as possible, be taken into account in fixing their pensions, this should not be allowed to lead to a multiplicity of contracts which would result in a serious increase in the cost of administration; and

(c) that they cannot provide breakdown benefits in the form of pensions for life on the same scale as for age pensions.

Nevertheless, it will be seen that any of the schemes listed under Types I and II above would be suitable for administration through a Life Office. The majority of Life Office schemes, however, are normally of the following types (the first two of which it will be noted correspond to Types II(b) and (c) above):

Life Office schemes: pension related indirectly to salary.

(a) 'Money purchase' scheme: usually operated by means of a 'blanket' policy covering the whole staff of a particular employer.

(*b*) 'Deferred Annuity' scheme: here also a blanket policy is usually issued.

(*c*) An endowment assurance scheme: this consists, in essence, of a series of endowment assurances, carrying an annuity option at the normal retirement age, although it may also be operated by a blanket policy.

2.4. Effect of financial considerations

It is now proposed to consider in greater detail the circumstances in which each of the types of pension benefit set out in the foregoing classification could be suitably adopted. Before doing so, however, it must be emphasized that the pension benefit to be provided depends in the last resort upon the extent to which the employer is prepared to finance the scheme. Accordingly, it will be found in practice that considerations of finance may result in the adoption of a different type of pension basis from that which would appear most suitable having regard only to the needs of the employees concerned. At one extreme there is the State which feels justified in meeting the cost of a standard of pensions which it considers to be reasonable for Civil Servants, employees of Local Government Authorities and other related services. The situation is similar in the case of many well-established commercial concerns such as banks and insurance companies, although financial considerations must weigh more heavily with them as they depend ultimately upon their trading profits to cover the employer's share of the cost of pensions. At the other extreme are employers who, for financial or other reasons, are only prepared to undertake a pension liability within strictly defined limits, and in these cases the suitability of the pension basis ceases to be the primary consideration.

2.5. Application and suitability of various types of pension benefit

The application and suitability of the various types of pension benefit noted in paragraph 2.3 are outlined below.

A. Privately financed schemes.

I. Pension benefit independent of salary.

(*a*) Fixed pension.

Suitable for a group of workers whose rates of pay vary little according to age, who have little prospect of promotion to a higher income status, whose ages at commencement of service are confined to a relatively small range, or whose earnings fluctuate widely, e.g. workers remunerated by commission.

Reasons: The income standard likely to be attained by the workers at retirement is known within fairly narrow limits and the amount of pension can be fixed accordingly. This arrangement is extremely simple to operate and finance.

(*b*) Fixed pension for each year of service.

Suitable for wage-earning grades of workers (as above) who enter employment over a wide range of ages.

Reasons: It is possible to differentiate between workers with relatively long and short periods of service rendered up to the normal pension age. This arrangement also is simple to operate and finance.

II. Pension benefit indirectly related to salary.

(*a*) 'Savings Bank' type of scheme.

Suitable for female employees.

Reasons: Numerous withdrawals are to be anticipated in consequence of marriages. The amount standing to the credit of the employee could be repaid as a marriage dowry without affecting the financial stability of the fund. The amount of pension is not, however, known until the date of retirement, and it is, therefore, not so satisfactory from the employees' point of view.

(*b*) 'Money Purchase' scheme.

Suitable for wage-earning employees in the normal case but may be adapted to suit most types of employee.

Reasons: By relating the amount of pension directly to the contributions paid each year according to a fixed table, this arrangement attempts to secure freedom from financial instability arising as a result of variation in wage scales. It is, however, still affected by other factors such as variations in the interest yield, mortality, etc., and, for this reason, it does not secure complete financial stability. The contributions can be fixed by reference to salaries in such a way as to secure pensions comparable to those under an 'average salary' scheme (see below).

(c) 'Deferred Annuity' scheme.

Suitable for a small staff of clerical and administrative workers.

Reasons: Similar to those for a 'money purchase' scheme but more complex in operation. Salary increases involve the setting up of additional annuity contracts, and the scheme is not, therefore, suitable for a very large staff.

III. Pension benefit directly related to salary.

(a) Average salary scheme.

Suitable for manual workers and other wage-earning employees whose earnings as they approach the normal retirement age do not greatly exceed the average earnings during service.

Reasons: There is generally a reasonably close relationship for these types of workers between the standard of living reached near the retirement age and a pension calculated on this basis. Long service and promotion to a higher wage grade secure enhanced pensions, whilst a reduction in earnings late in service due to impaired efficiency or a change to lighter work would not entail a serious reduction in the pension. This latter point might become material in the case of heavy industrial workers.

If, however, the members of the fund include salaried staff where the salaries attained towards the end of service may cover a wide range, it is not possible to adjust the pension scale so as to avoid either (i) a relatively low pension in relation to final salary in the case of the higher paid staff, or (ii) a relatively high pension for the lower paid staff. The hypothetical and by no means extreme cases given in Table 2.1 illustrate this point. (To simplify the figures, it has been assumed that salaries increase continuously at a uniform rate between successive decennial ages and that retirement occurs at exact age 65.)

TABLE 2.1

Examples of pension benefits
from an 'average salary scheme'

Attained age	Assumed salary career	
	Case A	Case B
	£	£
20	150	150
30	250	300
40	325	500
50	350	750
60	350	850
65	350	850
Total salary (20–65)	13,500	24,750
Pension scale 1¾% of total salary		
Amount of pension	236	433
Ratio: pension/final salary	·67	·51

Although these drawbacks can be avoided by basing the pension on the earnings immediately before retirement, many employers prefer the average salary basis in all cases where it is reasonably suitable. At any given date, the pension in respect of past service is fixed and does not vary with changes in wage scales. The risk of financial instability arising from such changes is, therefore, considerably less than in a 'final salary' scheme, although it is not entirely removed, as in the case of the schemes of Types I and II above.

The average salary scheme may thus be said to form a compromise between the employer's desire for financial stability and the employee's desire for continuity of living standard upon retirement.

(b) Final salary scheme.

Suitable for salaried staff.

Reasons: In a scheme of this type the pension is directly linked with the standard of living attained by an individual immediately before his retirement: this applies equally when earnings vary widely both between individuals and with age. In consequence, any hardship which might arise owing to a reduction in income is borne in equal measure by all members after a given length of service, whatever the level of salary they have attained. The employer may, therefore, feel at liberty to retire an employee at or near the normal pension age, paying regard not to the individual's circumstances but only to the efficiency of the staff as a whole. The employee who reaches a higher salary level and who, presumably, has proved of greater value to his employer, receives a pension which reflects this value, but there is no distinction between the employee who is promoted early in service and one who, although promoted late, reaches the same final level of salary.

There is thus the financially objectionable feature that an employer may be tempted to give a relatively large increase in salary shortly before retirement, not as a recognition of immediate worth, but merely to enhance the pension. It would obviously be very difficult, if not impossible, to provide in advance for the additional liability thus incurred, and, in consequence, it is usual to suggest in these cases that the employer should give an undertaking to be responsible for the extra liability arising from such special increases.

As already indicated, schemes of this type involve an inherent risk of financial instability owing to the fact that a general rise in salary levels would immediately result in an increased liability for pensions in respect of past service which would not be covered by the increased value of future contributions. A financial guarantee by the employer is thus desirable for the successful working of the scheme, and all employers may not be ready to undertake the liability thus involved. For this reason, schemes of this type are usually confined to salaried staffs for whom an 'average salary' scheme might involve a serious break in living standards at date of retirement.

(c) Final average salary scheme.

    Suitable for salaried staff.

    Reasons: This type of scheme is a variant on the 'final salary' scheme, designed to avoid certain drawbacks of the latter type of scheme. By basing the pension on the average earnings of the last few years of service, the effect of an employer granting a large increase of salary shortly before retirement is considerably reduced. This method is also helpful in cases where earnings are fluctuating or where an employee may be called upon to accept a lower income level in the last few years before retirement owing to waning powers. (The latter case may sometimes be dealt with by allowing the employee concerned to reckon his maximum salary for pension purposes.) It is, however, subject to practically the same risk of financial instability as applies to a final salary scheme.

It may be said generally in regard to pensions directly related to salary that in practice the difference between bases (*a*), (*b*) and (*c*) is usually small for wages grades unless, e.g. as a result of inflation, there is a general rise in wage levels. As a matter of convenience, however, it may be desirable to express the pension in terms of total wages, particularly if these are liable to fluctuate from time to time or to decrease in a few cases late in service.

B. Schemes financed through a Life Office.

In general, the relative application and suitability of schemes financed through a Life Office are similar to those of the corresponding types of privately financed scheme. For the reasons already indicated, the benefits obtainable through a Life Office are necessarily of a more rigid character than those possible in a private fund. In particular, as will be seen later, the benefits provided on premature retirement owing to a breakdown in health are usually unsatisfactory, and the scheme may be more costly in the long run, since the premium rates presumably include a loading for expenses and some margin for profit to the Office.

On the other hand, the benefits are guaranteed by the insurance company and the cost is (or ought to be) fixed, although the company may, of course, revise its rates as regards fresh contracts and perhaps also as regards increases of pension due to salary increases of existing staff already in the scheme. Further, although the employer is still responsible for a certain amount of administration, he is freed from the responsibility of looking after investments and administering the fund, both of which are done by the Insurance Company.

For a small fund arranged with a Life Office there is the additional advantage which arises from the larger scale of insurance company operations. The Life Office would be free from the embarrassment which may be incurred by the small fund as the result of fluctuations in the experience of members and pensioners and in the values of securities. The broader basis arising from large funds and probably greater skill in the matter of investment should, in most cases, enable the Life Office to secure a higher rate of interest than a small private fund. Any loadings or margins in the premium basis to provide for expenses and profits may thus be partly offset.

Consideration of the relative suitability of the two systems (i.e. privately financed schemes and schemes financed through a Life Office) in a particular case ought to be made in relation to:

   (i)   the size of the staff,

  (ii) the type of employer and what he is able and prepared to do, and (to some extent)

 (iii) whether the matter is considered from the point of view of the employer or from that of the employee.

The size of the staff is probably the most important criterion in the majority of cases. Considering first the two extremes:

   (i) it is evident that a small business with only a few employees cannot hope to run a private fund successfully, and that the only means by which some provision could be made for retirement would be through insurance contracts;

(ii) the case for a private fund is obvious for a large and well-organized company, with the services of financial experts ordinarily at its disposal, and with a substantial number of employees.

Between these two extremes the respective cases for and against the two systems will vary with the circumstances. The minimum number of members required for the successful operation of an independent fund depends to some extent on the homogeneity of the conditions of service, etc., of the staff. Further, there will be borderline cases where the issue is doubtful and the balance will be decided by what the employer is able and willing to undertake. Thus, in the case of a wealthy company with a moderately sized staff, if the company is prepared to guarantee solvency and a certain amount of fluctuation in cost will not embarrass it, a private fund would be preferable since it could be made to conform exactly to the requirements of the case, to the advantage of all concerned. If, however, the employer cannot face the prospect of having to bear the full burden of a deficiency himself and the fund would have to be self-supporting, with the possibility that the benefits or the employees' contributions might have to be revised, a larger staff would be required to enable a successful private fund to be maintained.

The popularity of insurance office schemes may perhaps seem to be due in some measure to the probability that some of the employers concerned are not fully aware of the advantage of the private type of scheme. At the same time it is to be recognized that the employer's main concern is his business—not the specialized problems of finance connected with superannuation to which he may be disinclined to devote the necessary time or of which he may lack the necessary knowledge. It may be presumed that the employer is well accustomed to the payment of insurance premiums of various kinds and knows that the companies hope to make profits. An insurance office scheme in which the premiums are fixed and are not considered unreasonable, taking into consideration the risks attaching to a private scheme, will thus have an appeal in many cases where the employer likes to know exactly 'where he stands' and is satisfied that the scheme broadly solves the main problem of providing pensions to aged employees.

Finally, to conclude this summary of what is possibly a controversial question, it may be added that in some cases, in the desire to achieve the best of both possible worlds, contributions may be accumulated in a private fund during service, and the burden of maintaining, among others, the anticipated centenarians thrown on the broad shoulders of an insurance company by the purchase of annuities out of the proceeds of the fund when retirements take place.

CHAPTER 3

BENEFIT ARRANGEMENTS: PENSION SCHEMES

3.1. In the preceding chapter the various systems which are in common use for the determination of pensions have been considered in some detail. It is now proposed to discuss the regulations governing retirement, and also the various subsidiary benefits which are granted by the majority of funds upon the happening of other contingencies.

3.2. Normal pension age

The primary purpose of a pension scheme is, of course, the provision of pensions on retirement in old age from active service, and particular care must be taken in fixing the normal pension age. It will be clear that whatever age is fixed, there will be a number of employees who still remain capable of useful work. It is, however, possible to fix the age at such a point that the majority of employees will then have reached the end of their effective working lifetime, whilst, by allowing earlier pensions in the event of ill-health and possibly an option to retire during a small number of years before the normal retiring age, the needs of those employees who cannot remain in work up to the normal age can be met.

Bearing in mind these general considerations, the particular circumstances of each scheme must be allowed for. In a particular commercial concern or trade there may be a well-established rule which has been reached as a result of long experience, but, more generally, in the absence of a definite scheme, no retirement age will have been fixed. The employer will then wish to fix the normal age at a reasonable level both from his own point of view and from that of his employees, provided no difficulty arises from financial considerations. In some occupations, the nature of the work will dictate a somewhat earlier pension age owing to the importance of a high state of physical fitness, or the existence of special hazards (e.g. firemen and police); otherwise, the standards now generally accepted are a retirement age of 60–65 for males and 55–60 for females. These are frequently associated (especially where the later age is adopted) with an option either to the employee or to the employer for the retirement of an individual member to take place within the five years preceding the normal pension age (see §§ 3.4 and 3.5). If the basis of the pension varies with the number of years' service, the majority of funds set a maximum of 40 years to the service which ranks for pension.

3.3. Early retirement on grounds of ill-health

Many pension schemes include arrangements permitting the payment of an immediate pension to an employee who is forced to retire, or whom the employer deems it desirable to retire, on grounds of breakdown in health. In a scheme which is not merely an aggregation of individual deferred annuities, it is normal to provide a substantial benefit on ill-health, the cost being borne under the collective arrangements as part of the general risk. Thus a scheme providing on normal retirement a pension of a fixed percentage of the total salary received during active service would also provide the same percentage of total salary as a benefit on retirement due to ill-health. Similarly, a scheme based on a percentage of pensionable salary for each year of service would normally also grant the same scale, based upon actual years of service rendered, on ill-health retirement (subject to a minimum qualifying period for pension purposes of perhaps 10–15 years' service). Some schemes provide a minimum pension related, for example, to 20 years' service on ill-health retirement. As indicated above, the provision of such a benefit will usually increase the total cost of the scheme.

As an alternative, with the object of reducing the cost and providing as high a benefit on normal retirement as possible, the scheme may provide for a reduced scale of ill-health benefits. The reduction may either be on a somewhat arbitrary scale or such that, broadly speaking, it gives a benefit based upon the accumulated joint contributions. The scale of pensions is usually appreciably lower than on normal retirement, even where, in converting the accumulated contributions to a pension equivalent, some recognition is given to the retiring employee's reduced prospects of longevity; where retirement occurs more than 10 years before the pension age, the benefit is often quite inadequate.

3.4. Early retirement at option of employee

As already indicated, some schemes include arrangements which allow the member at his own option to retire within 5 years of the normal pension age, subject to the completion of, say, 40 years' service, and in this event he may be allowed to receive a pension on the full scale. Alternatively, an employee may have the option of retiring at any date within 10 years of the normal pension date; the pension would then be calculated on a scale lower than the normal, the reduction being usually determined so that the exercise of the option does not involve the employer or the scheme in any appreciable financial strain.

In certain schemes optional retirement may be granted even earlier than 10 years from normal retirement age, although it is not as a rule allowed more than 15 years before that age. An employee retiring under such a proviso obviously cannot be regarded as an impaired life, and the benefit must, therefore, be directly related to the actuarial reserve in hand in order to protect the fund and prevent the withdrawing member from involving the fund in a valuation strain. The benefit would not necessarily be taken in the form of an immediate pension, as, in some cases, it is more suitable for a deferred pension to be granted commencing at the normal pension age. (If the approval of the Inland Revenue is sought, they now usually require that an early retirement pension payable on grounds other than ill-health shall not commence more than 10 years before the normal pension age.)

3.5. Early retirement on grounds of redundancy

The employer sometimes desires to have the option to retire an employee on grounds of redundancy. If the pension granted on such a retirement is calculated on the normal basis, it is clearly impossible to provide for it in advance by an actuarially calculated contribution, since the frequency with which the benefit is allowed obviously depends upon considerations which are quite independent of the financial state of the fund. The maximum pension which can be provided by the fund alone must be that based upon the actuarial reserve in hand for the employee at the time of retirement, and a pension calculated upon this basis will usually involve too drastic a cut in the retirement benefit which the employee has been expecting, unless he is very near the retirement age. The employer will, therefore, normally provide additional resources, either through the fund or outside it, to enable the pension granted to a member retired for redundancy reasons to be calculated upon a more adequate basis. (The amount of such provision may have to be limited if Inland Revenue approval is sought.)

The need for these special financial arrangements should not, however, be regarded as a sufficient reason for eliminating a benefit of this type from a scheme. The employer may rightly feel that the conditions of his particular concern or of the trade in which he is engaged are such that it is essential to preserve a high degree of flexibility in a retirement scheme operating for the benefit of his staff.

3.6. Deferred retirement

In some schemes a member may be permitted to remain in the fund for a few years after the normal retirement age, at the option of the employer. Generally, contributions would cease, and there would be no further increase in the pension granted for the additional years of service, although some compensation by way of increased benefit may be allowed in respect of the benefit which has not been paid between the normal retirement date and the actual retirement date.

3.7. Other retirement benefits

In certain schemes the retirement benefit may consist partly of a pension and partly of a lump-sum benefit paid immediately upon retirement. The lump sum may represent either part of the normal retirement benefit or may take the form of an optional commutation of part of the pension. As an example, mention may be made of the non-contributory scheme for Civil Servants which provides on retirement a benefit (based upon the average annual salary received during the last 3 years of service) consisting of a pension equal to $\frac{1}{80}$th plus a lump sum equal to $\frac{3}{80}$ths for each year of service.* Again, many schemes arranged through insurance companies on the deferred annuity principle include a cash option at retirement, whilst others take the form of endowment assurances with annuity options. Here again, the proportion of the benefit which may be granted in the form of a lump sum is subject to severe restrictions where Inland Revenue approval is sought.

The lump sum was fairly popular in schemes set up in recent years, but it is open to strong objections except for very highly paid staff where considerations of the incidence of taxation may be decisive. The primary purpose of a pension scheme is, of course, to make satisfactory provision during the lifetime of an employee after his retirement, and there is no guarantee that a lump-sum payment will not be dissipated unwisely. This may lead to appeals after a few years for the supplementing of pensions, thus rendering the purpose of the scheme largely nugatory.

3.8. Subsidiary benefits—otherwise than upon retirement

The majority of schemes at present in operation provide, in addition to the main retirement benefit, ancillary benefits in the case of those employees who die or withdraw from the service of the employer before becoming entitled to a pension. The scale of these ancillary benefits is normally not fixed at a level appropriate to the various contingencies, their purpose being merely to mitigate the hardship which would otherwise be experienced by those employees who do not secure the full advantage of the main purpose of the scheme. In fixing this type of benefit, the aim is generally to grant what it is conventional to style a 'return'† at least equal to

---

* The earliest retiring age is 60 and, until recently, the number of years of reckonable service could not exceed 40. Under the Superannuation Act, 1949, service in excess of 40 years, up to a maximum of 5 years, is reckonable provided it occurs after age 60.

† It has long been customary, in the rules of pension funds, to describe a benefit of a sum equal to the member's contributions (with or without interest), payable on withdrawal or death, as 'a return of contributions'. Strictly, on insurance principles, contributions cannot be 'returned'. Such a benefit is obviously contingent, like any other insurance benefit, and is payable only on the occurrence of an event, viz. withdrawal or death. The use of the expression 'return' is open to the objection that it tends to obscure the essential nature of a fund, namely, that it is a mutual insurance scheme. Benefits of this nature can most usefully be regarded as increasing contingent assurances, the sum payable being, for convenience, related precisely to the contributions paid to the fund up to the date of withdrawal or death.

the total contributions paid by the employee. Any benefit granted in excess of this sum is usually kept to a minimum, so that the resources available for the provision of the main pension benefit may not be dissipated.

3.9. Withdrawal from service

If the employee terminates his service in circumstances which do not entitle him to a pension benefit, it is usual to provide a benefit equal to the whole of his own contributions, with or without interest, sometimes with a deduction on account of expenses. As will be seen later, the fund is liable to pay income tax at a modified rate on such 'returns', but this liability is sometimes passed on to the member himself. In the case of female staff, where one of the chief causes of withdrawal is marriage and the staff are likely to be more concerned with the more immediate benefit than with the remoter provision of an old-age pension, the withdrawal benefit may be supplemented by the addition of a proportion of the employer's contribution, thus providing in effect a marriage dowry.

In the case of the Local Government pension scheme, a transfer value may be paid where the employee leaves the service of one authority and joins another; the transfer value payment entitles the employee to count all his prior service with his former employer and thus mobility within the service is facilitated. This scheme is being extended to preserve general continuity of pension rights in cases of transfer between other superannuation schemes within the various public services and nationalized industries. A similar arrangement might be made for a group of associated companies, even though the pension arrangements for the several companies within the group may differ materially. In such a case it would be necessary to limit the amount transferable to the actuarial reserve in the case of the first employer's fund, whilst the corresponding benefits secured in the fund of the second employer would have to be determined as the actuarial equivalent of the sum brought over.

Occasionally an employer desires the withdrawal benefit to include a 'return' of the joint contributions of himself and the employee. If a withdrawal benefit is granted in this form, the fund will not secure Inland Revenue approval, but the Revenue will not raise objections if the employer's contribution is allowed in the form of a paid-up deferred pension (which may be commuted for a lump sum if trifling in amount). Such a provision would meet the objection sometimes held against pension schemes that they tend to reduce mobility of labour. On the other hand, it is not very satisfactory for a fund to remain liable for the payment of a pension to a person who may have left the employer's service many years before.

3.10. Death in service

Generally a sum equal to the member's own contributions, with interest, is paid on his death before retirement on pension, but quite frequently a larger benefit is provided up to the joint contributions of the employer and employed, with interest. Some schemes go further and provide for a minimum return of half or one year's salary, thus adding, in effect, a temporary decreasing assurance, whilst others include an additional temporary life assurance benefit roughly proportionate to salary attained. An additional benefit on the latter lines is a very common feature of schemes arranged through insurance companies.

3.11. Death after retirement on pension

With the object of providing reasonably consistent treatment between the employee who dies in service and one who dies very soon after retirement on pension, it is usual to provide a minimum benefit to the pensioner. This minimum is frequently fixed at the amount of the benefit which would have been paid had death occurred immediately before retirement. Thus where, owing to early death, the total pension payments are less than this minimum, the difference would be payable upon death. Alternatively, the pension payments may be guaranteed for a fixed number of years certain (e.g. 5 years) with the object of achieving a similar effect.

3.12. Pension to wife

Where no formal widows' fund has been established, partial protection for members' wives is often secured by including in a pension scheme an arrangement whereby the member may exercise an option to convert part of his own pension into a reversionary annuity to his wife. Sometimes there is also separate provision for pensions to the widows of members who die in service, thereby securing fairly complete protection at a relatively low cost to the employer.

The reversionary annuity would be actuarially equivalent to the pension surrendered, and, therefore, the option would not impose any strain on the fund, provided that the assumptions involved in the formula are realized. The basis of conversion may, of course, have remained unaltered for a long time, and, in consequence, may be out of accord with the latest experience; if this is so, the actuary may have to allow in his valuation for the cost of the option until a revised scale is introduced. If, however, as in recent years, the mortality of *both* males and females has shown a steady improvement, the terms upon which the option is allowed may not be seriously wrong, even though the rates of mortality may have altered considerably.

In order to safeguard the fund against adverse selection, the rules may require the member to declare the option a number of years before the normal retirement date. In this case the conversion could only be cancelled if either the wife or the husband died before the normal retirement date. Selection against the fund would thereby be reduced to a level which, in practice, may be ignored or covered by a nominal loading in the contributions. Alternatively, the member may be required to submit himself to medical examination when the option is declared on or very shortly before retirement. The disadvantage of the second method is that the option would be ruled out for those whose health is doubtful and who, therefore, stand in the greatest need of the arrangement. As a further alternative it would, of course, be possible to arrange for the cost of any selection which might be exercised by individual members to be borne by the scheme as a whole, by means, for example, of a suitable loading to the contributions payable. Whichever procedure is adopted, a reversionary benefit to the wife of a member who retires prematurely on account of ill-health can only be granted if further resources are made available to the scheme or if the contribution rates provide accordingly.

CHAPTER 4

BENEFIT ARRANGEMENTS: WIDOWS' AND ORPHANS' SCHEMES

4.1. Widows' benefits

The possible variations in schemes designed to provide for dependants of employees are even more numerous than in the case of retirement pension schemes, although the same general pattern may be discerned in most cases. The main benefit to the widow or dependant is usually one of the following:

(a) a fixed pension;

(b) a pension varying with the number of years' service;

(c) a pension of a fixed proportion of the pensionable salary;

(d) a pension varying with the number of years' service and with salary;

(e) the aggregate of a series of reversionary annuities secured by annual or single premiums. (Analogous to the 'money purchase' basis for pension funds.)

The payment of the benefit normally commences on the death of the employee, whether this should occur during active service or after his own retirement. As in a retirement pension scheme, the pensionable salary brought into account when the widow's benefit is dependent upon salary may be the final salary, the average salary throughout service, or some form of final average. In some schemes either the first £X of salary or any salary in excess of a specified level is excluded in calculating the pensionable salary. In addition, a minimum pension may be specified in order to secure reasonable cover in the event of early death.

The widow's pension will usually terminate in the event of her remarriage, although, if children's benefits are also provided, it may continue wholly or partly for the benefit of the children. In either case, the full amount of the pension may be revived by subsequent re-widowhood. Since the cost for a given age of the husband will depend upon the age of the wife, it is often provided for the benefit to be adjusted according to the age difference of husband and wife. The adjustment may take the form of a percentage deduction (or addition) where the age of the wife differs by more than, say, 3 or 5 years from that of the husband and consequently would only affect cases which fall beyond this range. An adjustment on these lines has the double purpose of protecting the scheme from additional liabilities over and above those provided for in the premium basis (which may occur, e.g. through an elderly member marrying a young wife) and of preserving an element of equity between individuals covered by the scheme.

It is usual for the wives of second and even of subsequent marriages to be eligible for the widow's benefit, although marriages contracted after the member has retired and, possibly, those contracted within a limited number of years before the normal retiring age, may be ruled out. In the case of second marriages, the adjustment on account of age disparity referred to above is often substantial.

Although the widows' scheme may exist quite independently of a retirement pension scheme, it may, on the other hand, be parallel to such a scheme or even an integral part of a comprehensive scheme covering old age as well as dependants. In the latter case, pensions to the widows of members who die after retirement may be provided for (as mentioned in paragraph 3.12) by an option to the member to convert part of his own pension or other retirement benefit into a reversionary annuity. Further, the normal benefit of a 'return' of contributions on death in service may be set off against the widows' benefit.

4.2. Children's benefits

Most widows' schemes provide also for the payment of a benefit to children left after the death of the father, and the benefit granted is sometimes higher after the death of both parents. The benefit may be an annuity for each child ceasing at 16 or 18 years of age, with a maximum to the number of eligible children or, alternatively, it may be a collective family benefit. In the latter case, the amount may be governed by the number of surviving children below a specified age, or it may be entirely independent of the size of the family.

The annuity granted to each child is usually a fixed amount, but it may be somewhat larger for the oldest child below the limiting age at any time. There is, however, no inherent reason why this benefit also should not be related to salary (as, for example, a proportion of a widow's benefit similarly calculated), and such a provision is sometimes encountered. There are other variations, such as, for example, a provision that the amount of the orphan's allowance shall increase by stages with age, since the expense of bringing up the child may be expected to increase.

4.3. Other dependants

Occasionally married members have the right to nominate a dependant to receive a benefit on their death where there is no wife, but the benefit may be on a lower scale than that provided for a widow. This right may also be extended to unmarried members. In such cases, it is usually necessary to introduce safeguards to prevent a strain on the finances of the fund in consequence of the nomination of a young dependant by a member who has reached a fairly advanced age.

4.4. Ancillary benefits

The inclusion of ancillary benefits under a widows' and orphans' scheme will depend largely on the extent to which the employee himself contributes towards the cost of the benefits. If the whole cost of the scheme is met by the employer, there may be no case for providing benefits other than those payable to the dependants. On the other hand, if the employee himself contributes, it is usually considered desirable to provide for the 'return' of part at least of the contributions in the event of his withdrawal from the service or of his death before marriage. Less frequently, a partial 'return' of contributions may be allowed even in cases where the member concerned has been 'at risk' for the widow's benefit but his wife has predeceased him.

4.5. Desirability of compulsory membership

In the case of a fund established for the benefit of the employees of a business firm or other undertaking employing a large staff, it will be necessary for membership to be compulsory, at any rate for future entrants, if the rates of contribution are to be assessed either as a fixed contribution per member or a fixed proportion of salaries (see Chapter 5). The necessity for this will be seen from the following considerations.

If membership were optional, it is clear that the only satisfactory method of finance would be to charge contributions appropriate to the risk in respect of each individual married member with due regard to his age and the age of his wife, and no real assurance of any unmarried members would be possible, since the risk in respect of a bachelor in these circumstances could not properly be assessed until he married. The results, therefore, would not be materially different from those obtainable by taking out reversionary annuity contracts with a Life Office.

If an attempt were made to run a fund in which membership were left entirely to the discretion of the individual but contributions were not related to individual risks, men already married and bachelors about to marry in the near future would be predominant among those who would join, since it is evident that there must be a tendency for those who have no present intention of marrying to remain outside the fund. It would therefore not be possible to arrive at any authoritative estimate of the varying probabilities of marriage at successive ages in the future, which are essential for the purpose of the calculation of the proper contribution rates and for the valuation of the liabilities and assets of the fund. Briefly, the admission of bachelor voluntary members to a widows' and orphans' fund at strictly appropriate rates of premium on an insurance basis is impracticable.

4.6. In this chapter the main types of benefit provided in widows' and orphans' funds have been outlined. In practice, there may be other detailed provisions, but these do not usually affect the character of the fund. For example, special conditions may be included, such as a requirement that marriages after retirement from the service shall not rank or that the widow shall not receive benefit if the member dies within a specified short period after marriage. When the bases and formulae for valuation are considered, it will be important to see that proper allowance is made for the effect of any such conditions, some of which may have a profound effect on the liability.

CHAPTER 5

METHODS OF FINANCE

5.1. As was indicated in Chapter 1, the development of pension schemes has been a slow process extending over a considerable number of years, and the financial structure of the schemes has undergone a parallel development. In the earliest days when old-age benefits existed in the form of casual payments in cases of particular hardship, the benefits were met out of current revenue or out of a fund built up arbitrarily without any actuarial basis. Subsequently, payments may have been made on some recognizable plan as precedents became established and, later still, as the shortcomings of the existing methods of finance became apparent, an attempt may have been made to seek actuarial advice and relate the available resources to the anticipated expenditure. The modern actuary may thus find himself called upon to give advice on arrangements which may range from the most primitive type to a fully actuarial scheme. It is now proposed to examine the underlying financial structure of some of the possible arrangements before considering the actuarial problems in detail.

5.2. Financial principles

One of the principles of sound finance now generally accepted is that the cost of retirement benefits for each generation of employees should be provided for during their working lifetime. The cost of pensions is thus set aside concurrently with the payment of salaries and wages, so that an employee who retires and ceases to contribute to the general welfare of the organization does not impose a burden upon the employer for the provision of his pension. It follows that the sums set aside to provide pensions to staff would be increased concurrently with earning capacity in the case of an undertaking which has expanded, even though outgo for pensions would not show any marked increase for some years. Conversely, if a company's payroll contracted over a period of years, it would not (apart from any outstanding back-service liability) have to provide out of current revenue for pension charges incurred during an earlier period of prosperity, and consequently disproportionate in amount to its current earning capacity. Similarly, any change in the composition of the staff which would ultimately affect the aggregate pensions to be provided (e.g. altered proportions of skilled and unskilled labour) should immediately give rise to an automatic change in the sums set aside to provide pensions.

There are, however, still in existence numerous funds whose financial structure does not follow these general principles. Broadly speaking, retirement benefit schemes may be classified, according to the method of financial provision, into (a) unfunded; (b) partially funded; and (c) fully funded.

5.3. Unfunded schemes

Under an unfunded scheme, the employer would meet the whole cost of retirement benefits out of current revenue, and the employee would not be called upon to contribute. Pensions may be determined on a casual basis according to need at the sole discretion of the employer, or they may be on a well-defined basis, having the sanction of established custom or even a formal legal framework.

Arrangements of this type may be set up for a variety of reasons. At the one extreme, the employer, although recognizing the need for adequate retirement benefits, may not be able to afford the current cost of a fully funded scheme. At the other extreme may be found institutions of great financial strength which prefer, as a matter of deliberate policy, to retain full control of their pension arrangements so that they may vary the scale of benefits in individual cases. Thus, they can retain a high degree of freedom in retiring their employees as part of their general staffing policy.

Arrangements of this kind are usually open to criticism from the members' point of view. The security for their old age is entirely dependent upon the continued financial strength of their employer as well as on the retention of his goodwill, and the amount of their pension might tend to vary with their employer's prosperity.

There are other serious grounds for criticism of unfunded schemes. The outgo on pensions under such a scheme may be quite nominal for some years after its establishment, but the charge ultimately rises to a much higher proportion of the payroll than in a funded scheme. The employer may, therefore, be tempted at the outset to fix a generous scale of pensions, since his immediate cost will, in any case, be small. At a later stage the increasing pressure of pension charges may force him to reduce the benefit to an extent which may lead to hardship.

5.4. Partially funded schemes

Under a partially funded scheme—rarely encountered in practice nowadays—the employee would usually pay contributions on a prescribed scale in order to secure benefits on a definite basis. The employer, on the other hand, would not pay a regular contribution in respect of each employee but would undertake to pay the balance of the cost of pensions over and above that provided out of the employee's contribution when the pension actually became payable. Such an undertaking might be implemented in one of two ways:

(a) Each member's own contributions could be invested and accumulated in an individual account and applied at retirement to purchase an annuity from a Life Office or through the Post Office. At the same time, the employer would purchase an additional annuity sufficient to make up the total pension to the amount to which the employee is entitled.

(b) The contributions of all employees could be accumulated in a single fund against which a part or the whole of pensions would be charged. The employer would be called upon out of current revenue to make up the pensions which could not be met out of the fund. If the charge against the fund were for the whole pension, the income from interest and employees' contributions would, after a while, be overtaken by the pension outgo and the fund would then gradually be exhausted. From that point onwards, the employer would be called upon each year to meet the whole of the excess of the pension outgo over the aggregate contributions paid by the members, and in effect the scheme would revert to the unfunded type.

A particularly unsatisfactory feature of the second of these arrangements is that if the employer were unable to meet his obligations there would be no complete safeguard even for that part of the pension provided by the members' own contributions. In addition, the employer would, for a considerable number of years, be relieved from making contributions. Thus, at the expense of the members, he would be placed temporarily in a more favourable financial position than the employer who had paid throughout his share of the cost concurrently with the members. Ultimately, however, because there would be no fund earning interest, his annual outlay would be much higher than if he had made contributions at the same time as the members.

5.5. State pension schemes

A special category of unfunded schemes comprises those established by the State either as employer or for the benefit of the general population. For example, in the scheme for the benefit of the main body of Civil Servants the benefits are payable according to a prescribed scale, but no contributions are paid by the employees and pensions are met out of the current national revenue. Again, the general scheme of pensions under the National Insurance Act, 1946, is also of the unfunded type. Both the individual members (who comprise practically the entire working population) and employers are called upon to make contributions. These contributions are applied towards the current outgo for benefits, and the balance of the cost emerges as a direct charge on the current national revenue. The criticisms of this form of financial provision expressed in the preceding paragraphs are generally considered not to be applicable to this special type of case, since the accumulation of a pension fund on normal actuarial lines would reduce to mere book-keeping if the accumulated funds were to be invested in government securities. It will be seen that, whether the resources available to meet the excess of outgo over current contributions are expressed as interest on an invested fund or as a direct charge on revenue, this sum must be raised by taxation of the general body of taxpayers.

It might be argued that some method analogous to the accumulation of actuarial funds should be applied to State schemes so that the cost of pensions for the present generation of workers should, as far as possible, be provided for by allocating and storing up a definite proportion of the national wealth. There are two objections to such a suggestion. In the first place, owing to the need to provide pensions for the existing elderly population who have not contributed in the past, there is normally no excess of income under such a scheme which could be used to finance such a process. In the second place, the method of accumulation would present problems which it would be difficult to solve. It is sufficient to remark here that the question may not be one of mere academic interest in a society faced with the possibility of a declining population.

5.6. Fully funded schemes

Fully funded schemes—which are those most commonly encountered—call for contributions from the employer, and usually also from the employee, which are paid concurrently with salary over the active-service lifetime. These contributions are set aside in a fund with the purpose that there shall be available a sum sufficient to cover the aggregate liability for pensions upon the retirement of each age-group of employees. One of the main objects of establishing such a fund is to satisfy the desire of the employer to give his employees the maximum security for their pensions. The aim is, as far as possible, to secure the payment of the pensions independently of the prosperity of the employer and to ensure that, by the time the member retires, a sufficient sum has been accumulated to provide the benefit in full without further contributions either from employer or employee.

It must be appreciated, however, that the security provided is not complete even in the sense in which a life assurance fund is said to be solvent. In this connexion there are two aspects which must be considered:

(a) The full provision of the pension to an individual must, of course, ultimately depend upon the continued sound financial position of the employer at least until the member retires. On the other hand, even if the employer finds that he cannot meet his full liability, the accumulated fund will at any rate provide some part of the active employees' pensions accrued in respect of services rendered to date in addition to the full pensions for retired members, once the initial liability at the inception of the scheme has been met. For this reason, it is important that the fund should remain outside the control of the employer, and preferably invested outside his business, either in the form of a trust fund, or in the hands of an insurance company if a Life Office scheme is adopted.

(b) The existence of a pension scheme implies the recognition by an employer of the desirability of enabling his employees to retire on a standard of living comparable to that which they enjoyed whilst in employment. Consequently, in a great number of schemes, the benefits are based upon salaries. A pension fund of this type is normally said to be solvent if the periodical valuations show that it can meet its obligations on the assumption of a continuance of the assumed experience rates, particularly the existing scales of salaries, adjusted for any foreseeable modifications. In practice there can, of course, be no guarantee of such continuance. In fact, in the recent past, the effect of two wars has been to cause a marked jump in the level of all salaries which has automatically created deficiencies in salary-based schemes, the most serious deficiencies arising in those cases where pensions are based on salaries at retirement.

These considerations lead to a rather different conception of the duties of the actuary than in the case of a life assurance fund. He should aim to advise and assist the employer so that the cost of pensions may be spread reasonably over the working lifetime of his employees in such a way that the pensions will be fully secured in the absence of unforeseeable salary fluctuations.

Where the pension is not based on salary the above difficulty is avoided, but the practical problem is not thereby solved. A general salary increase arising from economic conditions would face the employer with the difficulty that, although the pension fund is financially solvent, it no longer gives pensioners the desired living standard. Thus there would be pressure for increased pensions, and if this is yielded to the employer will have to face a liability in respect of supplementary benefits which is fundamentally very similar to the deficiency which automatically arises in the 'final salary' type of fund in these circumstances.

5.7. Contribution scales

Subject to the limitations referred to in the preceding paragraphs, it will be necessary in a funded scheme to fix a scale or scales of contributions such that the contributions payable by each individual or group of individuals will, in normal circumstances, be actuarially equivalent to the benefits provided, so that each group of entrants to the scheme will be self-supporting. Whatever the type of fund, the form of the contribution should follow the form of the benefit. For example, if the pension is of a fixed amount, or determined as a definite amount for each year of service and not affected by the salary of the individual member, the contribution scale should also be fixed independently of the individual salary. If, however, the pension is based on salary, the contribution should also be a percentage of the salary payable from time to time during service and, theoretically, the percentage should vary with the age at entry. In practice, however, the scale adopted in a private fund would sometimes be simplified, the percentage of salary being constant over age-groups; in a 'final salary' scheme it may indeed be possible to adopt a constant percentage for all normal entry ages. Such a practice leads to administrative convenience, and if, in fixing the scale, the expected spread of entry ages is carefully considered, it should be possible to ensure that, within broad limits, the value of contributions for each group of ages is equal in the aggregate to the value of a theoretical scale of contributions for the same ages.

In the case of a savings bank or 'money-purchase' type of scheme, a considerable variation in the form of contributions is practicable, since, owing to the constitution of the fund, the form of the benefit will automatically correspond to the contributions made. Thus the contributions may be a level cash sum, a varying cash sum, or a percentage of salary determined mainly by convenience of operation and the ability of members at different salary levels to meet the cost. A money-purchase fund may thus provide pensions approximating quite closely to those in a fund of the average salary type.

If the contributions are fixed without consideration of the points referred to in the preceding paragraphs, the effect may be to introduce an avoidable instability into the operations of the fund which would create valuation difficulties and aggravate the problems arising from any general change in the level of earnings.

5.8. Payment of contributions

The total contribution required to provide the benefits may be entirely met by the employer, but it is much more common for the cost to be divided between the employer and employee. The basis of the division will be affected by considerations such as the generosity of the employer and the practical limits to the ability of the employee to pay contributions. The most usual method in the case of a salary-based private fund is for the normal contribution to be divided equally, or nearly equally, between the employer and employee. Where, however, a fund is being established for the benefit of a staff which includes members at fairly advanced ages, the contribution required in respect of the older members may be too heavy for such a subdivision. This difficulty is often met by setting a maximum to the rate of contribution payable by the member and calling upon the employer to meet the whole balance of the cost. In addition, if benefits are being provided in respect of service before the establishment of the fund, this is usually done entirely at the employer's expense.

The true effect of such subdivisions of the cost will be considered in more detail later. The fact that the normal contribution for a new entrant is divided equally between employer and employee does not necessarily mean that each individual will pay for 50% of his own pension. For example, in funds where the employee's contribution is 'returned' on withdrawal but that of the employer is retained in the fund, the proportion of pension ultimately provided by the employer's contributions may be substantially in excess of 50%.

5.9. Specimen contribution scales

It may be helpful at this stage to consider Table 5.1, in which, on the assumption of equal contributions by employer and employee, are compared the total or combined contributions required to secure at age 65 a pension of $1\frac{1}{2}$% of total salary (a) when the contribution is fixed as a percentage of salary under the normal average salary scheme, and (b) upon the money-purchase basis.

TABLE 5.1

Annual contribution required to secure a pension of $1\frac{1}{2}\%$ of total salary from age 65

Age attained	Salary career	(a) Contribution as a fixed percentage of salary (7·36%)		(b) Contribution on money purchase (annual premium) plan	
		Additional contribution per £10 salary increase	Total annual contribution payable	Additional contribution per £10 salary increase	Total annual contribution payable
	£	£	£	£	£
20 (entry)	200	·736	14·7	·663	13·3
30	360	·736	26·5	·801	24·9
40	480	·736	35·3	·966	35·5
50	540	·736	39·7	1·163	41·9
60	580	·736	42·7	1·413	47·1
64	580	—	42·7	—	47·1

Basis. 3% interest. On death before pension age: payment of a sum equal to the accumulation of the employee's own contributions with 3% compound interest. Salary assumed to proceed by equal steps between the ages shown. Withdrawals ignored.

Two important points emerge from the consideration of this table. In the first place, it will be seen that under the money-purchase scheme the cost of a unit of additional pension purchased for an employee at an advanced age may be very high in relation to the salary, and the major part of the cost at that age may have to be thrown on the employer. Secondly, it will be seen that, whilst both schemes are fully funded in the sense explained in § 5.6, the cost is spread more evenly throughout service when the contribution is fixed as a level percentage of salary than under the money-purchase plan. Thus, in the first case the portion of the full pension at 65 secured by contributions paid

up to age 35 is £115,

up to age 45 is £194.

In the second case (money purchase plan) the corresponding figures are

up to age 35—£107,

up to age 45—£186.

These differences would be greatly accentuated if the pension is based upon final salary instead of total or average salary.

It should, perhaps, be emphasized that the contributions quoted in Table 5.1 are, of course, given for comparative purposes only; they would not be suitable for use in connexion with any particular fund. As will be seen from Chapter 6 the rate of contribution required for a given benefit will depend to a considerable extent upon the decremental rates appropriate to the fund and upon the rate of interest at which it is assumed the fund will accumulate from time to time. The rate of interest is particularly important, since the period of accumulation between the payment of contributions and the disbursement by the payment of pensions can be very long. Thus, in the example given above, the rate of contribution fixed as a level percentage of salary would be reduced from 7·36% of salary to 6·81% of salary if it were possible to assume a rate of interest of $3\frac{1}{4}$% instead of 3%.

5.10. Widows' and orphans' funds

The general principles outlined in this chapter in relation to pension funds apply also in relation to widows' and orphans' funds. In those funds where the employees share part of the cost, they may pay periodical contributions which may vary with marital status or length of service or both. These contributions may be expressed as percentages of salary or as a series of fixed amounts. They may cease on retirement from the service, or may continue thereafter, possibly at a reduced rate, but continuation after retirement usually applies only if the member himself receives a pension. In addition to periodical contributions, lump-sum payments on marriage may be required, the amount of which may vary with the age of the member at marriage and that of his wife, whilst separate contributions may be required in respect of children. A higher scale also may be imposed if the member marries after retirement. Entrance fees, also, may be exacted. In practice there is a great variety of conditions, ranging from complete mutual assurance in all respects, where all members pay the same scale of contributions, to the other extreme where the contributions purport to relate strictly to the liabilities in respect of the individual.

CHAPTER 6

ACTUARIAL STRUCTURE OF FUNDS: GENERAL

6.1. It is now proposed to consider the actuarial aspects of the funds and the duties of the actuary in relation thereto. This can be conveniently discussed under two main heads, viz. the establishment of a new fund and the valuation of an existing fund, although there are naturally a considerable number of points common to both. The following is a brief outline of the actuary's duties as they will be considered in this and the following chapters.

6.2. The establishment of a new fund

The type of scheme to be set up must be discussed with the employer in the light of the particular type of staff employed by him, the needs of his business and any special conditions peculiar to it. The object of these discussions is, of course, to decide what will be the most suitable arrangements in regard to benefits, contributions, retirement conditions, etc.

When the outlines of the scheme have thus been tentatively fixed, the actuary must estimate the contributions required to meet the benefits for new entrants, and also the initial liability which will be incurred if it is decided to grant pension rights in respect of past service or to allow existing members of the staff who entered the fund at advanced ages to pay rates of contribution lower than those which would apply to their actual ages. As already explained the latter provision may be necessary in order to avoid calling for rates of contribution at such a high level as to give rise to hardship.

In the drafting of the trust deed and rules, the actuary has an important role to play in co-operation with the legal advisors of the employer. It is usual, and in any event desirable, before the deed is finally executed to submit a draft for the provisional approval of the Inland Revenue. With taxation at its present high level the financial advantages of approval to schemes are considerable, and therefore it is essential before any fund is finally established that the actuary should satisfy himself that the trust deed and rules governing the operations of the fund fully comply with the statutory requirements and regulations. In recent years the provisions of the Income Tax Acts in relation to pensions and widows' and orphans' funds have assumed such complexity as almost to form a subject of study in themselves, but an outline of the present position as regards taxation and conditions of approval is given in Chapter 17.

6.3. The valuation of an existing fund

In the case of most existing schemes a quinquennial valuation is a statutory requirement or is specifically required under the trust deed. Such valuations serve the double purpose of acting as checks on the estimate of future conditions on the basis of which the fund was established and of affording an opportunity for adjustment to changing circumstances. It is an especially important duty of the actuary to advise either upon the action to be taken in the event of a surplus arising, or upon the steps necessary to deal with a deficiency.

In addition to the above, the actuary should expect to give advice upon suggestions for variations in the scheme which may emanate either from the employer or from the members, especially where financial adjustments are involved. Where it is impracticable, apart from questions of cost, for the suggestions to be adopted, the actuary must be prepared to explain the reasons in non-technical language which will prove convincing to persons unaccustomed to dealing with such matters. He must also be prepared to offer advice upon the adjustment of a scheme to meet eventualities which could not be foreseen when it was established, such as a general inflation of wage levels or the introduction of universal State pensions. Further, the trustees of many funds are accustomed to consult the actuary in regard to investment of the funds and other problems of day-to-day administration.

6.4. Actuarial basis

The first and most important step, whether in connexion with the establishment of a new fund or the valuation of an existing one, is to determine the actuarial bases on which the calculations are to be made. In life assurance work actuaries are normally concerned only with three elements—mortality, interest and expenses—since withdrawal or cessation is rarely taken into account. In dealing with pensions or widows' and orphans' funds, on the other hand, the actuary may, in addition, have to allow for the effects of retirement from active service for various causes, withdrawal from service, mortality after retirement, and for salary changes. In the case of widows' and orphans' funds, allowance may also have to be made for marital status and the number of children who may become entitled to benefit after the member's death. The marital status may involve either explicitly or implicitly a consideration of marriage and remarriage rates, of the relative ages of husbands and wives, mortality rates of wives and widows, remarriage rates of widows, and of mortality rates of married men and of widowers and bachelors. The valuation of orphans' benefits may involve consideration of family statistics, issue rates, and mortality rates of children. The large number and varied character of these elements account for the complexity of the preliminary work and of the formulae used, and indicate the wide scope which exists for the application of reasoned judgement. In determining the actual basis to be adopted the utmost care is necessary, and the actuary must as far as possible keep clearly in mind the financial effect of variations of the experience of the fund from the assumptions which he makes. The circumstances of different funds may vary so widely that the statistics derived from one fund cannot be used for another, however similar superficially, without the most careful investigation to ensure that they are suitable. The reasons for this will be apparent when each element of the valuation is dealt with individually.

6.5. Service table

Before dealing with the various elements, it is proposed to give brief consideration to the multiple decrement or service table which is normally necessary as the foundation of the estimates of liability for members in employment. Such a table would be based upon the probability, at successive ages, of withdrawal, of death and of retirement on pension for reasons of ill-health or age. The student will already be familiar with this extension of the more usual single decrement or life table, but a brief recapitulation may be helpful.

If l_x represents the number surviving in the service at exact age x, and w_x, d_x, i_x, r_x the numbers out of l_x who, at age x last birthday, withdraw, die, retire on ill-health pension, and retire on age pension, respectively, the probability that a member now aged x will die in service in the year of age $x+t$ last birthday will be represented by d_{x+t}/l_x. The multiple decrement table is built up from probability ratios in such a way that

$$\frac{l_{x+1}}{l_x} = 1 - \frac{w_x}{l_x} - \frac{d_x}{l_x} - \frac{i_x}{l_x} - \frac{r_x}{l_x}$$

or

$$l_{x+1} = l_x - (w_x + d_x + i_x + r_x).$$

6.6. Decremental rates

In the following chapter the various probability rates will be considered individually in detail, and for the present it will be assumed that the scheme under consideration is very large so that it provides a sufficient volume of data to enable the actuary to examine in detail the various rates he wishes to employ. Subsequently, there will be a discussion of the practical steps necessary when, as frequently occurs in respect of one or more of the rates, these ideal conditions are not encountered. It should be particularly noted that, except where the contrary is indicated, these probability ratios are for the sake of brevity referred to as rates; the remarks are in general equally applicable to rates derived from a 'family' of single decrement tables, but the latter are not so readily adaptable to pension fund work and are consequently rarely employed directly. Another point which should be emphasized is that the rates required are in principle forecast rates suitable for the calculation of liabilities which will normally emerge over a long period in the future, and it is necessary to bear in mind the financial effects of making any adjustments on this account to any rates derived from the recent past experience of the scheme.

CHAPTER 7

ACTUARIAL STRUCTURE OF FUNDS: DECREMENTAL RATES

7.1. Introductory

The decremental rates which normally have the greatest financial effect upon the valuation of a pension fund are the rates of mortality experienced by pensioners and the rates of retirement from active service and it is accordingly proposed to deal with these first. Withdrawal rates, although they may appear substantial by comparison, are not usually so important financially as they normally operate only at the younger ages at which the reserves are, in any case, small.

7.2. Pensioners' mortality: normal retirements

The mortality of pensioners who have retired on reaching the final age limit for active service is usually very light, particularly for clerical and other non-manual employees, who show rates approximating to those of annuitants. Where there is an option to take either part or the whole of the benefit in the form of a lump sum, the mortality of pensioners who do not exercise the option may be exceptionally light—at any rate for a few years following retirement—as a result of selection. In general, there are significant differences between well-defined sections of the membership, e.g. males and females, clerical and manual workers, and, as would be expected, the mortality of manual workers is usually the heaviest. It should be borne in mind, however, that the mortality rates finally adopted for pensioners should, if anything, be slightly lower than those likely to be experienced, thus providing a small margin for fluctuations.

Unless the fund is very large, the data will usually be insufficient to justify the construction of a special life table for pensioners based upon the actual experience of the fund. In most cases it will be advisable to compare the actual deaths experienced over a period of years with those expected according to a suitable standard table and to adapt that table for use by rating the ages up or down if necessary. In deciding the mortality to be used for the valuation of future pensions to existing active-service members, it must be remembered that the liability for payment of pensions will gradually emerge over a long period in the future, and that consequently it will be necessary to anticipate some improvement in mortality compared with that of incumbent pensioners. Such a course is particularly desirable in the calculation of rates of contribution for future entrants.

7.3. Pensioners' mortality: ill-health retirements

The mortality experience of members who retire before the normal retiring age owing to breakdown in health is often very heavy and shows a marked degree of reversed selection. The mortality rate immediately after retirement is particularly heavy, but as the most seriously deteriorated lives are removed by death the mortality rate of the survivors tends to become less heavy. Although the data for a particular fund are not likely to be conclusive, this feature is generally observed where the fund is sufficiently large. The degree and extent of the initial period of selection and the excess of the ultimate rates over the normal mortality of pensioners would, of course, depend upon the standards set in the administration of the fund and the general management policy of the employers. The rates would, therefore, be closely linked in this respect with the rates of ill-health retirement from service, and the overall rates of mortality brought out by applying the adopted rates of mortality in service, ill-health retirement and mortality after retirement should approximate to those which would be expected in a normal body of lives of the same class which had not been subjected to a process of segregation into active and retired classes.

In a scheme providing the normal type of benefit the reversed selection would generally be more marked at the younger ages for two reasons. Firstly, the employer is likely to be more lenient in permitting retirements upon pension at, say, age 55 than at age 35. Secondly, the member himself would suffer a much more severe reduction in income on retirement at the younger age and a much higher degree of disability would be necessary before he applied for a pension. As a result, it is often found that the rate of mortality immediately after retirement decreases as the age at retirement increases. The annuity values derived from such rates will vary little over a wide range of ages at retirement, and, in some cases, it has been found appropriate to employ a constant annuity value for all ages of ill-health retirement. It must, however, be emphasized that, before doing so, the actuary must endeavour to satisfy himself that such a course is reasonable for the particular scheme under consideration. This procedure will, of course, not be suitable in the case of incumbent ill-health pensioners, since the surviving pensioners will have partly or wholly emerged from the initial period of selection.

The data available for determining the rates of mortality of ill-health pensioners are likely to be even more scanty than in the case of age retirements. Consequently, no elaborate investigation is usually practicable, and it is necessary to determine the rates to be adopted by comparing the actual deaths in broad groups with those expected on the basis of suitable rates derived from a larger fund.

7.4. Pensioners' mortality: optional retirements

It has already been stated that in some funds members are given the option of retiring within a fixed number of years before the compulsory retirement age. Where compulsory retirement takes place at age 65 and optional retirement is permitted after age 60, there is often no material reduction of pension apart from the fact that, where pension is dependent upon the number of years' service, the ranking years of service may be smaller unless the member has already completed the maximum of, say, 40 years' service which is permitted to rank for pension. If optional retirement is permitted at earlier ages, there is, as already indicated, usually some reduction in the pension allowed.

The mortality of members who take advantage of such an option may be expected on general grounds to be intermediate between that of normal and of ill-health retirements. In some funds the actual mortality may possibly reflect such factors as the amount by which the pension may be reduced and the type of occupation (e.g. if heavy physical labour is involved, a higher proportion of members may take advantage of the option). For these reasons, particular care must be taken in determining the mortality rates to be employed for such retirements. For this purpose, a careful investigation should be made of such experience as may be available and, in addition, inquiries made of the employer with a view to ascertaining whether it is normal practice for employees to retire as soon as they have completed the maximum number of years of ranking service or whether retirements before the final retiring age tend to occur mainly amongst members whose health is not of the best. In practice, normal retirement mortality would generally be assumed as a measure of safety, unless there was fairly conclusive evidence that heavier rates would be justified.

7.5. Retirement rates: normal

If retirement takes place at a fixed age, there is, of course, no problem in the determination of retirement rates. If, however, optional retirement is permitted on the basis indicated in § 7.4, or if the scheme provides for a pension benefit on retirement 'on or after age x', care must be exercised in determining the proportion of members who retire at each age. This is particularly so where the arrangement is coupled with the requirement that the member must complete a specified number of years of service in order to qualify for the maximum rate of pension. Provisions of this type are met with in a variety of funds, including those governed by the Local Government Superannuation Act, 1937, under which members may, at their own option, retire on pension upon completion of 40 years' service at any time between the ages of 60 and 65.

The rates of retirement employed for schemes involving any such options are particularly important, since small variations in the rates may lead to relatively large differences in the liability. This will be clear from the fact that a lower retirement age involves both a reduction in the number of contributions assumed to be payable by both employer and employee and a reduction in the age at which the pension commences. Where, as in the normal type of scheme, the benefit is calculated by reference to years of service and salary, the assumption that the members will retire at the earliest possible optional age will normally bring out the maximum liability. Such an extreme assumption would, however, be inappropriate unless definitely supported by the experience of the fund.

In the particular case where there is a minimum qualifying period of service to enable a member to retire before reaching age 65 other than on grounds of ill-health (e.g. Local Government funds), the age retirement rates would vary appreciably between different groups of members according to ages at entry into service, and it would be necessary, if the data permit, to examine the retirement experience and possibly to conduct the valuation in a select form throughout. Table 7.1 shows the *form* which the rates of retirement (excluding ill-health cases) would take in a fund where the qualifying period is 40 years (the rates, of course, being given for illustrative purposes only).

TABLE 7.1

Form of rates of age retirement in a fund with a 40-year qualifying period

Age at entry	Pension age					
	60	61	62	63	64	65
18–20	·6	·1	·15	·20	·25	1·0
21	0	·65	·12	·17	·23	1·0
22	0	0	·7	·15	·20	1·0
23	0	0	0	·75	·17	1·0
24	0	0	0	0	·8	1·0
25 and over	0	0	0	0	0	1·0

The figures in Table 7.2 provide a simplified illustration of the profound effect which differences in the assumed rates of retirement at optional ages would have upon the valuation.

In the light of the figures given in Table 7.2, it will be seen that any attempt to aggregate the membership and value by a single service table would involve the risk of serious inaccuracies. Theoretically, such a course would only be possible if the flow of entrants had been distributed in constant proportions between the various entry ages during the whole period since present active members first entered the service. Even if this requirement were ever satisfied, the aggregate retirement rates shown by the recent experience might be inappropriate for the valuation of future liabilities owing to the financial immaturity of the fund (see § 7.7 for an amplification of this point) and may thus require modification.

TABLE 7.2

Effect of variation in assumed retirement rates

Attained age	Prospective reserve		
	Assumed retirement rates		
	63–1·00 64– ·00 65– ·00	63– ·50 64– ·50 65–1·00	63– ·00 64– ·00 65–1·00
20	4·0	2·5	0·0
30	17·2	15·2	11·7
40	35·3	32·4	27·6
50	60·4	55·9	49·7

Basis. Interest, 3 %; mortality in service, A 1924–29 light; mortality after retirement, $a^{(m)}$. Ill-health retirements and withdrawals ignored.

Age at entry: 20. Joint contribution: 1·0 per annum. Pension at retirement: £10·2 per annum. Benefit on death in service: one-half of the joint contributions, with 3 % compound interest.

Among other considerations which may affect retirement rates may be mentioned the possibility that the higher paid staff in a salary-based fund may tend to exercise the option to retire early less frequently than the lower paid staff, with a consequent bias in financial estimates if the retirement rates are derived in the normal manner by reference to units of membership. This feature may be particularly noticeable in an average salary scheme or some deferred annuity schemes, since the benefit provided for those higher paid members who have progressed more rapidly than the average would be relatively small in relation to the retirement salary, leading such members to defer retirement as long as possible. A correction for this feature could to some extent be made by basing the rates of age retirement on units of salary instead of units of membership.

In any scheme where the benefit on optional retirement (see § 3.4) is calculated as the actuarial equivalent of the reserve held it will be sufficient to calculate the liability at the normal retirement age only, ignoring the possibility of optional retirement. If the benefit does not approximate to that which could be provided by the reserve on the valuation basis adopted more involved methods would be necessary.

7.6. Retirement rates: ill-health

Although the financial effect of variations in ill-health retirement rates is less marked than in the case of age-retirement rates, no less care is necessary in fixing them, since they are particularly influenced by the circumstances of the individual fund. The rates may be directly affected by the generosity or otherwise of the scale of benefits provided, as well as by the policy and administrative action of the employer. They will be closely correlated with the mortality rates in service and after retirement, since, for example, stringent regulations in regard to ill-health retirement would tend to produce a low retirement rate, coupled with high rates of mortality in service and of mortality of ill-health pensioners. It should be borne in mind that the mortality of active and retired members taken together will usually be somewhat lighter than that shown by a population table for a similar social class, because of the initial exclusion from an employed group of many of the worst lives in the general population. The difference is likely to lessen as age increases.

In addition to these special features, ill-health retirement rates will, of course, vary with age, sex, type of work and social class. The possibility of a gradual change over a period of years should also be considered before the rates to be employed are finally fixed. The latter feature could theoretically be allowed for by the use of rates of retirement dependent upon age attained at the valuation date as well as upon age at retirement, but such a course would rarely be adopted in practice, particularly as the rates appropriate to liabilities emerging in the more distant future must in any event be somewhat uncertain. The normal practice would, therefore, be to employ aggregate rates (dependent upon age attained only) derived from the recent experience, subject to a suitable margin and, if necessary, adjusted to take account of the financial immaturity of the fund.

In the case of a private scheme providing for a full-scale benefit on ill-health retirement, it is important not to under-estimate the risk of earlier retirement, since an undue proportion of ill-health retirements, i.e. an excess of 'actual' over 'expected', would normally create a strain on the fund. A similar position would arise in a money-purchase type of scheme if the full pension purchased to date is allowed on ill-health retirement before the normal pension age.

There are a number of other minor points which must be watched, among which the following may be mentioned.

A test of fitness may be imposed on entry to the service, thus involving some degree of selection of the staff as a class. As there is normally a considerable qualifying period for an ill-health pension, any special initial effects of selection may be expected to have worn off before the qualifying period has expired. Therefore, it is usual to incorporate 'aggregate' ill-health retirement rates in the valuation basis, commencing at the age at which the qualifying period for an ill-health retirement benefit is completed. If the spread of entry ages is narrow, it is usually satisfactory to relate completion of the qualifying period for this purpose to the average entry age. If the spread is wide, it might be necessary to subdivide the members who have not completed the qualifying period into groups of narrow ranges of entry ages and to treat each group separately. The very few members who leave the service for reasons of ill-health before completing the qualifying period can reasonably be regarded as withdrawals for all practical purposes.

Occasionally there is a tendency for an employer to use the ill-health provisions of a pension fund as a vehicle for getting rid of redundant or unsatisfactory employees. Apart from this, the rules of some funds actually permit the retirement of employees upon 'rearrangement of staff', although this may have repercussions on the tax position. It is clearly not practicable to allow for either of these features by the introduction of corresponding retirement rates into the valuation formulae except on an arbitrary basis. The only course which is open to the actuary is to call the attention of the employer to the fact that no allowance for such retirements is made in the valuation, and to point out that the additional liabilities resulting therefrom may lead to a deficiency which will call for special contributions.

7.7. Mortality in service

The benefits payable on death during service vary so much from one fund to another that it is important to consider in each fund whether the death benefit is likely to exceed the average valuation reserve in typical cases and if so, over what ranges of ages and/or divisions of membership. The rates of mortality in service incorporated in the valuation basis should be fixed with due regard to the opinions formed. In the majority of pension funds the benefit payable on death is smaller than the average accumulated reserve, and it is therefore important that the rate of mortality in service should not be over-estimated, since an undue proportion of deaths, i.e. an excess of 'actual' over 'expected', would imply a release of liability.

In widows' and orphans' funds an undue proportion of deaths among the married members, i.e. an excess of 'actual' over 'expected' deaths, would create a strain on the fund. It is, therefore, important not to under-estimate the rate of mortality in service, especially as this factor is normally one of the most important in determining the amount of the reserve. In the special case where a single fund covers both retirement and widows' benefits, the mortality used should be determined by reference to a suitable standard for the combined benefit, i.e. if, as will usually be the case, the liability for the widow's pension is substantially greater than the release of reserve in respect of the pension fund, then care should be taken not to under-estimate the mortality. This course can be adopted since the mortality profits in respect of one benefit can be set off against losses on the other. If, however, there are two separate funds, each of which must stand by itself, this is not feasible. In spite of the apparent inconsistency of using two different mortality standards for the same staff, it may be necessary to do so in these circumstances in order to provide a margin in each fund.

In both types of fund the death rates in service are often found to be very light, since deteriorated lives will be removed from the service by the grant of ill-health pension benefits or, if no such benefit is allowed, by inability to remain in active employment. It will be seen that the degree of incapacity necessary to enable the benefit to be claimed will have important repercussions on the mortality in service. For example, the standard set for the granting of ill-health pensions to female staff is generally less severe than for males, with the result that the mortality rates in service may be very light indeed. Again, the adequacy or otherwise of the scale of ill-health pensions would be reflected in the ill-health retirement rates and, hence, in the rates of mortality experienced by those who remain in the service. In this connexion it may be noted that in the case of a recently established fund where full credit is not given for past service in calculating pensions, the actual benefit payable on ill-health retirement in an average case will for some years be less than that which will ultimately be available and, consequently, members may be reluctant to claim an ill-health pension. A similar situation could arise even in an old-established fund if the pension is calculated on the money purchase or average salary basis where, for example, a sharp rise in wage levels such as has occurred in recent years would for a time render the retirement benefit inadequate in relation to the new wage level. The relatively heavier rates of mortality in service that might result from such special conditions would tend to decrease in the future, quite apart from any general improvement in the longevity of the population as a whole.

Again, as previously indicated, some employers require a good standard of fitness before engaging staff, resulting in mortality rates which are very light at the young ages and of a 'select' nature. The rates of mortality will also tend to reflect the nature of the employment, e.g. a group of workers in a heavy industry would generally show heavier rates than a clerical group, particularly on account of the accident risk. Deaths arising from the latter cause, however, should be treated with caution, as their number may fluctuate widely in successive periods. Any deaths resulting directly from war conditions would normally be excluded from the experience.

7.8. Mortality according to marital status

For the valuation of a widows' fund it will be necessary to consider the mortality of the wives of members and of widows who are in receipt of pensions. Theoretically small differences may be anticipated between the rates of mortality of these two groups, but, in practice, it is usually found that the same mortality table can reasonably be adopted for them both. As in each case death will lead to a reduction in liability, it is important not to over-estimate the rates of mortality. In addition, it may be necessary to treat bachelors, married men and widowers as separate groups, since, owing to the selective effect of marriage, the mortality of married men is normally found to be somewhat lighter than of the other two groups.

7.9. Withdrawal from service

Particular care is always necessary in deciding the allowance to be made for withdrawals both in a valuation and in determining the rates of contribution to be charged. It is especially desirable to determine the withdrawal rates in the light of the experience of the particular fund under consideration, since it will be found that funds which are apparently similar in other respects will vary widely both as to the number of withdrawals and to their distribution according to age and length of service. General factors such as the rate of labour turnover in the particular industry, and local factors such as the availability of alternative employment will affect the rates of withdrawal as between different funds, whilst variations in economic conditions and other similar factors may result in a great degree of variability from time to time in the rates experienced by a particular fund.

In the case of male staffs, the rates of withdrawal are normally found to be at their highest immediately after entry into service. As the employee settles down in his work and acquires more experience and a growing 'stake' in his employment the withdrawal rates decrease steadily. During the early years of service the loss of accrued pension rights on withdrawal probably has little effect, but, as service increases, the potential loss tends to have an increasing weight in discouraging withdrawals.

Similar factors influence the level of withdrawals amongst female staffs, but in this case the rates are principally affected by the incidence of marriage, which is normally a function of age rather than of service. It is usual to employ a composite withdrawal rate to cover such exits from all causes including marriage, but, in doing so, the actuary must always bear in mind that the shape of the underlying curve for the rate of withdrawal on marriage is quite different from that of ordinary withdrawals. In addition, there is perhaps a greater stability in the marriage rate, and so it is practicable to take credit for a higher proportion of the anticipated number of exits if membership terminates on marriage.

As indicated above, ordinary withdrawal rates are generally more affected by duration from entry than by age attained, so that an examination of the probabilities according to age alone will not usually be sufficient to enable suitable rates to be determined, unless entry is confined to a fairly narrow age-group. For example, if entry to the service normally occurs at age 18, a special temporary influx of new entrants between ages 30 and 40 will probably result in a temporary increase in the rates of withdrawal at and above those ages. Similarly, in a fund in which entries normally occur over a wide range of ages, the aggregate withdrawal rate at advanced ages is likely to be considerably in excess of the rate which will apply to the younger members as they pass through those ages. Accordingly, a valuation which introduces an allowance for withdrawals on the basis of such an aggregate rate may seriously overestimate the release of liability arising from this cause.

7.10. Withdrawals: subdivision of data

In order to meet these difficulties, it is helpful to examine the withdrawal rates according to duration in service, the rates being examined separately for two or three entry age-groups unless entry occurs over a very narrow range of ages. A further subdivision into consecutive periods of time may yield valuable information as to the extent of fluctuations with time. If the range of entry ages is fairly wide, it would be theoretically desirable to derive from these subdivided data withdrawal rates which vary both according to age at entry and age attained. In practice, the size of the fund and the financial effect upon the liabilities rarely justify the additional labour involved in such a valuation and, as the financial effect of withdrawals is in any case only of importance at the younger ages where the liability is least, the expedient is often adopted of using rates appropriate to entrants at a weighted mean entry age. The use of the same decrement table to value a relatively few entrants into the service at ages above the normal would tend to be on the stringent side, since the actual withdrawals among such a group are likely to be more numerous than those indicated by a table appropriate to entrants at the younger ages.

In this discussion, it has been assumed that we are dealing with the normal type of fund where the benefit payable on withdrawal is almost invariably an amount equal to the member's own contributions with or without interest, the fund being left with an amount equal to the employer's accumulated contributions. Consequently, any withdrawals in excess of those allowed for in the valuation will, normally, give rise to a profit, but, if actual withdrawals fall short of the expectation, the fund will fail to realize an anticipated gain taken credit for in advance. Unless, therefore, the withdrawal rates during the period examined have been particularly steady and no change in general conditions is anticipated, the rates adopted should be well within those shown by the recent experience of normal entrants.

7.11. Withdrawal: special circumstances

The actuary should watch for any special circumstances which may have led to an abnormal number of withdrawals. For example, a reorganization or reduction of staff may result in a number of special withdrawals which would normally be excluded before the calculation of the withdrawal rates. Special treatment may also be necessary when the staff is expanding at a relatively rapid rate. This may result in an unusually wide range of entry ages, or perhaps, as a result of a relaxation of standards, it may be accompanied by a general increase in the withdrawal rates measured according to duration from entry. It would, however, be unwise to give too much weight to a possible temporary increase of this nature until it had been confirmed by the experience of a more normal period. Other special conditions, such as a general increase in the level of unemployment or the operation of war-time and similar restrictions on the movement of labour, may have upset the normal course of withdrawal rates. Apart from such temporary circumstances, there may be special reasons in particular funds leading to withdrawals of a different character. An example of this is the transfer provisions of funds established under the Local Government Superannuation Acts. Members of these funds who withdraw upon transfer to another local authority are entitled to have a transfer value paid from the original fund to that of the new authority and to receive a corresponding credit in the new fund for past service. A similar situation may arise where one employer maintains separate funds for employees of the officer and workman type, if transfer may take place from workman to officer status. In such cases it will usually be sufficient to exclude transfers before deriving the withdrawal rates; if the transfer value is appreciably less than the reserve held under the valuation a proportion of transfers could be included with withdrawals for the purpose of determining the withdrawal rates.

7.12. Withdrawals: widows' and orphans' funds

The general considerations which affect the determination of withdrawal rates for widows' and orphans' funds are similar to those which apply in the case of pension funds. The financial effect of withdrawals is, however, generally less, as, relatively speaking, the reserves held are smaller. There is, however, one particular type of withdrawal which should be specially considered, namely, the withdrawal of the more mobile unmarried members who may be more likely to accept a change of employment involving either a change of residence or some loss of security. The reserve for such members is less than the average, and may even involve hidden negative values (i.e. cases where the value of future contributions is greater than the value of future benefits). Withdrawals may, therefore, in effect, involve the loss of a potential profit, in which case some allowance for possible future withdrawals of such members should be made.

CHAPTER 8

ACTUARIAL STRUCTURE OF FUNDS (CONTINUED)

8.1. Interest

The rate of interest assumed in the calculation of contributions to and in the valuation of a pension fund or a widows' and orphans' fund is of prime importance in view of the long period which normally elapses between the payment of contributions and the receipt of the benefits; it should therefore be conservatively estimated. Even where part of the retirement benefit is receivable in the form of a lump sum, interest is still of paramount importance, although the average period during which resources will be accumulating at interest is not so great as when the whole of the benefit takes the form of a pension.

A full discussion of the considerations which affect the valuation rate of interest to be assumed will be found in Chapter 17.

8.2. Salary scales

When the benefits and contributions payable under a pension scheme or a widows' and orphans' scheme are calculated with reference to the rate of earnings of the individual members, it is necessary to obtain estimates of the future progress of such earnings. The methods to be adopted in making these estimates by the use of salary scales are fully discussed in Chapter 13, but in reading the intervening chapters the following introduction to the subject may be helpful.

Three possible methods of incorporating a scale of earnings in the calculations have been suggested. These may be described as follows:

(i) *The absolute scale method*: a fixed scale is used which it is assumed will apply on the average to all members as they pass through successive years of age.

(ii) *The relative scale method*: a scale is used to measure the ratio of future earnings to present earnings.

(iii) *The scale of increments method*: a scale is used which it is assumed will represent the average future increment of earnings in each year of age.

Thus, under method (i), if s_x represents the scale salary at age x, n_x members now aged x will be assumed to receive, in total, salaries of $n_x s_x$, and the estimate of their aggregate future salaries t years hence, *if all survive*, is

$$n_x s_{x+t}.$$

Under method (ii), for n_x members with salaries now aggregating ΣS_x, the corresponding forecast of the total salaries t years hence is

$$\Sigma S_x s_{x+t}/s_x.$$

Under method (iii), if Δs_x represents the scale increment receivable between age x and $(x+1)$, the corresponding forecast of salaries after t years is

$$\Sigma S_x + n_x \sum_{r=0}^{t-1} \Delta s_{x+r}.$$

It should be noted that, under each method, the forecast does not relate to individual salaries but to the aggregate salaries of a group of members. The salary career of particular members will, in general, diverge from the forecast, but the estimate will nevertheless be accurate if the average salary per member coincides with the forecast according to the scale. Again, it is the normal practice to employ a single scale which is applied to the whole of the present membership. Theoretically, separate forecast scales could be employed for different present age groups of the membership, or even for each individual present age, but this would involve greatly increased labour in the construction of the valuation factors and, except in special circumstances, would scarcely justify the theoretical increase in precision, particularly when it is borne in mind that the forecast of salaries must inevitably be speculative in practice.* These three methods of forecasting average earnings are illustrated numerically in Table 8.1.

* See, however, the paper on Pension Funds in *T.F.A.* vol. XIX, by Heywood and Marples, in which a development of the normal salary-scale technique is mentioned; the method there outlined would, in effect, enable different scales to be employed for each attained age or age-group at the valuation date by the use of two sets of factors only, one incorporating a normal salary scale and the other a constant salary scale. The effective scales of increase of salary thus allowed for as regards the members at different attained ages would of course all be related to the same normal salary scale.

The first method is only suitable in special circumstances. It is open to the objection that it discards information available as to variations between the actual average earnings and the salary scale employed, and it is therefore only suitable where such variations are sufficiently small to be negligible, as may occur, for example, in the case of a group of workmen.

TABLE 8.1

(A) Members aged 30 with average salary £290.
(B) Members aged 40 with average salary £370.

Attained age	Salary scale assumed		
	Absolute scale	Relative scale	Increments scale
	(i)	(ii)	(iii)
30	300	1·00	
40	360	1·20	Average 6·0 p.a. 30–40
50	405	1·35	Average 4·5 p.a. 40–50
60	435	1·45	Average 3·0 p.a. 50–60

Attained age	Estimated average earnings					
	Method (i)		Method (ii)		Method (iii)	
	A	B	A	B	A	B
30	300	—	290	—	290	—
40	360	360	348	370	350	370
50	405	405	391	416	395	415
60	435	435	421	447	425	445

The other two methods both take full and direct account of the information available regarding the current level of earnings of each individual member of the scheme. Accordingly, they are strictly accurate so far as such current earnings are concerned, and only introduce estimates in order to deal with future increments. As a result, the second and third methods give successive adjustments from one valuation to the next for any differences between the actual salaries and the previously estimated amounts as such differences emerge.

Under the first method, no distinction in the forecast of future salaries would be made for a group of members if the present average level of salaries were below normal as measured by the scale. Under the second method, a group for which the average salary career to date had been subnormal would be assumed to fall progressively further below the average in the future. Under the third method the difference between the average present level of salaries for the group and the normal level for the same age would be assumed to persist unchanged in the future as the group advanced in age. The reverse position would of course hold in the case of a group whose average salary career to date had been above the normal. The second method therefore seems to accord most closely with general experience in distinguishing between members who have in the past progressed less or more rapidly than the average; if anything, the future divergence in salaries may indeed be expected to be somewhat greater than that allowed for by this method, but on the whole the assumptions underlying the second method are thought to give the best approximation to actual experience that can be achieved in practice.

The second method (i.e. the relative scale method) is most commonly used, both for the reasons given in the preceding paragraph and because it lends itself to a valuation procedure under which present salaries and future salary increments are treated together. The third method, on the other hand, involves the evaluation of benefits and contributions separately in respect of present salaries and future increments.

Although the majority of salary scale problems can be handled by one of the methods above indicated, the student should remember that each fund must be considered with an open mind, and that cases may arise for which special methods must be adopted.

8.3. Shape of salary scale

Whatever method is used in incorporating the salary scale in the calculations, it will generally be found that the actual scale will conform to one of two common types.

The first type is commonly found amongst a clerical or administrative staff whose earnings commence at a low level. Individual salaries increase fairly rapidly up to about age 35 or 40, and more slowly for another 10 or 20 years. In addition, a few members may attain very large incomes as high-salaried officials. The salary-scale curve for a staff of this type would be parabolic in shape, increasing rapidly in the early years and tending to level off in the latter half of the working lifetime. It may be conveniently referred to as an *officers' scale*.

Among manual workers, on the other hand, the average wage tends to reach a figure equal to the full adult wage at quite a young age, say 25, after a series of fairly rapid increases. There would be little variation thereafter, and the only increases in earnings which would normally occur would arise upon promotion to the position of foreman or overseer. These promotions would be relatively infrequent and would have only a small effect upon the scale of average salaries. The curve representing the salary scale in such a case would thus rise rapidly for a few years but, after age 25 or thereabouts, would be almost level. Such a scale may be referred to as a *workmen's scale*.

It will be apparent that, for either type of scale, the actual level of the figures employed is immaterial if the scale adopted is a 'relative' scale. Some actuaries make use of figures which represent the actual level of earnings at successive ages, and in this case the practical expedient is usually adopted of dividing the earnings by 100 in order to reduce the magnitude of the figures involved in the commutation columns. A more satisfactory alternative, which underlines the point that the scale is not intended to represent average actual salaries, is to use a scale of ratios developed from a radix, e.g. a radix of unity at age 20. It will be noted that this is the second method indicated in the example in Table 8.1, and used in the *Actuarial Tables for Examination Purposes*.

8.4. Marriage status of members

The various factors so far discussed enter into the valuation of a pension fund. In the case of a widows' and orphans' fund all these factors may come into operation and, in addition, certain others arise. Thus, for the valuation of a widow's pension commencing on the death of a member, the actuary must take account of (*a*) the probability that the member may be married at the date of his death and (*b*) the likely age of his widow at that time. Where orphans' benefits have to be valued allowance must be made for the probability of children surviving the member and for the ages of such children. In practice, two methods are normally employed which are described fully in Chapters 14, 15 and 16.

CHAPTER 9

THE VALUATION OF AN EXISTING FUND: PREPARATORY WORK

9.1. Introduction

It is now proposed to consider in detail the procedure to be followed in the valuation of an existing fund and the formulae which will be used for that purpose. It may appear to be reversing the natural order of things to discuss the valuation of an existing fund before dealing with the establishment of a new fund and the consideration of scales of benefits and contributions. The latter, however, is a difficult matter calling for considerable judgement, in which the experience gained in the valuation of an existing fund should be very helpful.

Throughout the ensuing chapters it will be necessary to emphasize the need for accuracy and care in the technical process of valuation. The results of such a valuation however cannot, in any sense, be regarded as exact. It is an estimate of future progress which events may or may not prove to have been approximately correct and which must stand or fall by the soundness of the underlying assumptions based largely on the considerations discussed in the preceding chapters. It cannot, therefore, be repeated too often that, whilst every care must be taken to ensure that the processes of valuation are carried out accurately, the purpose of such care is to ensure that the basic assumptions are correctly translated into numerical form. This numerical accuracy introduces into the results no greater degree of exactitude than is justified by the underlying assumptions. On the other hand, any unjustified approximations which may be introduced into the technical processes would be open to the serious objection that they might largely vitiate the care and judgement given to the choice of suitable bases. This consideration should not, however, lead the student to an elaboration of formulae which is not justified by either the financial importance of the benefit to be valued or the limitations of the data available.

It has already been indicated that individual funds may vary widely in respect to the nature and details of the benefits which they provide, and of the financial arrangements for meeting the cost of such benefits. The basic principles of valuation are, however, the same for all funds. These principles will be discussed in this chapter, and consideration of minor variations will be left to a later stage. Accordingly, this chapter is mainly concerned with a straightforward type of scheme providing benefits, etc., on the lines outlined in the next paragraph.

9.2. Specimen scheme of pensions

Let it be assumed that the scheme is compulsory and applies to the permanent clerical and administrative staff of a large industrial company (for staff employed at the date of inception, however, membership would be optional). The essentials of the scheme are as follows:

I. Retirement benefit: a pension of $\frac{1}{60}$th of the pensionable earnings for each completed year of pensionable service. Pensionable service is defined as the full period of membership of the fund plus one-half of the period of service rendered with the employer before the inception of the fund. Pensionable earnings are defined as the average annual earnings (excluding overtime payments) for the last five years immediately preceding retirement. The maximum pension allowed is two-thirds of such average earnings.

II. Retirement conditions: pensions are granted provided 10 years' service has been rendered,

   (a) on breakdown in health of sufficient severity to render the member (in the opinion of the employer) permanently incapable of working;

   (b) on the attainment of age 65, when retirement is compulsory.

III. Contributions:

By the members: a fixed percentage of their earnings (excluding overtime payments), varying with age at entry into service.

By the employer:

(a) a normal contribution of an amount equal to the contributions paid by the members; and

(b) a yearly contribution of a fixed amount payable for a limited number of years. The latter contribution would represent the deficiency contribution assessed when the fund was established as the amount required to liquidate the initial liability which arose owing to (i) the granting of back-service pensions to existing employees and (ii) the fact that they were then permitted to contribute for future service benefits at the contribution rates appropriate to their ages at entry into service instead of into the fund.

IV. Subsidiary benefits:

(a) On the death of a member in service, a payment equal in amount to the member's own contributions, with $2\frac{1}{2}\%$ compound interest thereon to the date of death.

(b) On death as a pensioner within five years after retirement, the pension to be continued to the member's widow or other dependant until five years' payments in all have been made.

(c) On voluntary withdrawal from the service before becoming entitled to a pension or on ill-health retirement before completion of 10 years' service, a payment equal to the contributions paid by the member, without interest.

V. Expenses: to be met by the employer.

9.3. Preliminary inquiries

Before any other steps are taken in regard to the valuation of such a fund, careful preliminary inquiries must be made in order to secure all available information about the past history of the fund and its present position. The following are points to which particular attention should be given.

A copy of the trust deed and of the rules, including all amendments to date, which govern the operation of the fund should first be obtained. These must be studied carefully, and if there is any ambiguity in the provisions with regard to benefits and contributions this must be resolved, attention being given if necessary to the interpretation adopted in practice. The general outline of the method of valuation must be carefully considered in the light of these documents before any decision is reached upon the particulars which will be required in regard to each member and pensioner, and the form in which this information is to be supplied. Any decisions made at this stage must, however, be regarded as only tentative, as it is possible that the proposed valuation method may have to be modified when the full data become available.

At the same time, copies of the fund accounts, including balance sheets, covering the period since the last valuation, and a list of the investments held by the fund upon the valuation date should be obtained. The information contained in these documents is essential to the determination of the valuation rate of interest. This is a matter which requires the most careful judgement. The considerations which influence this decision are too numerous to be dealt with here, but a full discussion will be found in Chapter 17.

The accounts will give a preliminary indication of the extent of the movements in the fund in regard to withdrawals, deaths, retirements, etc., and, at a later stage, can be used as a check on the information furnished to the actuary in regard to such movements. A similar check can be placed on the valuation data in regard to the total contributions payable by members and the amount of pensions payable to retired members.

The actuary should also call for copies of the preceding valuation report or, if this is the first valuation, of the reports submitted in connexion with the inauguration of the fund. In addition, it would be helpful to have copies of earlier valuation reports if they are available.

9.4. Valuation data

The next step is to obtain from the employer full details of the present membership of the fund and of employees who have been members of the fund at any time during the period over which it is proposed to investigate the experience. This period must be fixed in the light of the size of the fund and of the subdivision of data which will be necessary. It should be long enough to give sufficient data to enable satisfactory rates of decrement to be deduced, but short enough to avoid the introduction of heterogeneity arising from the employment of data associated with a past period during which the conditions in which the fund was operating may have been markedly different. The period selected would not normally exceed 10 years, as the additional data introduced by using a longer period is unlikely to be suitable owing to changes in the experience. Special care is necessary where the period includes an abnormal occurrence such as a war, which may render it extremely difficult to obtain rates which could be applied with any confidence in estimating future liabilities. In such circumstances it may prove necessary to reject in whole or in part the recent past experience of the fund, and to adopt rates determined in the light of the earlier experience of that fund or of some other fund, modified to allow for such information in regard to present circumstances as is available. Again, the experience of a given period may be abnormal for reasons entirely due to the domestic circumstances of the fund, and the results of the investigation should be carefully watched for any abnormalities of this kind arising from causes of which the actuary would not be aware without explanations from the employer.

9.5. Valuation record cards

If the employer is already maintaining an individual valuation card record of the members, the actuary should call for specimens and consider whether these can be utilized for the valuation. Otherwise the actuary should design a card, but, in any case, it will usually be desirable before reaching a final decision on the lay-out of the card to consider the form in which the internal accounts and records of the fund are kept, so as to facilitate the transfer of the particulars to the actuarial cards.

The design of the card must be carefully considered in relation to each individual fund. The card illustrated on pages 70 and 71 should prove suitable for the scheme outlined in § 9.2. It will be noted that, in addition to spaces for the insertion by the employer of full particulars in regard to each member, the card also contains spaces for the actuary to insert the various ages and other particulars required in carrying out the valuation.

When the form of card is decided upon and forwarded to the employer, it must be accompanied by precise instructions in regard to its completion. It must be realized that the cards may be prepared by clerks who have no technical knowledge of the requirements of an actuarial valuation. If, therefore, there are any ambiguities or obscurities in the actuary's instructions it is possible that the cards will not be completed in accordance with his intentions. Errors of this kind can cause trouble and delay, especially if they are not detected until a considerable amount of work has been done upon the valuation. For this reason, it will usually be found very well worth while to discuss the instructions in detail with the officials of the fund at the outset to ensure that their purport is clearly understood.

9.6. Subdivisions of data

Although no final decision can be taken with regard to the subdivision of data until after an examination of the information furnished on the cards, the valuation card should be drafted in a form which will facilitate such subdivision. The following notes must be read in conjunction with the preceding chapters, which have already indicated the types of subdivision which are likely to be necessary.

The experience must, of course, be investigated in reasonably homogeneous groups, and the first division which is almost invariably necessary is according to sex, since males and females usually show widely differing experiences in regard to most of the decremental rates as well as salary scales and mortality after retirement. It is usually desirable to separate manual from clerical grades and, possibly, also outside staff from inside staff and technical from non-technical staff. Apart from differences in salary scales, these grades generally show differences in withdrawal and retirement experience, and may differ in respect to mortality also.

As in other fields of his work, the actuary will be faced with the problem of how far to carry this process of subdivision. The ideal would, of course, be to examine separately the experience of each group which exhibited or was likely to exhibit distinctive characteristics as regards one or more of the decremental rates or the salary scale. In practice, the extent of subdivision will depend upon

SPECIMEN CARD

FRONT OF CARD

Name of fund				
Name			Sex	
Grade	Ref. no.		Cont. rate %	

Date	D.	M.	Y.	For actuary
Born				
Entered service				
Entered fund				
Ceased to contribute				
Cause of cessation				
Amount paid on death/ withdrawal: £ : :				
PENSIONER—Amount p.a. £ : :				
Date of commencement				
Date of death				
Remarks:				

BACK OF CARD

	Name					Ref. no.			
Year	Salary at end of year	Contributions paid in year			Year	Salary at end of year	Contributions paid in year		
	£.	£	s.	d.		£	£	s.	d.
Total	—				Total	—			
Total	—				Total	—			
Total	—				Total	—			

the volume of data available, since, if the data in each subgroup are too scanty, the results will be unreliable. It is not practicable to meet the latter difficulty by extending the investigation over a longer period, since, as already indicated, heterogeneity can be introduced as readily by an extension in time as by an extension of the area over which the investigation is carried out.

The use of heterogeneous data involves the tacit assumption that the composition of the membership of the fund as regards the proportions of the different subgroups has always been the same and that this condition will hold in the future. If this assumption is not valid, differences in the future rates as measured against the past experience will arise even when there is no variation in the underlying facts. For example, in the case of a fund which covers both male and female members, the combined withdrawal rate will fall if the proportion of females falls, or even if the proportion at the normal marriage ages falls owing to a change in age distribution. A variation of this type in the combined rate may not be significant of any change in the underlying rates.

If the actuary is faced with the problem of whether or not to combine such groups of members owing to paucity of data, he may, in order to avoid the difficulty mentioned in the preceding paragraph, adopt rates derived from other sources which exhibit the special features which he wishes to take into account. Before doing so, he must, of course, satisfy himself that there is a sufficient similarity in conditions to suggest that the rates adopted are suitable for the purpose in hand. Although action on these lines is perforce frequently taken, it must be remembered that it involves an inherent danger, for each fund is in practice, as well as in theory, a law unto itself. The considerations set out in the preceding three chapters must, therefore, be given the fullest possible weight before a decision is reached. Before finally adopting the rates, the actuary should of course satisfy himself, by a comparison of actual and expected deaths, retirements, etc., that the limited data of the fund itself are reasonably consistent with the rates adopted.

It will be assumed that in the case of the fund now under consideration the data are sufficiently voluminous to permit of a full investigation which will be discussed in detail in the following chapter.

CHAPTER 10

THE VALUATION OF AN EXISTING FUND: FORMULAE AND NUMERICAL WORK

10.1. The investigation of the experience

To some extent it will now be necessary to recapitulate what has appeared in earlier chapters, but this course has been adopted in order to show the processes of valuation in true perspective. As already indicated, for the purpose in view it is necessary to derive a multiple-decrement service table which will be developed from probability ratios (not rates in the strict sense) of secession from the service, age by age, on account of withdrawal, death and retirement on pension, whether as a result of ill-health or on attainment of the limiting age. The crude probability ratios which will be obtained for each subdivision (namely, withdrawals, deaths, ill-health and normal retirements) will, in each case, be a ratio of the number of exits during the year of age x to $x+1$ to the number of members entering that year of age adjusted for movements (E_x). As the student will realize from previous consideration of ratios of this type, these probabilities are, strictly speaking, interdependent, and if, in the process of graduation and adjustment, it becomes necessary to reduce any one probability substantially, it is theoretically necessary to make corresponding adjustments in the other probabilities. Except in the case of withdrawal rates at the young ages, however, the decremental rates are usually so small at the ages concerned that the adjustments would be negligible in effect and may be ignored in practice. This difficulty can be met by the use of central rates, and some actuaries prefer to undertake the small amount of additional work involved.

10.2. Derivation of rates: active members

The method normally adopted for the construction of the service table for each separate subdivision of active members may now be briefly described.

In determining the ages, it is usually found most convenient to take for *age at entry* the age nearest birthday at the date of entry. In the case of the members on the active list at the beginning of the period the then age nearest birthday should be taken, and similarly for members on the active list at the end of the period.

To obtain the *age at exit* in the case of members who were on the active list at the beginning of the period, the subsequent curtate duration must be added to the age at the beginning of the period; in the case of members who entered during the period, the curtate duration since entry must be added to the age at entry.

The various ages will be inserted in the appropriate positions on the valuation cards, which will then be sorted and tabulated to give the following data for each age of member:

b_x Survivors on the active list brought under observation from antecedent entrants.

n_x New entrants during the period.

w_x Withdrawals during the period.

d_x Deaths during the period.

i_x Retirements on pension during the period owing to ill-health.

r_x Retirements on pension during the period on attaining pensionable age.

e_x Existing on the active list at the close of the period.

The *Exposed to Risk* at each age is derived from these data by the formula

$$E_x = E_{x-1} + (b_x + n_x) - (w_{x-1} + d_{x-1} + i_{x-1} + r_{x-1}) - e_x.$$

The decremental probability ratios are then calculated by the formulae

$$\frac{w_x}{E_x}, \quad \frac{d_x}{E_x}, \quad \text{etc.}$$

10.3. Derivation of rates: pensioners

Similar methods will be adopted for deriving the rates of mortality of pensioners, except that, normally, the only cause of decrement is death. The formula for the *Exposed to Risk* for the probability of death for pensioners who retire on attaining the limiting age will, therefore, be similar to that given for active members, with the exclusion of other causes of exit.

In the case of pensioners who retire owing to ill-health the methods will be similar, except that, as already indicated, it is desirable, if possible, to subdivide the data according to broad groups of retirement age and duration since retirement, in order to obtain the results in a select form which will exhibit the effect of duration since retirement upon the rates of mortality. The size of the age groups to be investigated will, of course, be dependent upon the volume of data available. For members who retire between the ages $x - t$ and $x + t$ (say $\bar{x}$), the formula for the *Exposed to Risk* between durations n and $n + 1$ will be

$$E_{\bar{x}+n} = E_{\bar{x}+n-1} + (b_{\bar{x}+n} + n_{\bar{x}+n}) - (d_{\bar{x}+n-1} + e_{\bar{x}+n}) \; .$$

The select investigation would be continued up to a sufficiently high attained age for the effect of selection at retirement to have worn off. From that point the investigation would be carried out according to age attained only, in exactly the same way as for age retirements. In practice such an investigation would only be justified if the volume of data were sufficiently extensive.

10.4. Graduation

In the case of the majority of pension funds met in practice, the crude rates will show wide fluctuation from age to age owing to the small amount of data available, and considerable care will be necessary in graduation to obtain the rates for actual use in valuation. Before graduation it may be desirable to group the data in quinquennial age groups, whilst graduation by a graphical method will normally be adequate for the purpose in view. It will be helpful at this stage to recapitulate the main points which must be watched in the process of graduation.

Withdrawal rates are likely to be heavy shortly after entry age and to decrease rapidly with duration unless there are special causes of withdrawal such as marriage of female staff or transfers to other grades. If the range of entry ages is wide, care must be taken to ensure that the graduated rates are not too high owing to the effect of the inclusion of new entrants in deriving aggregate rates. In such cases, if the data are sufficiently extensive, it may be necessary to carry out some modified form of select investigation. If any special exits such as transfers are not to be included in the decremental rates, the *Exposed to Risk* formula should be modified so as to give them only half a year's exposure on the average.

Ill-health retirements should not be under-estimated, as this would involve a strain on the fund which may be substantial. The qualifying period of 10 years may, where the range of entry ages is wide, affect the rates of ill-health retirement brought out by the normal *Exposed to Risk* formula and, if necessary, an adjustment for this should be made.

Rates of mortality both in service and after retirement, on the other hand, should not be over-estimated, since each death will involve an appreciable release of liability. Care should be taken to see that the rates of mortality in service are consistent with the rates for ill-health pensioners, and that these rates, taken together, give a reasonable measure of the mortality expected for the particular class of lives involved.

10.5. The service table

When the actuary is satisfied that he has obtained series of decremental rates which represent as satisfactorily as possible the experience of the fund, adjusted if necessary for anticipated future trends, they should be compared with the rates used at the preceding valuation if these are available. If the differences between the two sets of rates are only small and do not suggest a definite change in the underlying conditions, it will not be necessary to make any change in the valuation basis. If, however, the new rates show marked variations from the old, it will be necessary to decide whether this is due to temporary fluctuations arising from accidental causes or special conditions operating during the inter-valuation period, or whether there has been a definite change in the forces operating within the fund which may be expected to continue in future years. If the latter conclusion is reached, it will be necessary to prepare a new service table by the formula

$$l_{x+1} = l_x - (w_x + d_x + i_x + r_x),$$

where l_x = the number of active members surviving in service at exact age x; w_x = the number of members withdrawing in the year of age x to $x+1$ out of l_x in service at age x; with corresponding meanings for d_x, etc. A suitable radix would be adopted for l_x at the earliest entry age.

10.6. Salary scale

The retirement pension in the illustrative fund is based upon the earnings of the last five years of service and, accordingly, it is of particular importance that the salary scale adopted should represent as closely as practicable the anticipated future course of salaries. The limitations which must apply to any forecast of this kind have already been indicated, and a full discussion of the methods which can be adopted to derive a suitable salary scale will be found in Chapter 13. The formulae given in this chapter will incorporate a salary scale of the relative type (see §8.2).

The data supplied by the officials of the fund will usually give the actual earnings of each member during the 12 months preceding the valuation date, although in some cases the rate of salary on the valuation date may be given. The valuation formulae incorporate a salary scale s_x under which the following relationship holds:

s_{x+t}/s_x = the ratio of the average earnings in the year of age $x+t$ to $x+t+1$ to the average earnings in the year of age x to $x+1$.

Accordingly, it will be necessary to include in the valuation formulae ratios of the form s_{x+t}/s_{x-1}, $s_{x+t}/s_{x-\frac{1}{2}}$ or s_{x+t}/s_x, according to whether the earnings given are for the year preceding the valuation date, the rate of earnings on the valuation date, or the rate of earnings expected in the year following the valuation date.

In addition, enquiry should be made as to the dates upon which salary increases are given. If this reveals that the assumption implicit in the above formula (viz. that increases are evenly spread over the year of age) is invalid an appropriate adjustment may be desirable.

10.7. Scheduling of data

The next step will be to summarize the valuation data in schedule form. A draft heading for schedules which would be suitable for the fund under consideration (see §9.2) is as follows:

Schedule for males/females

Valuation date..................

Salary grade............

Member's ref. no.	Valuation age	Effective duration to valuation date	Contribution rate %	Annual salary current valuation date	Total member's contribution to date	$(3) \times (5)$	$\dfrac{(4) \times (5)}{100}$
(1)	(2)	(3)	(4)	(5)	(6)	(7)	(8)

Note. The members in each sex and salary grade would be scheduled in order of valuation age, subsorted within each group under effective duration or contribution rate, according to which is thought to be more convenient. The effective duration to the valuation date would make allowance where appropriate for any non-contributory service prior to entry to the fund, and for the fact that in the specimen fund being considered only the curtate period of effective service ranks for pension purposes. Totals for each age of columns (5), (6), (7), (8) would be required for valuation purposes.

10.8. Formulae and commutation columns

The algebraical construction of the formulae required for the evaluation of pensions and similar benefits has been previously studied. When practical work in the subject is commenced, however, it is of particular importance to keep in mind the arithmetical processes involved in their application. It is frequently possible to develop two formulae which are of equal accuracy algebraically, but one of which may be quite unsuitable owing to practical difficulties of application. Before deciding to adopt any particular formula, therefore, it must be carefully considered in the light of the following principles, which are of general application:

(*a*) it must, of course, interpret the valuation bases adopted as accurately as possible;

(*b*) the use of averages which combine elements which may vary independently can only be justified if an alternative formula which introduces those elements independently would be too complex to be warranted by the size of the fund, the statistical basis underlying the calculations, or the relative importance of the particular item being valued;

(c) it must be capable of expression in the form of commutation functions so as to produce factors for the full range of ages by a straightforward process;

(d) the tabulations required should be kept to a minimum, e.g. if the required degree of accuracy can be achieved by the use of formulae which call for classifications according to age attained only, one which demands tabulation of the data by both age attained and age at entry should not be used.

10.9. System of notation

The International Actuarial Notation published in July 1946 does not cover the full range of symbols required for the valuation of pension funds; the notation used for this purpose is constructed in accordance with the principles set out below. It will be seen that these are analogous to the general principles enunciated in the International Notation for general actuarial purposes.

(a) To each fundamental symbolic letter are attached signs and letters each having its own signification.

(b) The lower space to the left is reserved for signs indicating the age or status at which a title to a payment first began to accrue, e.g. the age at entry where it is necessary to evolve functions dependent upon both entry age and age attained.

(c) The lower space to the right is reserved for signs indicating the age or ages at the date under consideration.

(d) The upper space to the right is reserved for signs indicating (i) the conditions the satisfaction of which results immediately in a benefit becoming payable; and (ii) the type of benefit (if other than a single cash payment), e.g. the letters *ra* would be used to indicate that the benefit commenced immediately on retirement and was in the form of an annuity.

(e) The upper space to the left is reserved for signs indicating factors entering into the calculation of the amount of a payment (e.g. *s* for salary or *j* where the payment includes interest accumulations), or indicating a status necessary to qualify for a payment (e.g. h where only married men can qualify for benefit).

(f) The only consideration of periodicity normally arising is where payments, etc., are made momently, which is indicated by placing a bar over the principal letter.*

(g) The final factors are expressed in the form of a ratio of commutation functions, unless it is necessary to use a single letter to express such a ratio for the purpose of incorporating it in further commutation functions.

It will have been observed that in dealing with multiple decrement tables the expressions l_x, d_x, etc., have been used instead of $(al)_x$, $(ad)_x$, etc. This is in accordance with the well-established custom in practical work on pension and widows' and orphans' funds. For the purposes in view, confusion between multiple-decrement and single-decrement tables is unlikely to arise, whilst the use of two letters for a single concept might lead to confusion in the consideration of complex monetary functions.

10.10. Valuation formulae

The general types of formulae which are required for the valuation of pension and similar benefits will already have been studied. It is important to realize that, in dealing with this type of benefit, all formulae should be derived from first principles, since otherwise there is a serious risk of error creeping in; the 'look' of the formulae can, in fact, be very misleading. The number of possible variations met in practice is such that it is virtually impossible to adopt a set of symbols for the valuation factors each of which has a single meaning. For this reason, the standard notation employed in this volume for pension funds does not include any symbols representing the actual valuation factors, these being expressed simply as the ratios of commutation columns. In the paragraphs that follow, the full

---

* A bar indicates, when placed over functions involving D_x or N_x, that payments are made continuously, when placed over M_x that the benefit comes into force continuously during the year of age x to $x+1$, and when placed over R_x that the benefit increases continuously. Symbolically, the meaning of the bar may be defined by the relationship $\bar{F}_x = \int_0^1 F_{x+t} \cdot dt$. This use of the bar is in accordance with the International Actuarial Notation in the case of D_x and N_x, but not in the case of M_x or R_x.

derivation of the formulae from first principles is given in a small number of specimen cases only.

In life assurance work, the basic functions for the values of assurances and annuities are normally calculated for a benefit of 1 payable at the end of the year of death or the value of an annuity of 1 per annum payable yearly, and the values of benefits payable at other times and intervals are derived therefrom. In pension fund work, on the other hand, it is usual to proceed in the first place on the assumption that all benefits are paid immediately on the happening of the event which gives rise to the payment, i.e. on the average in the middle of the year. It is also assumed that contributions which are generally payable at short intervals are due on the average in the middle of the year; for practical purposes this is equivalent to the assumption that payments are made continuously. It will be noted that, unless the contrary is expressly stated, all the formulae given in this book are based on these assumptions which are more convenient in practical work and are satisfactory for the purpose, since the necessity to derive therefrom the values of benefits payable at other times or intervals does not normally arise. Modifications to the formulae should be made if necessary to give effect to variations in any particular case. The formulae given in the ensuing sections are those required for the fund briefly outlined in §9.2.

10.11. Valuation of pension benefits: past-service pension

When the pension benefit is based upon salaries earned in the final years of service the valuation formulae lead conveniently to a subdivision of the pension benefits into those which are granted in respect of service prior to the valuation date (referred to as past-service pensions) and those in respect of service subsequent to the valuation date (future-service pensions).

The formula for the valuation of past-service pension may be derived as follows.

The value on retirement at age $y(y<65)$ of a pension of 1 per annum guaranteed for 5 years is

$$\bar{a}_{\overline{5}|} + \frac{D_{y+5}}{D_y}\bar{a}_{y+5} = \bar{a}_y',$$

based upon the table appropriate to ill-health pensioners.

The value at age x of a pension of 1 per annum commencing upon retirement owing to breakdown in health at age y last birthday is

$$v^{y-x+\frac{1}{2}}\frac{i_y}{l_x}\bar{a}'_{y+\frac{1}{2}},$$

which may be written as

$$\frac{C_y^{ia}}{D_x},$$

where

$$C_y^{ia}=v^{y+\frac{1}{2}}i_y\bar{a}'_{y+\frac{1}{2}} \quad \text{and} \quad D_x=v^x l_x.$$

The *relative* earnings for the year of age y to $(y+1)$ according to the salary scale are s_y and, accordingly, the corresponding pensionable earnings (average salary for the five years immediately preceding retirement) in the event of retirement at exact age y will be

$$\tfrac{1}{5}(s_{y-5}+\ldots+s_{y-2}+s_{y-1})=z_y.$$

The pension receivable on retirement at age y last birthday, in respect of n completed years of service, all ranking for full pension, prior to age x, by a member aged x on the valuation date whose earnings for the year of age x to $(x+1)$ amount to S_x will, accordingly, be on the average

$$\frac{n}{60}S_x\frac{z_{y+\frac{1}{2}}}{s_x}.$$

The present value of that pension will be

$$\frac{n}{60}S_x\frac{z_{y+\frac{1}{2}}}{s_x}\frac{C_y^{ia}}{D_x}=\frac{n}{60}S_x\frac{{}^zC_y^{ia}}{s_xD_x}, \quad \text{say.}$$

The value of a pension to be awarded upon breakdown in health at any time after age x can then be obtained by summation from the preceding formula and may be written as

$$\frac{n}{60}S_x\frac{{}^zM_x^{ia}}{{}^sD_x},$$

where

$${}^zM_x^{ia}=\sum_{t=0}^{64-x}{}^zC_{x+t}^{ia} \quad \text{and} \quad {}^sD_x=s_xD_x.$$

For the whole group of members scheduled at age x at the valuation date, the value of the past-service pension would thus be

$$\frac{(\Sigma nS_x)}{60}\frac{{}^zM_x^{ia}}{{}^sD_x},$$

the summation extending over the whole group of members aged x.

(*Note.* In computing n, allowance would, of course, be made for one-half of any period of service prior to entry to the fund ranking for pension purposes.)

By similar reasoning, the corresponding formula for the value of the past-service pension arising upon compulsory retirement at exact age 65 may be written as

$$\frac{(\Sigma n S_x)}{60} \frac{z_{65} D_{65} \cdot \bar{a}'_{65}}{{}^sD_x},$$

where $\bar{a}'_{65}$ would be calculated by reference to the life table adopted for normal retirement pensioners.

10.12. Valuation of pension benefits: future-service pension

For each year of service completed subsequent to the valuation date the member will become entitled to an additional pension of $\frac{1}{60}$th of the pensionable salary as at the date of retirement. The value at age x of a pension arising on breakdown after age $(x+t)$ in respect of the year of service rendered between the ages $(x+t)$ and $(x+t+1)$ will, therefore, be represented by

$$\frac{1}{60} \frac{S_x}{s_x} \frac{v^t l_{x+t}}{l_x} \frac{{}^z M^{ia}_{x+t} - \frac{1}{2} {}^z C^{ia}_{x+t}}{D_{x+t}}.$$

The pension being based upon completed years of service, the total past service on the valuation date would, on the average, be $(n+\frac{1}{2})$ years, of which n years have been taken into account in the formula for back service pension. Accordingly, a further year's service will not be completed until age $(x+\frac{1}{2})$, and this fact is allowed for by the deductive item in the above formula.

This formula reduces to

$$\frac{S_x}{60} \frac{{}^z M^{ia}_{x+t+\frac{1}{2}}}{{}^sD_x},$$

whence $\qquad \dfrac{S_x}{60} \sum_{t=0}^{64-x} \dfrac{{}^z M^{ia}_{x+t+\frac{1}{2}}}{{}^sD_x} = \dfrac{S_x}{60} \dfrac{{}^z R^{ia}_{x+\frac{1}{2}}}{{}^sD_x}, \quad$ say,

represents the value corresponding to the present salary S_x of the pension arising upon breakdown retirement in respect of all future service, and the value of the future-service pension for all members now aged x would be $\dfrac{(\Sigma S_x)}{60} \dfrac{{}^z R^{ia}_{x+\frac{1}{2}}}{{}^sD_x}.$

By similar reasoning, the corresponding formula for the value of future-service pension arising upon compulsory retirement at exact age 65 may be written as

$$\frac{65-x}{60}(\Sigma S_x)\frac{z_{65}D_{65}\bar{a}'_{65}}{{}^sD_x}.$$

10.13. The formulae provide for the separate evaluation of the pension arising on ill-health retirement and on retirement at age 65, but generally it is not necessary to make such a subdivision. If ill-health and age retirements are treated together,* the valuation factors per unit of present salary corresponding to those given in §§ 10.11 and 10.12 are

(a) past service:

$$\frac{n}{60}\sum_{t=0}^{65-x}\frac{{}^zC^{(i+r)a}_{x+t}}{{}^sD_x}=\frac{n}{60}\frac{{}^zM^{(i+r)a}_x}{{}^sD_x}$$

The summation is now extended to age 65 and ${}^zC^{(i+r)a}_{65}$ is defined as $z_{65}v^{65}r_{65}\bar{a}'_{65}$ ($={}z_{65}D_{65}\bar{a}'_{65}$ since $r_{65}=l_{65}$).

(b) future service:

$$\frac{1}{60}\sum_{t=0}^{64-x}\frac{{}^zM^{(i+r)a}_{x+t}-\tfrac{1}{2}{}^zC^{(i+r)a}_{x+t}}{{}^sD_x}$$

$$=\frac{1}{60}\sum_{t=0}^{64-x}\frac{{}^zM^{(i+r)a}_{x+t+\frac{1}{2}}}{{}^sD_x}=\frac{1}{60}\frac{{}^zR^{(i+r)a}_{x+\frac{1}{2}}}{{}^sD_x}$$

It should be noted that the summation of ${}^zC^{(i+r)a}_{x+t}$ in (a) is extended to age 65, but the summation of ${}^zM^{(i+r)a}_{x+t+\frac{1}{2}}$ still terminates at age 64, since no additional pension rights can accrue after the 65th birthday in the scheme under consideration.

10.14. In the case of entrants below age 25 it will be necessary to introduce an adjustment for the limitation of pensions to a maximum of two-thirds of pensionable salary. The age at which this maximum is reached is $x+40-n=m$ (say).

---

* In such a case the symbol r is frequently used to denote retirements on account of ill-health and age together, i.e. it is taken as equivalent to $(i+r)$ as used in this chapter, in order to make the formulae somewhat simpler. It should be noted that this simpler system of notation has been used later in the book in the chapters devoted to widows' and orphans' schemes and emerging costs.

For a particular member the amount of the deduction from the total liability for past- and future-service pension as set out in §§ 10.11 and 10.12 will be calculated by the formula

$$\frac{S_x}{60}\left[{}^zR^{ia}_{x+\frac{1}{2}}+(n-40)\,{}^zM^{ia}_x+\{(65-x)+(n-40)\}\,z_{65}D_{65}\bar{a}'_{65}\right]\bigg/{}^sD_x,$$

when $n > 40$, and by the formula

$$\frac{S_x}{60}\left[{}^zR^{ia}_{m+\frac{1}{2}}+(65-m)\,z_{65}D_{65}\bar{a}'_{65}\right]\bigg/{}^sD_x,$$

when $n \leqslant 40$.

In practice, the terms involving $(n-40)$ in the first formula may be allowed for at the stage of scheduling by limiting n to a maximum of 40. The remainder of the adjustment would, if the cases are few, be calculated individually. Otherwise the adjustment would be calculated by aggregating members according to valuation age, with a subsidiary division according to the maximum age m.

It will be noted that in the formulae of this and preceding sections the 10 year qualifying period for pension purposes does not appear explicitly; as already explained in §7.6 this would be normally allowed for in determining the ill-health retirement rates and the subsequent construction of the service table and valuation factors.

10.15. Valuation of contributions

Where the contribution of each member is a fixed percentage of salary the contribution will, of course, increase throughout service proportionately with salary, and the same salary scale may be used for estimating future contributions.

For the valuation of future contributions payable by the members, we therefore require columns of

$${}^s\bar{D}_x \quad \text{and} \quad {}^s\bar{N}_x,$$

where
$${}^s\bar{D}_x = s_x D_{x+\frac{1}{2}} = s_x (D_x + D_{x+1})/2,$$

$${}^s\bar{N}_x = \sum_{t=0}^{64-x} {}^s\bar{D}_{x+t}.$$

We then have

${}^s\bar{N}_x/{}^sD_x =$ the value of an annuity payable during future active service commencing at 1 and increasing in proportion to the salary scale.

By multiplying this function by the total contributions to be paid in the year following age x by all members of that age, the value of the future contributions payable by them can be obtained. The value of the normal contributions by the employer will be an equal amount, unless they are payable in one sum at a later date than those of the employees, in which case an appropriate adjustment (involving interest only) will be made.

The deficiency contribution, if any, payable by the employer as a fixed amount payable for a limited number of years, would be valued by a suitable annuity-certain factor.

10.16. Valuation of death benefits: past contributions

The benefit payable on the death of a pensioner has been provided for in the formula for the valuation of pension benefits.

It is now necessary to derive the formulae for the valuation of the benefit payable on the death of a member in service, and for this purpose it will be assumed that the rate of compound interest at which the member's contributions are accumulated in order to calculate the amount of this benefit is not the same as the valuation rate of interest. In cases where these two rates are identical or where no interest accumulation is added, some simplification of the formulae is possible, as will be seen later.

As in the case of the pension benefit, it is convenient to value the death benefit in two parts corresponding to past and future contributions.

The value of a unit to be paid with compound interest from the present time at the rate j on the death whilst in service of a person now aged x is

$$\frac{1}{l_x} \sum_{t=0}^{64-x} d_{x+t} \frac{(1+j)^{t+\frac{1}{2}}}{(1+i)^{t+\frac{1}{2}}} = \frac{1}{(1+j)^x D_x} \sum_{t=0}^{64-x} C_{x+t}^d (1+j)^{x+t+\frac{1}{2}}$$

$$= \frac{1}{{}^j D_x} \sum_{t=0}^{64-x} {}^j C_x^d = \frac{{}^j M_x^d}{{}^j D_x},$$

where ${}^j C_x^d = (1+j)^{x+\frac{1}{2}} C_x^d$ and ${}^j D_x = (1+j)^x D_x$.

If we assume a rate of interest J such that

$$(1+J) = (1+i)/(1+j),$$

the factor can be expressed in the form

$$\frac{1}{l_x(1+J)^{-x}} \sum_{t=0}^{64-x} d_{x+t}(1+J)^{-(x+t+\frac{1}{2})} = \frac{M_x^d}{D_x} \quad \text{calculated at rate } J.$$

In practice the introduction of the rate J, which will be an awkward rate not available in published tables, will not facilitate the calculations, although it was probably a useful device when computation was generally performed with the aid of logarithmic tables.

If the total amount of past contributions of members aged x accumulated with compound interest at rate j to the valuation date is available from the records of the fund, the present value of the death benefit arising in respect of such past contributions can be immediately calculated by multiplying by the above factor.

In the absence of individual records of past contributions with interest accumulations, the total of past contributions without interest should normally be available from the records of the fund and a reasonably accurate approximation can be obtained as follows. Calculate (a) the total amount of past contributions without interest on the basis of the salary scale, and (b) the total amount of the scale contributions accumulated at compound interest to date. The actual past contributions can then be multiplied by the ratio (b)/(a) in order to estimate the amount of such contributions accumulated at interest to the valuation date. By this method, full use is made of the information available as to the actual amount of contributions, the area of approximation being limited to the assumption made as to the distribution of such contributions over past years.

The factor (b)/(a) would be of the form

$$\sum_{y=x_0}^{x-1} s_y(1+j)^{x-y-\frac{1}{2}} \bigg/ \sum_{y=x_0}^{x-1} s_y,$$

where x_0 is the age at entry into contributory membership. For convenience of calculation this can be expressed as

$$(1+j)^{x-\frac{1}{2}} \Sigma^j s_y / \Sigma s_y,$$

where $\qquad {}^j s_y = s_y(1+j)^{-y}.$

As the liability now being valued will generally form only a small part of the total liability it may be possible in practice to assume an average value of x_0 for the group of members now aged x and, hence, to apply a single adjusting factor $(b)/(a)$ to the whole group at age x.

If, as occasionally happens, information regarding past contributions with or without interest is not available, it is possible to proceed from the present contribution on the assumption that salaries in the past have increased in accordance with the scale. The factor to be applied to the present contribution payable from age x to $(x+1)$ would be

$$(1+j)^{x-\frac{1}{2}} \sum_{y=x_0}^{x-1} {}^is_y \Big/ s_x.$$

This assumption would, however, be unsound in many cases, particularly if the general level of salaries has altered since contributions commenced. It would be desirable in such circumstances to make a further adjustment in the light of any general information available regarding salary levels in the past.

10.17. Valuation of death benefits: future contributions

The value at age x of a benefit equal to a contribution of 1 % of the scale salary payable for the year of age $(x+t)$ to $(x+t+1)$ with compound interest thereon at rate j in the event of death occurring in service subsequent to age $(x+t)$ is

$$\cdot 01\, s_{x+t} \frac{v^{t+\frac{1}{2}}}{l_x} \{\tfrac{1}{2}d_{x+t} + d_{x+t+1}(1+j)/(1+i) + \ldots\}.$$

The above expression may be written in the form

$$\cdot 01 s_{x+t} \frac{v_j^{x+t+\frac{1}{2}}}{v^x l_x} \{\tfrac{1}{2}(1+j)^{x+t+\frac{1}{2}} C_{x+t}^d + (1+j)^{x+t+1\frac{1}{2}} C_{x+t+1}^d + \ldots\}$$

$$= \cdot 01 s_{x+t} \frac{v_j^{x+t+\frac{1}{2}}}{D_x} \{{}^jM_{x+t}^d - \tfrac{1}{2}{}^jC_{x+t}^d\} = \cdot 01 s_{x+t} \frac{v_j^{x+t+\frac{1}{2}}}{D_x} {}^j\overline{M}_{x+t}^d.$$

The factor for the valuation of a death benefit of 1 % of all scale salary receivable after the valuation date, which may be obtained by summing the above expression for all values of t, is, therefore,

$$\cdot 01 \sum_{t=0}^{64-x} \frac{s_{x+t}v_j^{x+t+\frac{1}{2}}\,{}^j\overline{M}_{x+t}^d}{D_x} = \cdot 01\, \frac{{}^{sj}\overline{R}_x^d}{D_x}, \quad \text{say.}$$

The corresponding expression for the value of a benefit of 1 % of salaries which commence at S_x and increase according to scale is, therefore,

$$\cdot 01 S_x {}^{sj}\Big/ \overline{R}_x^{ds} D_x.$$

It should be particularly noted that the denominator in this factor is ^sD_x, incorporating v^x at the valuation rate i only, not $v^x(1+j)^x$ as in the factor for that part of the benefit related to past contributions.

Again, the unusual structure of $^{sj}\bar{R}_x^d$ should be noted; it arises from the fact that interest accumulations on future contributions only commence from the date of payment and not from the present age x.

An alternative form for the factor is

$$\frac{1}{^sD_x} \sum_{t=0}^{64-x} s_{x+t} D_{x+t+\frac{1}{2}} \frac{^jM_{x+t+\frac{1}{2}}^d}{^jD_{x+t+\frac{1}{2}}},$$

as will be readily understood when it is noted that

$$^jM_{x+t}^d - \tfrac{1}{2}{}^jC_{x+t}^d = \tfrac{1}{2}{}^jM_{x+t}^d + \tfrac{1}{2}\left({}^jM_{x+t}^d - {}^jC_{x+t}^d\right)$$
$$= \tfrac{1}{2}{}^jM_{x+t}^d + \tfrac{1}{2}{}^jM_{x+t+1}^d$$
$$= {}^jM_{x+t+\frac{1}{2}}^d.$$

The function $\dfrac{^jM_{x+t+\frac{1}{2}}^d}{^jD_{x+t+\frac{1}{2}}}$ which appears in this form of the factor is that which appeared in § 10.16 for age $(x+t+\frac{1}{2})$, and if this function is first prepared the factor related to the future contributions may, therefore, be constructed from it.

A similar relationship may be shown to exist between the factors for past and future service pensions given in §§ 10.11 and 10.12.

10.18. Valuation of withdrawal benefits

The formulae for the valuation of the benefit payable in the event of withdrawal from the service before retirement on pension may be derived by similar methods.

When the benefit is equal to the contributions without interest the formulae to be employed are as follows:

(*a*) The factor for valuing the benefit in respect of contributions paid prior to the valuation date is

$$M_x^w/D_x,$$

where
$$M_x^w = \sum_{t=0}^{x_1-x} C_{x+t}^w, \quad \text{and} \quad C_x^w = v^{x+\frac{1}{2}} w_x.$$

The summation of C_{x+t}^w extends to age x_1, the highest age at which the withdrawal decrement appears in the service table.

(*b*) The value of a withdrawal benefit of 1% of salaries which commence at S_x and increase according to scale is

$$\cdot 01 S_x {}^s\overline{R}_x^w / {}^s D_x,$$

where $\quad {}^s\overline{R}_x^w = \sum_{t=0}^{x_1-x} {}^s\overline{M}_{x+t}^w, \quad$ and $\quad {}^s\overline{M}_x^w = S_x(M_x^w - \tfrac{1}{2}C_x^w).$

10.19. Death and withdrawal benefits where the rate of accumulation coincides with the valuation rate

The factors required when $j = i$ may be conveniently given here.

(*a*) *Death benefit—past contributions*

On reference to § 10.16 it will be seen that when $j = i$, $(1 + J) = 1$ and the factor reduces to $\dfrac{1}{l_x} \sum_{t=0}^{64-x} d_{x+t} = \dfrac{\lambda_x^d}{l_x}$, i.e. the value at age x of a benefit of 1 accumulating with interest at the same rate as is used in reducing to present values is equal to the total probability at x of death occurring whilst in the service.

(*b*) *Death benefit—future contributions*

Corresponding to the formula ${}^{sj}\overline{R}_x^d / {}^s D_x$ of § 10.17 the factor now required may be expressed as

$$^{si}\overline{R}_x^d / {}^s D_x,$$

where $\quad {}^{si}\overline{R}_x^d = \sum_{t=0}^{64-x} s_{x+t} v_i^{x+t+\frac{1}{2}} (\lambda_{x+t}^d - \tfrac{1}{2}d_{x+t}).$

(*c*) *Withdrawal benefit*

The factors for the withdrawal benefit are built up in the same manner as for the death benefit.

10.20. Variations in interest accumulation procedure

In the absence of any evidence to the contrary, it is reasonable to assume that interest accumulations will accrue continuously and the formulae given in §§ 10.16 to 10.19 are all based on this assumption. The rules of the fund usually specify the manner of calculating interest accumulations, a variety of methods being met in practice. Thus it may be laid down, largely as a matter of convenience, that interest shall accrue yearly in arrear so that no interest would be allowed for the broken period of the year in which a particular contribution is paid nor for the broken period of the year in which death occurs. The valuation factors related to past and future contributions would under such a rule require to be multiplied by $(1+j)^{-\frac{1}{2}}$ and $(1+j)^{-1}$ respectively, or these adjustments could be incorporated in an early stage of the construction of the factors.

10.21. Incumbent pensions

These will be valued on appropriate pensioner's mortality tables, select for recent breakdown retirements, and with allowance for the unexpired portion of the guarantee period of 5 years in the case of new pensions which have arisen during the quinquennium ended on the valuation date.

10.22. Expenses

In the fund being considered, expenses are paid by the employer. In the less usual case where the expenses are met out of the fund a suitable reserve must be set up. It would generally be sufficient to base this reserve on a suitable percentage of the value of future contributions, together with a percentage of the value of pensions (prospective and incumbent). These percentages, which would not necessarily be the same, would be determined after an examination of the accounts and an assessment of the incidence and probable level of expenses of collection of contributions and payment of pensions.

CHAPTER II

THE VALUATION OF AN EXISTING FUND: THE VALUATION REPORT

11.1. Final checks

Before writing the valuation report the actuary must give the most careful consideration to the results as a whole and apply checks wherever this is practicable. The checks which would normally be applied are the following.

(*a*) *Data.* The accuracy of the data employed in the valuation should, as already indicated, be checked by comparison with the corresponding items in the accounts of the fund. For example, the total present contributions valued may be compared with the actual contributions received during the final year of the inter-valuation period, the total pensions valued with the pensions actually paid, and an approximate check placed upon the exits by an examination of the benefits paid upon withdrawal, etc. The total membership and the detailed movements in the membership during the valuation period should also be checked against any figures which may be quoted in the annual reports of the fund. It is also desirable to check that the interest yield corresponds with the investment portfolio and that proper income tax recoveries have been made.

(*b*) *Valuation results.* An approximate analysis of the profits and losses arising from each source during the valuation period should be made wherever possible, as this affords a most valuable independent check on the valuation as a whole. The degree of accuracy to which such an analysis is carried will, of course, vary with the size of the fund. In view of the number of elements involved in the valuation and the interplay of these elements, as well as the complex nature of the valuation formulae employed, it is seldom practicable to carry this analysis as far as is commonly done in dealing with life assurance data. Great care should be taken to ensure that any approximations introduced in the profit and loss analysis are reasonable and do not distort the results to a material extent. This matter is dealt with in more detail in Chapter 19.

(*c*) *Contribution scales and negative values.* No valuation should be regarded as complete without an examination of the scale of contributions, by reference to the valuation basis, to ascertain whether the contributions payable by new entrants are adequate to meet the cost of the benefits. It may be found that, although, taking all entrants together, the contributions are adequate, at some ages the existing rates are greater and at others less than those actuarially required. In such circumstances 'negative values' will arise in the valuation. Ordinarily, the sound course would then be to eliminate them by reducing the value of contributions by the amount of the excess. If the negative values are left in and credit is taken for the full value of the future contributions, a potential asset will be lost if the exits from the fund (e.g. by withdrawal) amongst the persons affected are greater than the number allowed for in the valuation; this point must be borne in mind in fixing the rates of withdrawal. This difficulty would normally be avoided by eliminating the negative values, but the latter course may involve an over-valuation and an unreal strain if, for example, shortly before the valuation there were an abnormal number of new entrants, some paying more and other less than adequate contributions. The actuary would then be faced by the dilemma that, if the valuation results are to be strictly interpreted, there may be a call for further contributions to meet a strain which will probably be self-liquidating as the negative values are realized.

If the examination of the scale of contributions reveals that these, as a whole, are inadequate, this should be pointed out in the report and appropriate recommendations made.

11.2. Valuation results

When considering the advice which should be given upon the results of the valuation, the actuary must always remember that it is undesirable for the financial basis of a pension fund to be disturbed at frequent intervals. Such a fund is not a suitable subject for periodical 'bonus distributions', as the benefits provided are designed to meet specific needs. For this reason, no action would normally be taken to deal with a surplus unless it were relatively large and unlikely to be required as a margin against future adverse fluctuations in the experience, etc. Valuations are usually made at quinquennial intervals and the surplus or deficiency arising during the inter-valuation period is unlikely to be large in relation to the total liabilities, unless there has occurred a sudden financial strain resulting possibly from a change in the valuation basis or from a change in the general level of salaries. Consequently, in normal circumstances, violent changes in the benefit and contribution arrangements to deal with a surplus or deficiency will not be required.

If the valuation reveals a surplus, the sources of that surplus must be carefully studied before deciding upon the advice to be given to the employer. If, for example, it is due to favourable experience in respect to interest yield, mortality, etc., and the contributions payable by new entrants are more than adequate, it may be justifiable to distribute the surplus by reducing future contributions, if there is no reasonable doubt that future experience will not deteriorate. If, however, the contributions for new entrants are not more than adequate to meet the cost of the benefits to which they will be entitled, the best course would be to retain the surplus by carrying it forward either unallocated or allocated to a contingencies reserve, if it were of a reasonable amount for the purpose. Alternatively, a large surplus arising in a fund in which the employer is paying a deficiency contribution may be used to reduce that contribution. In any event, no cash return may be made either to the employer or to the members as objections would be raised to such a course by the Inland Revenue authorities.

In the event of a deficiency of more than a nominal amount being disclosed, it would generally be extremely unwise to postpone remedial measures as otherwise the financial position may be expected to deteriorate still further with the passage of time. The actuary may decide, in the light of any contingency or other margins in his valuation basis, that it is not essential to remove the whole deficiency at once. In any case, however, it would be desirable to ensure that the deficiency will not be increased by reason of the admission of new members at inadequate rates of contribution.

11.3. Apart from administrative action, which may take the form of imposing stricter conditions for the grant of ill-health benefits or broadening the basis of investments so as to secure a higher interest yield, the possibilities of dealing with a deficiency are generally limited to alterations in one or more of the following:

(i) The contributions payable by the members and/or the employers.

(ii) The pension benefits.

(iii) The retiring age.

(iv) The ancillary benefits.

The methods of dealing with a surplus can be similarly classified.

11.4. Deficiency

(i) *Alteration of contributions*

If the scale of contributions for new entrants is adequate, it will not be practicable or desirable to increase to any material extent the contributions payable by recent entrants, although it might be possible to increase the contributions of other members. If the contribution payable by the employer is increased with the increase in the members' contributions, the employer would thereby meet part of the deficiency. The employer may be willing, or required under the trust deed, to meet the whole of the deficiency by the payment of a capital sum, an equivalent annuity-certain or some other form of increased contribution related, for example, to salaries. Occasionally, it may be decided to increase the rate of contribution payable on salary in excess of a certain figure on the ground that, broadly, the higher salaried staff are mainly or wholly responsible for the deficiency.

(ii) *Alteration of pension benefits*

In general it is not desirable and sometimes it is not permissible, except in extreme financial circumstances, to adjust pensions which have already vested. Any alteration in the prospective pensions to members nearing retiring age should, where possible, avoid a sharp disparity of treatment between such members and those who have already retired. If the deficiency is due to a sudden special increase in the level of salaries it may be possible to deal with the deficiency by basing the pensions in respect of past service on the salary excluding the special increase and only allowing the increase to rank for pension purposes in respect of future service during which contributions on the augmented salary will be received. Whilst such an arrangement would be broadly equitable, it should be remembered that the relationship between the pensions and the total salaries receivable will be disturbed, to the greatest extent in the case of those members retiring in the near future and to a diminishing extent for younger members. This may, in turn, have repercussions on the experience of the fund as regards the rate of ill-health retirement as well as optional retirement if allowed under the scheme; this point has already been noted in Chapter 7. Consequently it may not be necessary to remove immediately the whole deficiency by the method suggested, as a part of the deficiency may well be eliminated by a change in the future experience. Other courses of action sometimes suggested are to alter the pensionable salary by excluding salary over a certain level or to change it from final salary to average salary received over the last 5 or 10 years. That part of the deficiency removed by reduction of pensions will of course fall wholly upon the members.

(iii) *Alteration of the retiring age*

If the pension age has been fixed below that normally operating for the class of members covered by the fund, it might be appropriate to suggest that the retiring age should be increased, although of course the general establishment policy of the employer in this respect will be the deciding factor. If optional retirement is allowed, some modification of the rule or even the total abolition of optional retirement before normal pension date may afford a practical solution.

(iv) *Alteration of ancillary benefits*

As the primary purpose of the scheme is to provide benefits on retirement, a suggestion to reduce the ancillary benefits payable on death or withdrawal may be more acceptable than a change in the contribution or pension arrangements, although it is unlikely that the members will be agreeable to the benefit payable on death or withdrawal before the pension age being reduced below a sum equal to the member's own contributions without interest. In any case, as the liability in respect of these benefits is only a small part of the total, action under this heading would only meet the case where the deficiency is relatively small.

11.5. It will be clear that there is no generally suitable method which may be applied in every case. The actuary must consider the sources of the surplus or deficiency and the circumstances of the particular fund and, in the light of these, recommend a suitable scheme. Any proposals will generally have to be on fairly broad lines if they are to be acceptable and workable in practice, but subject to this a reasonable degree of equity should be maintained between the different categories of members of the fund. Any proposals which are made must of course be in accordance with the trust deed governing the operations of the fund; this document very often gives precise instructions and thus limits the field of action open to the actuary. Before any final decision is taken it will be desirable to consult the trustees or management committee of the fund and through them the employers, and possibly, in addition, representatives of the members. A specimen valuation rule is given at the end of this chapter.

11.6. Valuation report

The valuation report must, of course, be written with the object of conveying to those responsible for the operation of the fund a clear picture of the condition of the fund at the time of the valuation and of its future prospects. Although the report is necessarily of a technical nature, it should be written as far as possible in non-technical language. It is desirable that a reasonable amount of explanation regarding the valuation should be incorporated with statistics to show how the fund is progressing. It is important, however, to avoid introducing matter the implications of which can scarcely be understood without an actuarial training. With these points in mind, the following is an indication of the principal matters which would be dealt with in a report on the quinquennial valuation of a fund of the type which has been considered in the previous chapter. Obviously, the actual contents of any such report will vary with the circumstances of the particular fund concerned.

(a) The report would commence with brief particulars of the data upon which the valuation has been based, indicating the progress of the membership and the fund during the inter-valuation period.

(b) An indication should then be given of the bases adopted for the valuation, showing the extent to which these have been based upon the actual experience of the fund itself. If it has been necessary to depart from that experience, the reasons should be set out. It would not, however, usually be desirable to quote the actual rates of decrement used, since a judgement upon the suitability of these is dependent on technical considerations which would not be appreciated by the officials of the fund.

(c) The rate of interest assumed in the valuation should be set out with a brief explanation of the considerations which have led to its adoption. The basis upon which the value of the assets comprising the fund has been arrived at should also be stated.

(d) The succeeding paragraphs would set out the results of the valuation, stating the amount of the surplus or deficiency revealed. They should include a valuation balance sheet showing the principal subdivisions of the liabilities and assets on the following general lines:

Valuation balance sheet as at......

To present value of:	£	By present value of:	£
Current pensions		Members' future contributions	
Prospective pensions payable on retirement on account of age or ill-health in respect of:		Employers' future normal contributions	
(a) Past service ...		Employers' future additional contributions (if any) ...	
(b) Future service ...			
Benefits payable on withdrawal and death before retirement on pension ...		Amount of accumulated fund ...	
		Appreciation or other assets brought into account... ...	
Reserve for depreciation of investments or other liabilities brought into account...			
Reserve for expenses ...			
Balance (surplus)		Balance (deficiency)	

(*e*) On the basis of the analysis of surplus which has been carried out, a broad indication should be given of the sources of the surplus or deficiency.

(*f*) The report should also indicate whether the scale of contributions charged by the fund remains appropriate for new entrants, and the changes, if any, in the scale which should be made under current conditions.

(*g*) The report may conclude with the actuary's recommendations regarding the action, if any, to be taken for dealing with the surplus or deficiency.

11.7. Specimen valuation rule

The position of the fund shall be submitted to the actuary and investigated at least once in every five years from .... (the date of the first of such investigations). The actuary shall report to the Trustees in writing on the financial position of the pension fund and if such report shows a deficiency or anticipated deficiency in the pension fund the Trustees shall (subject to the approval of the company and with the consent of the actuary) determine what action (if any) shall be taken either by increasing the contributions or decreasing the pensions of members or otherwise to restore the solvency of the fund. If the said report shows a surplus beyond the requirements of the pension fund such surplus or any part thereof may at the option of the Trustees and on the written advice of the actuary (1) be carried forward by the Trustees or (2) be employed in either reducing the contributions or increasing the pensions of members to the fund or (3) be employed in reducing the age at which members shall be entitled to retire on pension.

CHAPTER 12

THE VALUATION OF AN EXISTING FUND: MISCELLANEOUS FORMULAE

12.1. In the course of the discussion in Chapter 10 on the valuation of a specimen scheme, the formulae required for the particular benefits of that scheme were given. It is now proposed to set out formulae for other benefits which are commonly encountered. The derivation of these formulae will not be given in such detail as in Chapter 10, but the methods there employed are equally applicable and the student should work out the derivations in full as an exercise.

12.2. Pension benefits: final salary pensions

The formulae already given are those appropriate to a pension benefit based on the average earnings of the last 5 years of service ('final average' basis). In the case where the pension is based on the rate of earnings at the time of retirement ('final salary' basis), the appropriate formulae are, of course, similar to those given in §§ 10.11–10.14, the component $z_{x+\frac{1}{2}}$ being replaced in each case by s_x for retirements at age x last birthday, i.e. at $(x+\frac{1}{2})$ on the average. If the pension were based on the earnings of the year preceding retirement, then $s_{x-\frac{1}{2}}$ would be used, and, generally, care must be taken to ensure that the salary factor incorporated agrees both with the assumptions made in constructing the salary scale and with the rules for computing pensions and their interpretation by the officials of the fund.

12.3. 'Average salary' pensions

If, on the other hand, the pension benefit is based on the average earnings throughout service the formulae will be quite different, and can be derived as follows, assuming, as before, that normal retirement takes place at age 65.

A pension of $\frac{1}{60}$th of the average salary throughout service for each year of service is equal to $\frac{1}{60}$th of the total salary received throughout service. Each payment of salary can therefore be regarded as carrying with it the right to a pension of $\frac{1}{60}$th of its amount, to be entered on when retirement takes place.

The *past salary pension* liability is then $\frac{1}{60}$th of the total actual past salaries $(TPS)_x$ multiplied by $M_x^{(i+r)a}/D_x$, where

$$M_x^{(i+r)a} = \sum_{t=0}^{65-x} C_{x+t}^{(i+r)a}$$

and
$$C_x^{(i+r)a} = v^{x+\frac{1}{2}} i_x \bar{a}'_{x+\frac{1}{2}} \quad (x < 65),$$

or
$$= v^{65} r_{65} \bar{a}'_{65} \quad (x = 65).$$

It will be noted that the salary scale is not involved in this formula, since the pension associated with earnings already received is finally fixed and cannot vary with the level of future earnings.

For *future salary pensions*, on the other hand, it is necessary to introduce the salary scale to estimate the future earnings upon which the pension will be based. Thus, if the actual present salary of a member aged x is S_x (receivable between ages x and $x + 1$), the salary to be received in the year of age $x + t$ to $x + t + 1$ is estimated by means of the salary scale to be $S_x . s_{x+t}/s_x$. The value at age x of each unit of pension receivable in respect of that salary will be $(M_{x+t}^{(i+r)a} - \frac{1}{2}C_{x+t}^{(i+r)a})\big/ D_x$ (or say $\bar{M}_{x+t}^{(i+r)a}\big/ D_x$), thus allowing for the fact that, on the average, members retiring in the year $x + t$ to $x + t + 1$ will only have received a half-year's salary for that year.

The value of the pension associated with the salary assumed to be receivable in that year is thus

$$S_x . s_{x+t}(M_{x+t}^{(i+r)a} - \tfrac{1}{2}C_{x+t}^{(i+r)a})\big/ 60\, {}^s D_x$$

$$= S_x\, {}^s \bar{M}_{x+t}^{(i+r)a}\big/ 60\, {}^s D_x, \quad \text{say.}$$

To obtain the value for all future years of service the latter expression must be summed for values of t from 0 to $64 - x$. Thus, writing $\sum_{t=0}^{64-x} {}^s \bar{M}_{x+t}^{(i+r)a} = {}^s \bar{R}_x^{(i+r)a}$, the value is $S_x\, {}^s \bar{R}_x^{(i+ra)}\big/ 60\, {}^s D_x$.

If necessary, these expressions could be subdivided to give the values of ill-health and age pensions separately, as was done in Chapter 10.

12.4. Limitation of pension

If the number of years of service ranking for pension is limited to, say, 40, an adjustment must be made to the ordinary formulae in which no such limit operates. The appropriate adjustment for pensions based on final average salary has already been given in § 10.14. If the pension is based on average salary, the adjustment takes a quite different form according to the way in which the pension limitation operates.

In the first place, the rule may provide that salaries earned more than 40 years before retirement shall be disregarded in computing the pension. It is then necessary to separate members who entered before age 25, and to calculate and deduct the amount of pension liability included in the ordinary formula given above which arises from the excluded earnings. For a member aged x who entered pensionable service at age x_0 (x_0 being less than 25 and x less than $x_0 + 40$), the amount to be deducted will be calculated by the formula

$$\{S_{x_0} . \overline{M}^{(i+r)a}_{x_0+40} + S_{x+1} . \overline{M}^{(i+r)a}_{x_0+41} + \ldots + S_{24}\overline{M}^{(i+r)a\}}_{64}\Big/ 60D_x.$$

If x is less than 24, it may be necessary to estimate the values of S_x up to age 24 by means of the salary scale, whilst if x is greater than $x_0 + 40$ the above formula would need to be modified. On the other hand, the rule may stipulate that the maximum pension shall be $\frac{40}{60}$ths of the average earnings throughout service. In passing, it may be noted that such a rule is unsatisfactory in practice, since under it a member who enters, for example, at age 20 and retires at age 65, may receive a smaller pension than a similar member who enters at age 25, even though their salary careers from age 25 may be identical. If, however, such a provision is encountered, the necessary adjustment can be made as follows.

If the entry age is $x_0 (< 25)$ the unadjusted formulae given in § 12.3 will value a pension on retirement between ages $x_0 + 40 + t$ and $x_0 + 41 + t$ equal to $\frac{1}{60}$th of

(total salary from age x_0 to age $x_0 + 40\frac{1}{2} + t$)   or $\frac{1}{60} {}_{x_0}E_{x_0+40\frac{1}{2}+t}$

say, whereas, according to the rules of the scheme the benefit should be

$$\frac{40}{60} . \text{(average salary)} = \frac{40}{60} . {}_{x_0}E_{x_0+40\frac{1}{2}+t}\Big/ (40\frac{1}{2} + t).$$

Similarly for retirements at exact age 65, the normal unadjusted formulae would provide for a pension of $\frac{1}{60}$.(total salary from age x_0 to age 65), whereas the amount required is

$$\tfrac{40}{60} \cdot {}_{x_0}E_{65}\big/(65 - x_0).$$

The maximum of $\frac{40}{60}$ths may thus be allowed for by using special sets of factors for entry ages x_0 less than 25; these factors will be constructed in precisely the same way as the ordinary 'average-salary' pension factors, except that $C_{x_0+40+t}^{(i+r)a}$ would be replaced by $K_t C_{x_0+40+t}^{(i+r)a}$ where $K_t = 40/(40\tfrac{1}{2} + t)$ or $40/(65 - x_0)$ when $t = 25 - x_0$. In practice, some grouping of members entering below age 25 may be made, in order to reduce the number of special sets of factors required.

An alternative method would be to value all members by the ordinary factors without adjustment and to value the deduction as a separate item. Thus, for a member aged x, the deduction would be

$$(TPS)_x \frac{\dfrac{\tfrac{1}{2}}{40\tfrac{1}{2}} C_{x_0+40}^{(i+r)a} + \dfrac{1\tfrac{1}{2}}{41\tfrac{1}{2}} C_{x_0+41}^{(i+r)a} + \dots + \dfrac{25 - x_0}{65 - x_0} C_{65}^{(i+r)a}}{60 D_x},$$

$$= (TPS)_x \frac{\displaystyle\sum_{t=0}^{25-x_0} \phi C_{x_0+40+t}^{(i+r)a}}{60 D_x} \text{ say } = (TPS)_x \frac{\phi M_{x_0+40}^{(i+r)a}}{60 D_x},$$

associated with past salaries $(TPS)_x$ and

$$S_x\{(s_x + \dots + s_{x_0+39} + \tfrac{1}{2}s_{x_0+40})\, \phi C_{x_0+40}^{(i+r)a}$$
$$+ (s_x + \dots + s_{x_0+40} + \tfrac{1}{2}s_{x_0+41})\, \phi C_{x_0+41}^{(i+r)a} + \text{etc.}\}\big/ 60\, {}^sD_x.$$

associated with future salaries.

If we define σ_x as $\displaystyle\sum_{t=0}^{64-x} s_{x+t}$ the total adjustment could be written in the form

$$\left\{(TPS)_x + S_x \frac{(\sigma_x - \sigma_{x_0+40})}{s_x}\right\} \frac{\phi M_{x_0+40}^{(i+r)a}}{60 D_x}$$

$$+ S_x \frac{\displaystyle\sum_{t=0}^{24-x_0} s_{x_0+40+t}\left(\phi M_{x_0+40+t}^{(i+r)a} - \tfrac{1}{2}\phi C_{x_0+40+t}^{(i+r)a}\right)}{60\, {}^sD_x}$$

$$= \left[(TPS)_x + S_x \frac{(\sigma_x - \sigma_{x_0+40})}{s_x}\right] \frac{\phi M_{x_0+40}^{(i+r)a}}{60\, {}^sD_x} + S_x \frac{{}^{s\phi}\bar{R}_{x_0+40}^{(i+r)a}}{60\, {}^sD_x}$$

which could be valued fairly simply since the special M and R functions need only be calculated for the limited range of ages (x_0+40) to 65.

Where x the valuation age is $> x_0+40$ the function ${}^\phi C^{(i+r)a}_{x_0+40+t}$ would be omitted and $\sigma_x - \sigma_{x_0+40}$ would be taken as zero for $t < x - x_0 - 40$.

12.5. Money purchase schemes

The pensions already assured by past contributions under a money purchase scheme will be known exactly, as they will have been calculated according to the tables incorporated in the scheme which will show the amount of pension secured for each unit of contribution paid at each age. These accrued pensions can be valued by the same type of formula as for past service pension under an average-salary scheme. The service table used may or may not allow for ill-health decrements according to the method of calculating the benefit on ill-health retirement. If the table by which contributions are to be converted into pensions is based on the valuation assumptions, or is such that the pension is smaller than the contributions would provide according to the valuation basis, the value of future contributions and the corresponding future service pensions would usually be left out of account, since the net reserve in respect of them would be either zero or negative. This would be equivalent to ignoring any expected profit from future purchases of pensions by existing members, and allowing such profit to emerge gradually in the future if and when the contributions are paid.

It may be found, however, that the pensions granted exceed those which can be justified on the valuation basis. In such a case a specific reserve must be made for the future strain in respect of existing members. In order to determine the liability arising in respect of the future service of existing members, the future contributions payable under the scheme and the corresponding pensions must be valued (incorporating where appropriate factors allowing for future salary increase if the contributions are dependent on salaries). The value of future pensions will be calculated by a similar formula to that employed for an average salary fund (§ 12.3) adjusted as follows:

(*a*) if the contribution is independent of salary let

c_x = the contribution payable in the year of age x to $x+1$,

f_x = the pension secured by a contribution of 1 at age x last birthday.

Then the value of pensions to be secured by future contributions is

$$\sum_{t=0}^{64-x} c_{x+t} f_{x+t} \frac{M_{x+t}^{(i+r)a} - \tfrac{1}{2} C_{x+t}^{(i+r)a}}{D_x} = \frac{cf\bar{R}_x^{(i+r)a}}{D_x}, \quad \text{say.}$$

(*b*) If the contribution is a fixed percentage ($K\%$) of salary, the required value is

$$\cdot 01 K S_x \sum_{t=0}^{64-x} s_{x+t} f_{x+t} \frac{M_{x+t}^{(i+r)a} - \tfrac{1}{2} C_{x+t}^{(i+r)a}}{{}^s D_x} = \frac{\cdot 01 K S_x \, {}^{sf}\bar{R}_x^{(i+r)a}}{{}^s D_x} \quad \text{say,}$$

where S_x is the salary receivable by a member at age x.

12.6. Deferred annuity schemes

These are similar to money purchase schemes except that the contribution payable is regarded as made up of a series of annual contributions, each purchasing a certain amount of pension. Under such an arrangement, the pension valued would normally consist of the pension to be secured on the assumption that no increase in the contribution payable in respect of an individual member would occur in the future, credit being taken as an asset for a level future contribution. In the circumstances discussed in § 12.5, in which the scales of contribution are inadequate to provide the benefits on the valuation basis, a further reserve should be made to cover the strain arising as a result of future increases in contribution payable in respect of the existing members. This reserve would be calculated in a similar manner to that outlined in the previous section, except that c_x would now have to represent the estimate of future *increases* in the annual contribution, and f_x would be the corresponding pension secured thereby.

12.7. Lump-sum retirement benefits

These would be valued by precisely the same formulae as pension retirement benefits, except that the annuity value $\bar{a}_x'$ would be omitted in the construction of the commutation columns.

12.8. Optional retirements

Frequently, schemes provide for the retirement of members before the normal pension age, on grounds other than ill-health. As already indicated in §7.5 this may necessitate a valuation in select form, different sets of factors being used for different groups of members according to age at entry into the service or the fund. The form of the factors is the same as for those already given earlier in this chapter and Chapter 10, but the service tables on which those factors are calculated will incorporate rates of optional retirement depending to some extent on the age at entry.

Where the benefit payable on optional retirement is not calculated on the same scale as for normal or ill-health retirements, an adjustment must be made in the calculation of the pension factors. This adjustment would be similar to that discussed in § 12.4 above, $C_x^{(i+r)a}$ being replaced by $K_x C_x^{(i+r)a}$, where K_x is the proportion of the full scale benefit payable on retirement between age x and age $x+1$. If K_x depends upon the age at entry x_0 as well as attained age x, a select form of valuation may be necessary.

12.9. Subsidiary benefits

In §§ 10.16–10.19 the necessary formulae are given for the valuation of benefits, on death and withdrawal of an active member, equal to contributions paid without interest and with compound interest (the formulae for withdrawal benefit can be derived from the corresponding formulae for death benefit by substituting w_x for d_x, and accordingly the formulae here given will be for a death benefit only).

Occasionally the rules of a fund provide for a benefit on the death or withdrawal of an active member equal to contributions paid accumulated with *simple* interest. The appropriate formulae for valuing such a benefit are as follows:

(a) Past contributions

It is assumed that information as to total past contributions is available from the records of the fund, and that interest thereon to date is either available from those records or has been estimated by methods analogous to those set out in § 10.16 relating to compound interest accumulations. The factors for valuation are:

Past contributions and future interest thereon at rate j:

$$(M_x^d + j\bar{R}_x^d)/D_x,$$

where
$$\bar{R}_x^d = \sum_{t=0}^{64-x} (M_{x+t}^d - \tfrac{1}{2}C_{x+t}^d) = \sum_{t=0}^{64-x} \bar{M}_{x+t}^d.$$

Interest to valuation date on past contributions:

$$M_x^d/D_x.$$

(b) Future contributions

The value of a benefit of 1 % of the scale salary receivable in the year of age $x+t$ to $x+t+1$ with simple interest thereon at rate j may be written as

$$\cdot 01 s_{x+t} \frac{(M_{x+t}^d - \tfrac{1}{2}C_{x+t}^d) + j(\tfrac{1}{4}C_{x+t}^d + C_{x+t+1}^d + 2C_{x+t+2}^d + \text{etc.})}{D_x}$$

$$= \cdot 01 s_{x+t} \frac{\bar{M}_{x+t}^d + j(\bar{R}_{x+t}^d - \tfrac{1}{2}\bar{M}_{x+t}^d)}{D_x}.$$

The corresponding factor in respect of all salary receivable after the valuation date commencing at S_x and increasing according to scale is obtained by summing the above expression and multiplying by S_x/s_x, viz.

$$\cdot 01 S_x \frac{{}^s\bar{R}_x^d + j \sum_{t=0}^{64-x} (s_{x+t}\bar{R}_{x+t}^d - \tfrac{1}{2}{}^s\bar{M}_{x+t}^d)}{{}^sD_x},$$

where
$$ {}^s\bar{M}_{x+t}^d = s_{x+t}\bar{M}_{x+t}^d$$

and
$$ {}^s\bar{R}_x^d = \sum_{t=0}^{64-x} s_{x+t}\bar{M}_{x+t}^d.$$

12.10. Minimum death benefit

Sometimes the death benefit, normally equal to an accumulation of contributions as already discussed, is subject to a minimum of, for example, so many months' salary. This in effect provides for a supplementary death benefit which decreases with duration of service and ceases at a comparatively early age, dependent on the relation between the guaranteed minimum and the normal death benefit. This supplementary benefit normally represents only a small part of the liability, and it will therefore be sufficiently accurate in such a case to value the additional benefit as a decreasing temporary assurance for broad groups of members or possibly for all members together. The benefit 'at risk' valued at age x would be the total benefit payable if all existing members of that age should die forthwith, viz.

$$\Sigma(KS_x - (TAC)_x),$$

where K = the minimum fraction of one year's salary, and $(TAC)_x$ = total accumulated contributions, and the summation would extend over all members who would be paid a supplementary benefit on immediate death.

12.11. Death benefit after retirement

In Chapter 10 the formula was given for the valuation of a pension guaranteed for a minimum period of years. This provision is often introduced to ensure that, in the main, each member will be entitled to benefits at least equal to the contributions he has paid, and to avoid anomalies between the benefits payable on death immediately before and immediately after retirement. These objects are frequently achieved more directly by providing for a death benefit after retirement equal to the excess, if any, of contributions paid by the member (with or without interest) over total pension payments. Such a benefit may be valued by estimating the average number of years' purchase of the pension represented by the death benefit at the moment of retirement (say t years' purchase), and incorporating in the commutation columns annuity factors of the form (based throughout on the mortality of pensioners)

$$\bar{a}'_x = \bar{a}_x + (tA^1_{x:\,\overline{n}|} - (IA)^1_{x:\,\overline{n}|}).$$

The estimate of t will call for careful judgement after a number of trial calculations, as allowance must be made for such factors as

(i) past variations in the level of earnings;

(ii) the effect of differing entry ages and rates of contribution;

(iii) the existence of non-contributing service before the establishment of the fund.

It will be clear that there may be a fairly wide variation in the value of t for different members or groups of members, and further variation according to the age at retirement. It will therefore be necessary to decide, with due regard to the relative magnitude of the benefit, whether it will be sufficient to adopt an average value of t for all members retiring at a particular age, or whether to subdivide the members into more or less homogeneous broad groups, in each of which the variation in t is sufficiently limited to enable an average value to be employed.

CHAPTER 13

SALARY SCALES

13.1. Mention has been made of the methods of incorporating salary forecasts into the valuation estimates, and it is now proposed to describe the factors determining the salary scale in practice and the steps necessary to construct a scale suitable for use in the valuation. The purposes of incorporating a scale in the formulae should be kept well in mind, namely (*a*) to enable future salaries of present members to be estimated for the purpose of valuing future benefits and contributions and (*b*) to furnish an estimate of the probable salary career of new entrants so that a scale of contributions adequate to support the benefits may be determined.

13.2. Generation of scale curve

In most large undertakings, the greater part, if not the whole, of the staff will generally fall into various grades, each receiving a distinct scale of pay, which may be related to age and/or length of service in the grade. Promotion from grade to grade will occur from time to time according to the vacancies arising or, it may be, the efficiency attained. Moreover, in general, the management, consciously or otherwise, will aim at a definite ratio of numbers of staff in related grades which will be determined largely by the nature of the employment. This underlying structure of the staff would, over a period of years, tend to produce at successive age groups a certain pattern of staff classification and a corresponding pattern of average salaries. Even in a fairly small concern, in which definite grades and salary rates may not be laid down, general economic and other forces will tend to produce a somewhat similar pattern, although over a period of years fluctuations from the average position would be proportionately larger.

The way in which this pattern of average salaries is generated is illustrated in the following example.

Example 13.1. The staff consists of 70% in Grade I, 25% in Grade II, and 5% in Grade III.

Grade I salaries commence at age 20 (normal age of entry into service) at £200 per annum, and rise by annual increments of £15 to a maximum of £380 per annum.

Grade II is recruited by promotions from Grade I between the ages 28 and 32, the scale of pay in the grade commencing at £400 per annum and rising by annual increments of £20 to a maximum of £600 per annum.

Grade III is recruited by promotions from Grade II between the ages of 40 and 45, the salary scale in the grade being £650 per annum and rising by annual increments of £30 to a maximum of £950 per annum.

Table 13.1 shows a possible composition of a staff of 1000, subject to the service and salary conditions described above.

TABLE 13.1

Structure of staff of 1,000 (approximate)

Age group	Total staff	No. in grade			Average salary per member (all staff combined)
		I	II	III	
					£
20–4	129	129	—	—	230
25–9	121	115	6	—	310
30–4	118	78	40	—	394
35–9	115	69	46	—	444
40–4	112	67	39	6	469
45–9	108	64	32	12	489
50–4	104	62	31	11	503
55–9	99	59	29	11	504
60–4	94	57	27	10	504
Totals	1000	700	250	50	—

The final column of this table would in the ideal state show not only the average salary attained by members passing through various ages on a particular date but also the average future progression of salaries of each age group of members as the group advanced in age with the passage of time. Thus, if the age distribution were stable and salary increments and promotions always occurred automatically and strictly at fixed ages, it would be possible to state exactly the future average salary history of any age group of employees. Such an ideal state of affairs would not, of course, obtain in practice. Increments are by no means automatic, and promotions will depend largely on the occurrence of vacancies as a result of death or retirement and on the availability of suitable staff for promotion. It is therefore only possible to make an estimate of the future expectation of salary on a basis which, whilst giving a reasonably accurate picture of the future progress of the salaries of the staff as a whole, may show fairly wide fluctuations in the actual experience of individual age groups. Nevertheless, the actuary is normally concerned only with the ratio of increase in average salaries from age to age, so that, by applying to the actual salaries in each age group ratios obtained from the salary scale, a good estimate of the future position can usually be obtained.

13.3. Construction of scale: average salary method

To enable him to make his valuation the actuary will normally ask for particulars of the salaries of individual employees year by year to be inserted on the valuation cards. In addition, the general policy as regards salaries should be discussed with the employers and all information available obtained regarding scales of pay according to grade, the distribution of staff between the various grades and the ages at which promotions to higher grades usually occur.

The next step would be to calculate the average present salary for each attained age of members existing at the valuation date by aggregating individual salaries at that date and dividing by the corresponding number of members. The resulting series of values would usually show a very irregular progression from age to age owing to:

(a) An uneven age distribution of staff in the various grades.

(b) An uneven flow of new entrants and exits.

(c) Variations in the past in the ages at which promotions to higher grades have occurred.

(d) The existence of a few highly paid posts which because of their small number cannot be spread evenly over the ages at which such posts may be expected.

(e) Changes in salary rates which have not been fully reflected in the salaries of the present staff.

(*f*) Changes in the grade structure of the staff, due possibly to an increase or reduction of the total number of employees, or to a change in internal organization and methods.

A more tractable series of average salaries would be obtained by suitably grouping the ages, possibly into quinary groups or, alternatively, into unequal age groups chosen so as to include approximately equal numbers of members in each group. The resulting series would then be graduated. A graphical method is usually sufficient, although care must be taken not to give too much weight to salaries which represent only a small group of members. The same process could be repeated for members existing 5 years earlier, relating the salaries at that time with the ages then attained. As an alternative, provided there has been no change in general salary levels during the period, the information regarding individual salaries at the valuation date and 5 years earlier could be amalgamated to produce a single scale. If thought desirable to increase what would otherwise be a small body of data, individual salaries for each year of the period could be similarly amalgamated, the salaries appropriate to a particular age or age group being aggregated. The resulting scale or scales should be checked as far as possible against the information obtained from the employers, as regards scales of pay and proportions of staff in each grade.

It should be noted that the salaries shown at adjacent ages or age groups relate to different employees and, unless the composition of the staff in these adjacent age groups is reasonably consistent, the ungraduated scale will not give a satisfactory measure of the rate of increase from age to age, whilst the scale after graduation may also be unsatisfactory in this respect. Again, the scale of average salaries at the valuation date may show special features over a range of ages, in which case the scale derived from salaries in operation 5 years earlier would probably show similar features at ages 5 years less, and it would thus be difficult to reconcile the two scales. To meet these objections, an alternative method of examining the individual salaries has been suggested.

13.4. Construction of scale: ratio of increase method

The salaries of those members who have been employed during the whole of the 5 year period would be examined, and the ratio of the total salaries of such members now aged x to the total salaries of the *same* members 5 years earlier ($\Sigma S_x/\Sigma S_{x-5}$, say) would be calculated. As described earlier, the data may be grouped as a first step in the graduation and finally a graduated series, say $_5r_x$, produced by graphical methods. Starting with a suitable radix, s_0, at the lowest age, these ratios of increase would then be applied successively to produce s_5, s_{10}, ..., etc., and thence, by interpolation, the final salary scale.

A possible criticism of this method is that no use is made of information regarding the salaries of members who have not been members of the fund throughout the 5-year period, i.e. those who have joined or left during the period. As regards recent entrants, it is probable that their rate of progression of salaries is not representative, particularly for entrants at ages above the normal, and it is therefore on the whole better not to allow their experience to be reflected in the salary scale. Again, as the main liability to be assessed relates to those members who will survive to pension age, it can be argued that it is preferable to exclude from the experience the salaries of those who fail to survive in the service, since their rate of progression of salary is likely to be below the average.

13.5. Sometimes the employer is prepared to give an estimate of the expected final salary of individual employees, and the actuary may accept this information as affording an indication of the level to which the salary scale will increase at the advanced ages. Such information should, however, be treated with caution, as the employer may not allow or may only allow on an arbitrary basis for the chance of promotion to the higher grades, particularly in the case of the younger staff. At the best this information should be regarded as providing a useful check on the actuary's own salary estimates based upon the detailed salary records of the staff, and upon the general information available as regards scales of pay and grades of staff. The scales of pay in the lowest grades should provide a sound foundation for the lower end of the salary curve. The final salary, or the ratio of the final to the commencing salary in the scale, should be examined so as to ensure that it is reasonable in the light both of the actual earnings of older members and of the general information available as to salary prospects and policy in relation to younger members.

The final salary is particularly important in the case of a scheme providing pensions based upon 'final' salaries, whilst the general shape of the curve will have an important bearing on the value to be placed upon the future contributions receivable as well as upon

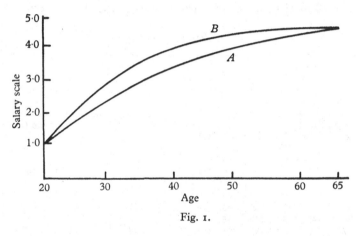

Fig. 1.

pensions based upon total or average salaries throughout service. Consider, for example, the results obtained under a final salary scheme by the use of the alternative scales A and B as shown in Fig. 1. At age 20 the liability in respect of retirements at age 65 will be the same, but the ill-health pension liability on the second basis will be larger; at ages above 20 the liability for age-retirement pensions will be larger on the basis of scale A, and except at the younger ages this difference will outweigh any difference in the opposite direction on the ill-health pension liability. For the whole membership the use of scale A in place of scale B would almost certainly result in a larger pension liability except for a very young staff. As regards contributions, scale B would produce a larger value up to some age about 40, but for members above that age the reverse would be the case, and for the total membership there may not be any great difference in the values of the future contributions on the two bases. Thus it will be seen that the net liability (value of benefits less value of contributions) is likely to be greater on the basis of scale A than on the basis of scale B.

The position is not so clear when the scheme provides pensions on an average salary throughout service basis; in this case the effect of substituting scale B for scale A would depend in large measure upon the distribution of membership at the valuation date.

Examples of the two methods of deriving the salary scale described in §§ 13.3 and 13.4 are summarized in Table 13.2.

TABLE 13.2

Central age of group x	Average salary per member		Graduated salary scales based on				Ratio of increase S_x/S_{x-5}	Graduated ratio of increase $_5r_x$	Salary scale based on (8)
	Year $Y-5$ (a)	Year Y (b)	(a)	(a)	(b)	(b)			
	(1)	(2)	(3)	(4)	(5)	(6)	(7)	(8)	(9)
22	220	200	220	1·00	210	1·00	—	1·30	1·00
27	270	300	275	1·25	280	1·25	1·36	1·21	1·30
32	325	320	320	1·45	330	1·57	1·19	1·14	1·57
37	345	370	355	1·61	365	1·74	1·14	1·105	1·79
42	390	380	380	1·73	390	1·86	1·10	1·08	1·98
47	405	420	405	1·84	415	1·98	1·09	1·06	2·14
52	420	430	430	1·95	435	2·07	1·06	1·04	2·27
57	465	450	455	2·07	455	2·17	1·05	1·02	2·36
62	470	470	470	2·14	465	2·21	1·01	—	2·41

Note. The ratio of increase S_x/S_{x-5} has been obtained above by dividing the average salary at age x in the year Y by the corresponding figure at age $x-5$ in the year $Y-5$; in practice the information from which S_x/S_{x-5} would be calculated would not be exactly the same as that employed in the calculation of scales (a) and (b), owing to the exclusion of new entrants and exits during the period.

13.6. The method of deriving a salary scale by means of a consideration of rates of increase over a recent period will, of course, break down if there has been any revision of grade rates of pay or adjustment of the general grade structure of the staff during the period of 5 years under examination. Again, the scale obtained by either method may have to be modified if the staff has not been approximately stationary in number during the period. When a staff is expanding, the proportion of higher paid posts usually falls, so that, for employees at the younger ages, the average salary which is to be expected late in service is likely to be below that now being received by employees at the advanced ages. Either the scale derived from the average salaries attained or the ratios of recent salary increases would then have to be modified in the light of recent variations in the size of the staff and the information available from the employers as to the extent of probable future changes. It may be found necessary in an extreme case to vary the degree of modification with the age attained at the valuation date; this might be done by subdividing the membership into a few broad age groups and adopting a different salary scale for each group, making allowance for this feature.

TABLE 13.3

The effect of employing an unadjusted salary scale derived from the salaries of a staff with an abnormal distribution

Age attained	Salary scale		Present age	Salary scale applied	Total future salary to age 60 per unit of present salary	Salary at age 60 per unit of present salary
	Normal (a)	Abnormal (b)				
20	200	200	20	(a)	68·5	2·1
30	300	300		(b)	67·5	2·1
40	360	340	40	(a)	21·9	1·17
50	400	400		(b)	22·9	1·24
60	420	420				

A similar problem may arise where the total numbers remain constant, if the age distribution of the staff is abnormal. Thus, an unusual influx of employees some years ago may now appear as a comparatively large number of staff at the middle ages with salaries at those ages somewhat below the average. As will be seen from Table 13.3, the direct inclusion of this feature in a salary scale of the relative type would lead to an underestimate of the total future salaries for the young employees, accompanied by an over-estimate of final as well as total salaries for those now in the middle ages affected by the abnormality.

One solution of this difficulty in a large fund would be to take out from the age group affected a proportion of the members representing the number in excess of those required to give a reasonable balance of staff. The remainder of the staff would then be treated on normal lines with a normal salary scale and the 'surplus' members would be valued separately with a salary scale flatter than normal to allow for the subnormal future salary career expected for this group. In a small fund more approximate methods might be considered to meet such a situation, e.g. for the age group affected an *ad hoc* adjustment to the net liability calculated on the basis of the normal salary scale.

13.7. Correspondence of salary scale with salary data valued

The salary scale, being derived by reference to the actual individual salaries received, represents either relatively, or occasionally as an absolute amount, the average salary received between ages x and $(x+1)$. Normal salary increments, apart from those arising on promotion, may for a particular fund be granted on the anniversary of entry to the service, or on the member's birthday or at a fixed date in the year. In the first two cases, individual increases may occur at any time over the financial year of the fund and, as the salary data would normally be aggregated for all members aged x nearest birthday at the valuation date, the average salary received over the previous year (if information were supplied in this form) would usually correspond to s_{x-1} on the salary scale; similarly, if the rate of salary payable at the valuation date were given, this would correspond with $s_{x-\frac{1}{2}}$.

In the third case, if the fixed date for increases falls on the last day of the financial year of the fund the salaries received over the past year would correspond to s_{x-1}; the rate of salary at the valuation date would correspond to s_x, but only approximately so, owing to the exclusion of increases on promotion which may occur during the ensuing year. If the fixed date for increases falls on the first day of the year, the salaries received over the past year would correspond to s_{x-1}, whilst the rate payable on the day following the end of the year would correspond to s_x approximately.

The salary data asked for would depend to some extent on the internal records kept by the employer, but, in whatever form they are supplied, it is necessary to ensure that the denominator incorporated in the valuation factors corresponds, i.e. $s_{x-1}D_x$, $s_{x-\frac{1}{2}}D_x$ or s_xD_x, as the case may be.

13.8. High-salaried officials

A staff comprising clerical and administrative grades normally includes a few employees with salaries well above the average. If these employees are recruited by promotion from the lower grades, the inclusion of their salaries in the body of data will give proper weight to the average salary expectation of members now below the normal ages of promotion to the higher paid posts. If, however, only a proportion of such senior posts is filled by promotion, and the remainder by outside recruitment, only a corresponding proportion of the senior officials should be included in the construction of the salary scale. The remainder may then have to be valued by a special salary scale if the normal scale is found to be inappropriate, and an additional reserve may be necessary to cover the strain which may arise on the appointment of their successors.

Even when all the senior posts are filled by promotion, the total number of such posts will be relatively small, and it will therefore frequently happen that the age distribution of the high-salaried officials at a particular valuation date is abnormal. For example, if some of the senior officials have recently retired and comparatively young men have been promoted to succeed them, the average age of the high-salaried officials may be somewhat lower at a particular valuation date than might normally be expected, and, in consequence, the average salaries of the staff may be higher, say, between ages 45 and 50 and lower between ages 50 and 55. This wave in the curve of average salaries would gradually move up to the highest ages as members grew older, and at a later date may be replaced by a fluctuation in the opposite direction. This is a special case of the abnormality discussed in § 13.6 and might be dealt with by redistributing the salaries of the senior officials so as to secure a more normal spread over the ages at which such officials are found, and adjusting correspondingly the salary scale or the data from which the salary scale is derived. It may be thought desirable in an extreme case to make a further adjustment for certain groups of members at the middle and later ages on this account so as to recognize the fact that, owing to the relative youthfulness of the senior officials at a particular valuation date, the other employees in these groups have a subnormal expectation of promotion.

An alternative method of dealing with high-salaried officials is to value them as a small separate group, or individually, using a special salary scale or scales. For the normal body of members, excluding the senior officials, the salary scale employed should in the first place be derived from the salaries of the members excluding the senior posts, but it will be necessary to make an adjustment to allow for expected promotions of younger members as successors to the present senior officials. This adjustment to the salary scale should strictly vary with the age at present attained by the members to correspond with the varying chance of promotion, but instead of employing a number of salary scales which such an adjustment would require it may be thought preferable to estimate separately the extra liability arising in respect of promotions to the senior posts from the present staff.

The extent of the adjustments indicated in the previous paragraphs will necessarily be somewhat arbitrary and must depend in the last resort upon the personal judgement of the actuary. As these adjustments are very troublesome, the senior officials should be included with the main body of the staff whenever this can be justified.

13.9. Grouped salaries

In Life Office types of pension schemes, contributions and benefits do not normally vary directly with the total salary but are fixed over certain ranges of salary, e.g. £250–299, £300–349, and so on. A similar situation may be met in a private fund as shown in Table 13.4.

Although the effective salary of an individual member may thus remain constant for a number of years and proceed by fairly large discrete steps, the progression of salaries for a group of members may be expected to show a gradual increase from age to age. It would therefore be legitimate to adopt the normal technique of incorporating the salary scale into the valuation formulae. The scale, which would increase from age to age as a smooth series, would be constructed in a manner similar to that described earlier in the normal case, except that the individual salaries initially tabulated would be the effective salaries brought into account. The valuation factors incorporating this scale would, of course, be used in conjunction with the effective salaries in arriving at the valuation liabilities.

TABLE 13.4

Actual salary	Corresponding effective salary for pension scheme purposes
£ 250–299	£ 275
300–349	325

13.10. Salary excluding first £x

Occasionally, under the rules of the fund, the effective salary on which contributions and pensions are calculated is the total salary less some constant amount. Such an arrangement may be made, for example, so as to avoid duplication with the State pension. Thus if the employer wishes to secure a *total* retiring allowance of one-half of retiring salary for an employee at age 65 after 40 years of service, the effective scheme salary or net salary might be defined as gross salary less £135. A member retiring after 40 years on a salary of £500 would then receive

$\frac{1}{2} \times$ £$(500-135) \eqsim$ £182 from the scheme

plus   £68 from the State (26s. per week as a single person)

Total   £250 = 50% of full salary of £500

Two methods of dealing with this situation are possible:

(*a*) Calculate the values of benefits and contributions:

 (i) on the basis of the gross remuneration before deducting the constant amount, by means of factors incorporating a salary scale appropriate to the gross remuneration; and

 (ii) on the basis of a fixed salary per member equal to the constant deduction by means of factors which do not involve a salary scale.

The final values would then be obtained by deducting (ii) from (i).

(*b*) Value benefits and contributions by reference to net salaries directly, using factors which incorporate a modified salary scale corresponding to the net salary.

If method (*b*) is employed, the salary scale should be derived from a consideration of individual net or effective salaries by the normal methods. It would not, in general, be correct to determine a suitable scale appropriate to gross salaries and to obtain the modified scale from this by deducting the constant amount, unless the scale corresponded closely in absolute amounts with the average actual remuneration over the whole range of ages of present members.

If the normal average salaries at ages x and $x+t$ are S_x and S_{x+t} respectively, the salary scale appropriate to gross salaries would show a ratio of increase between these ages of S_{x+t}/S_x, whilst the scale appropriate to net salaries (after excluding a constant amount c) would show a ratio of $(S_{x+t}-c)/(S_x-c)$.

If the actual average salaries of members now aged x is $(AS)_x$ the forecast of the average net salary at age $x+t$ would be, by method (*a*),

$$(AS)_x \frac{S_{x+t}}{S_x} - c$$

and by method (*b*)

$$\{(AS)_x - c\}\, (S_{x+t}-c)/(S_x-c).$$

These would be equal if

$$(AS)_x \left\{ \frac{S_{x+t}-c}{S_x-c} - \frac{S_{x+t}}{S_x} \right\} = c \left\{ \frac{S_{x+t}-c}{S_x-c} - 1 \right\}.$$

This equation reduces to

$$c\{(AS)_x - S_x\}(S_{x+t} - S_x) = 0.$$

Thus apart from the limiting cases where $c = 0$ or where $S_{x+t} = S_x$ (i.e. a constant salary) the two methods would only produce the same results if $(AS)_x = S_x$, i.e. if the actual average salary of members being valued at age x coincides with the scale. For example, if $S_x = 300$, $S_{x+t} = 600$, $c = 100$ and $(AS)_x = 280$, (a) would give a forecast at age $x + t$ of $280 \cdot \frac{600}{300} - 100 = 460$, (b) would give a forecast at age $x + t$ of $(280 - 100) \frac{500}{200} = 450$.

The two methods thus involve in general mutually incompatible assumptions in the forecasting of future salaries. On balance, method (a) is likely to give more satisfactory results, since it is less sensitive to variations in $(AS)_x$ from the normal average salary S_x.

Although, superficially, method (b) has certain attractions as compared with (a), in that fewer calculations are needed, it should only be used with extreme caution, as any error of judgement in the graduation of the scale would lead to a larger mistake in the final result than an error of an equal magnitude in the graduation of the salary curve based upon gross salaries. This consideration is of particular importance when the constant deduction is so large that the net remuneration at the younger ages is reduced to a relatively small amount. For example, if the constant deduction is £150, the commencing salary of members entering at the youngest age is £175 and the average retiring salary is £500, the ratio of final to commencing net salary under method (b) would be

$$(500{-}150)/(175{-}150)$$

or 14·0, whereas correspondingly under method (a) it would be necessary to make estimates of gross salaries ranging from £175 to £500, the ratio being $500/175 = 2{\cdot}86$ only.

Where estimates are required at the same time on the basis of the gross and the net remuneration, method (a) should obviously be employed, if only to ensure consistency. It should be noted that a constant percentage increase in salaries would leave unchanged the salary scale which related to gross salaries, whilst the scale applicable to net salaries after deduction of a constant amount would have to be amended.

13.11. Salary limits

Frequently in schemes in which benefits and contributions are related to salaries, there is an upper limit to the amount of salary which may count for purposes of the scheme. Where the limit is so high that it only operates in rare cases, it may be ignored in the valuation, apart from a modification in the values in respect of those members who have already reached or nearly reached the limit. Where, however, the limit is fixed so that an appreciable proportion of the staff is likely to be affected before retirement on pension, it will involve an important adjustment to the liability. Normally, the method of dealing with salary increases by means of the relative scale is independent of the actual level of salaries, but where a limit of salary is in operation the actual level of salaries in relation to that limit will affect the shape of the salary curve. Accordingly, it is necessary in such a case to keep in mind in determining a suitable salary scale not merely the ratios of increase which the salary scale will measure but also the actual level of salaries.

The procedure outlined in §§ 13.3–13.6 would again be followed, but the actual salary of an individual member would be replaced by the limit of salary if this has been reached. As in the case of the high-salaried officials discussed in § 13.8, it may be necessary to make an adjustment in fixing the scale, if the proportion of members already subject to the limit is abnormal at particular ages.

The scale derived from a consideration of the effective salaries operating in the scheme with a salary limit would be incorporated in the valuation factors in the normal way, and these factors would then be applied to the effective salaries of all members whether at or below the limit of salary at the valuation date. At certain ages, at which there are members who have already reached the limit, the valuation by means of factors incorporating a salary scale would seem to imply that the effective salaries of such members will increase beyond the limit. This apparent inconsistency disappears, however, when it is remembered that the salary scale is used to forecast not individual salaries but the aggregate salaries of a group of members of the same attained age.

If at a particular age there was a disproportionate number of members on the salary limit, the excess number (positive or negative) should be separated from the normal body of members and valued separately by means of factors with the salary element omitted; a corresponding adjustment to the data should of course have been made in collating the effective salaries of members for the purpose of deriving the salary scale.

In particular circumstances it may be practicable to use alternative methods. Thus, it might be possible to make the valuation in the first place by reference to salaries without limit (the salary scale being derived accordingly) and to make an adjustment by deducting estimates of the values based upon salaries at future ages in excess of the limit. If such an approach to the problem is made, it should be borne in mind that it will not in general be correct to forecast individual salaries by means of a salary scale and then to apply the limit. Similarly, it will not be correct to estimate, by the use of the salary scale, an age at which the salary limit is reached either in individual cases or on the average.

If more than one salary scale is required for forecasting in a particular scheme (e.g. where pensions and contributions are both related to salaries but in different ways), it is desirable that the scales adopted should be directly related to each other in some way, since they are required in order to forecast functions of the same underlying salaries. This might be done, for example, by determining one salary scale s_x and deriving another scale as $k_x s_x$. k_x would be obtained by reference to the basic data of the fund and suitably graduated. There would be a risk of inconsistency being introduced into the estimates if each scale were to be derived from the data and graduated independently.

13.12. In the case of a small fund it may not be possible to construct a satisfactory salary scale from the available information. In such a case it would be necessary to adopt a scale found to be suitable in the case of another larger fund covering a similar class of member. Even in such a case, however, it would be desirable to check as far as possible the suitability of this scale by a comparison of average salaries in broad age groups and the rates of increase actually experienced over recent years, with the corresponding figures implied by the salary scale to be adopted.

CHAPTER 14

VALUATION OF WIDOWS' FUNDS: REVERSIONARY METHOD

14.1. Reversionary method

Before the valuation of widows' funds is dealt with in detail the two alternative methods commonly employed will be considered in general terms.

Under the first method, generally described as the 'reversionary method', the probability of a member being married at the date of death is separately assessed for present married members, bachelors and widowers, and in respect of existing and any subsequent marriages. The main liability normally arises in respect of the reversionary benefit to present wives of members now married, and this is assessed with as high a degree of accuracy as desired by considering the joint status of each member and his wife allowing for the actual ages. For the remainder of the liability it is necessary to determine suitable rates of marriage of bachelors and of remarriage of widowers as well as the relative ages of husband and wife at date of marriage. The experience of different funds may show considerable variations in these rates, and it is therefore desirable that the rates should be derived as far as possible from the actual experience of the fund under consideration.

14.2. Collective method

Under the second method, known as the 'collective method', the valuation incorporates directly into the factors estimates of the expected proportion of members married at date of death and of the average age difference of husband and wife, all members being valued together irrespective of their individual present marital status or actual ages of present wives. The method is relatively simple, but it will only lead to reasonable results if it is possible to determine a series for the proportion married according to attained age (h_x) which will apply satisfactorily to the existing membership both at the present time and in the future as the members advance in age. Now the proportion married among members now aged x is the net result of rates of mortality amongst married and single members and their wives, of rates of marriage and remarriage and of differences between the ages at marriage of husbands and wives all operating over a number of years. As these factors are bound to have varied with the passage of time and changing economic and sociological circumstances, there must be a considerable element of doubt as to whether the proportion married among members now aged x will be reproduced in the future as members less than that age pass through age x. Despite the apparently sweeping assumptions thus implicit in the collective method, however, it has been found that the proportion married exhibits a considerable degree of stability over a number of years in a particular fund if the conditions governing membership have not varied, and this is apparently due to the fact that variations in the rates which enter into the determination of the emerging proportions married tend to operate in different directions and so tend to neutralize one another. Despite this reassuring feature, the actuary employing the collective method should realize that the method involves a considerable degree of speculation as to the future, since the fact that the proportions married age by age have been reasonably stable in the past cannot necessarily be taken as a firm assurance that this will hold good in the future.

14.3. Comparison of methods

The difference between the two methods may thus be summarized as follows: The reversionary method implicitly uses the proportions married which will arise if *current* experience as to marriage, mortality, etc., rates continues unchanged (apart from any modifications deliberately introduced in order to allow for future trends). The collective method, on the other hand, uses the proportions married which have resulted from the various rates which have operated over a past period of anything up to 40 years or more. Thus the collective method discards the available knowledge of the trends of the rates over many years, and its use is only justifiable if the actuary is satisfied that the changes in these various rates have been compensatory in character, and if a similar situation is likely to obtain in the future. It may be noted that in the case of a fund where the conditions of membership have changed, e.g. where membership was voluntary at the commencement but has been compulsory subsequently, the proportions married at certain ages may be unusually high and will not be suitable for the purpose of forecasting the proportions married in the future at those ages among the younger and more recent members.

Having regard to all the uncertainties involved in the method the actuary may well feel it advisable to employ in the valuation proportions married which are somewhat higher than those exhibited by the present membership.

14.4. From the foregoing, it will be realized that on theoretical grounds the reversionary method is preferable to the collective method since it proceeds by an analytical process of building up the liability from the various rates operating, and it is possible to allow directly for the most recent experience and for expected future trends in such rates. In practice, however, it is only in the case of large funds that sufficient data are available to enable all the rates required to be derived. In such circumstances, the actuary may have to decide whether more reliable results may be expected from the use of the reversionary method based upon rates derived from other funds or by the use of the collective method incorporating the proportions married of the particular fund being valued. Frequently a middle way is practicable and preferable, i.e. to value some of the major items of liabilities and assets by reversionary formulae and the remainder by collective methods.

14.5. Reversionary method: formulae

In subsequent paragraphs of this chapter the formulae under the reversionary method for a few specimen cases are derived.

Separate estimates are made of the liabilities in respect of: ·

(i) the existing wives of the members who are married on the valuation date,

(ii) the future wives of those of them who will become widowers and subsequently remarry, and

(iii) the future wives of bachelors and of widowers on the valuation date on their first, second, etc., subsequent marriage, each marriage being dealt with separately and the series taken up to a point at which the liability in respect of any further widowerhood and remarriage would be negligible and may be ignored.

An 'individual' valuation is not necessarily carried out, but the members of each status are valued together in groups according to age.

The series of formulae set out in the following paragraphs are built up in chain fashion, commencing with the factors appropriate to married members and their present wives. These are used to derive the value of a varying assurance on the marriage of unmarried* men, the factors for unmarried men are in turn employed to derive the value of a varying assurance on the widowerhood of present married members, and so on.

The first specimen case considered is relatively simple, but it will suffice to illustrate the principles involved. It should be noted that in the formulae developed in this and the following chapter it is assumed that fractions of years of service or membership will rank for benefit if the benefit depends upon years of membership. If complete years only were to rank some minor modifications in certain of the formulae would be required. An indication of this type of modification has already been given in the formulae derived for a specimen pension scheme in Chapter 10.

14.6. Example A

The scheme under consideration may be briefly described as follows:

Membership is confined to males employed in a certain profession. A benefit of £100 per annum is payable on the death of the member for the remainder of the lifetime of any widow left by him or until her remarriage. A fixed contribution per month is payable until age 65 estimated to be sufficient to meet the cost of the benefits.

---

* In Chapters 14 and 15 'unmarried' should generally be read as including widowers as well as bachelors unless the contrary is clearly indicated.

Tables required: The basic tables required for such a scheme are:

(i) A life table appropriate to males; different tables would be used for married and unmarried members if the experience or other relevant data rendered this necessary.

(ii) Marriage rates of bachelors and remarriage rates of widowers.

(iii) A life table appropriate to wives of members.

(iv) Mortality rates of widows.

(v) Remarriage rates of widows.

(vi) A table showing, for each age at marriage of a member, the average difference between the age of the member and that of his wife.

If withdrawal from the profession is an important factor, the life table (i) would be replaced by a double decrement table incorporating both mortality and withdrawal rates. It should be noted that, as the assurance to the widow presumably extends throughout the lifetime of the member, table (i) would be extended to the end of life.

Tables (iv) and (v) would be used to calculate a series of annuity values $\bar{a}_y'$ to a widow aged y commencing on the husband's death and terminating on the death of the widow or on her remarriage. As remarriage rates are essentially select in form it would not be possible to combine these two tables into a single aggregate double decrement table for widows from which all values of $\bar{a}_y'$ could be calculated directly. Values of the annuity would be calculated at a number of pivotal ages and intermediate values obtained by interpolation.

14.7. Present wives of existing married members

The valuation of the benefit in respect of the present wife aged y of a married member aged x is effected simply by means of a reversionary annuity, e.g.

$$^mB_{xy} = \frac{\sum\limits_{t=0}^{\infty} d_{x+t} D_{y+t+\frac{1}{2}} \bar{a}'_{y+t+\frac{1}{2}}}{l_x D_y}.$$

l_x and d_{x+t} would be based upon the table (i) appropriate to male married members, and D_y and $D_{y+t+\frac{1}{2}}$ on table (iii). It may be noted that if the widow's annuity is not terminable on remarriage and if the same mortality table may be used for wives and widows, the expression $^mB_{xy}$ reduces to the normal form of reversionary annuity, viz. $(\bar{a}_y - \bar{a}_{xy})$. $^mB_{xy}$ would theoretically allow for the actual present ages of the member and his wife, but in practice some grouping would be desirable.

Unless the spread of ages of the wives of members aged x is restricted within a narrow range, it is not satisfactory to assume an average age for the wives and to value all these members together. Complete tables for all ages of wives need not be constructed, however, and it will usually be considered sufficient to do a certain amount of grouping of the wives and so reduce the tables of factors required and the number of groups to be separately valued. If the spread of ages of the wives is wide and all members aged x were valued together on the assumption that all the wives were aged (say) z, being the average of the actual ages, the liability would be understated. Presuming that $x - z$ is positive, this difference will increase with the passage of time, since the older wives in the group will die first and the average age of the wives surviving jointly with their husbands t years hence will be less than $z + t$. The younger wives will be the more likely to survive their husbands and to become claimants on the fund, introducing a liability greater than that allowed for. The wider the range of wives' ages, the greater will be the scope for error. If, therefore, the members aged x are separated into groups, each group relating to members whose wives' ages are within a short range, and each group is valued separately according to the average age of the wives in the group, the error will be reduced to a minimum. The precise grouping to be adopted will depend on the age distribution of the members and their wives, and will be decided after examination of che data. For example, the method of procedure might be as follows:

Group together (tabulating according to age of member in each group):

(i) all members whose wives' ages are not more than 3 years less chan their own, investigate the average difference in this group (say 1) and value all these members on the assumption that the ages of their wives are 1 year less than their own;

(ii) all members whose wives are more than 3 years but not more than 6 years younger and value as if the difference were (say) 4;

(iii) all members whose wives are more than 6 but not more than 11 years younger and value as if the difference were (say) 8; and

(iv) all members whose wives are more than 11 years younger and value as if the difference were (say) 15.

There would thus be four series of factors to construct in this case (corresponding to $x - y = 1, 4, 8$ and 15). The percentage error increases with increasing age of the lives and also with a wider age-difference range. The effect of remarriage at ages where the rates are material would reduce the discrepancy, since the reversionary value to a younger widow would be reduced to a proportionately larger extent by reason of the heavier remarriage risk.

14.8. Future first wives of unmarried men

A double decrement table incorporating mortality rates appropriate to single male lives and marriage rates (table (ii)) would be constructed with columns $(bl)_x$, $(bm)_x$ and $(bd)_x$ representing the numbers of unmarried members surviving in this status at age x, the numbers marrying at age x last birthday and the numbers dying at age x last birthday respectively. If necessary a further decrement—withdrawal—would be incorporated.

The factor required to value the liability arising in respect of the future first wives of unmarried members now aged x is

$$
{}^m_b B_x = \frac{\sum_{t=0}^{\infty} v^{x+t+\frac{1}{2}} (bm)_{x+t} {}^m B_{[x+t+\frac{1}{2}]:\, y+t+\frac{1}{2}}}{v^x (bl)_x},
$$

where ${}^m B_{[x+t+\frac{1}{2}]:\, y+t+\frac{1}{2}}$ is a factor representing the mean value of benefits in respect of wives of married members aged $x + t + \frac{1}{2}$ on marriage.* This would be obtained by interpolation from the sets

---

* The select bracket is placed round age $x + t + \frac{1}{2}$ as an indication that the average value of the factor ${}^m B_{x+t+\frac{1}{2}:\, y+t+\frac{1}{2}}$ should be obtained by reference to the age distribution of husbands and wives on marriage. For simplicity the expression $(y + t + \frac{1}{2})$ in this and similar formulae is used to denote the average age of wives of husbands aged $(x + t + \frac{1}{2})$; this is not necessarily equal to y increased by $t + \frac{1}{2}$, where y is the average age of wives corresponding to husbands aged x.

of $^mB_{x:y}$ already calculated for present married members (see §14.7) having regard to the age distribution of wives at the time of marriage to members at age $x+t+\frac{1}{2}$. For the same reason as explained in §14.7 it would strictly be incorrect to use values $^mB_{x+t+\frac{1}{2}:y+t+\frac{1}{2}}$ corresponding to the arithmetical mean age difference of husbands and wives at the date of marriage.

As the marriage rates of bachelors and widowers are likely to differ very appreciably, separate calculations of the factors $^m_bB_x$ should strictly be made for these classes. In practice, however, the number of widowers may not be sufficient to justify such action.

14.9. Future wives of present married men

To estimate this liability, it seems hardly necessary to subdivide the members in groups according to the ages of their present wives. It should be sufficient to value on the basis of a double decrement mortality and widowerhood table, for which purpose the rate of widowerhood may conveniently be obtained by reference to the average ages and rates of mortality of the wives. The factor, applicable to all married men, is

$$\frac{\sum_{t=0}^{\infty} v^{x+t+\frac{1}{2}} (mw)_{x+t} \, {}^m_b B_{x+t+\frac{1}{2}}}{v^x \, (ml)_x},$$

where $(ml)_x$ = the number of married men alive at age x, shown by the double-decrement table, $(mw)_x$ = the number shown as becoming widowers between ages x and $x+1$ and $^m_bB_{x+t+\frac{1}{2}}$ is the factor representing the liability in respect of the future wife of an unmarried man aged $x+t+\frac{1}{2}$ (see §14.8). If it is considered necessary to deal separately with bachelors and widowers, the last-mentioned factor should be that appropriate to widowers.

14.10. Further marriages

The liability in respect of second wives to present unmarried members, third wives to present married members, etc., could be similarly computed, but these contingencies are sufficiently small to justify more approximate methods, or even some fairly arbitrary reserve to cover the further liability. As an indication of the reduction in the liability in respect of successive marriages it may be noted that in the recent valuation of the widows' fund of a Scottish Bank the liability in respect of second wives of married members represented ·055 of the liability in respect of present wives, whilst the ratio of the liabilities for second and first wives of present unmarried members was ·068 (see *T.F.A.* vol. XIX, pp. 149 et seq.).

14.11. Existing widows

The liability in respect of existing widows would be valued by means of $\bar{a}'_y$ where the values would not be the select values brought into the calculation of $^m B_{xy}$, but would be only partly select, or ultimate values of $\bar{a}'_y$, as the widows existing at the valuation date will have passed through part or the whole of the period during which the risk of remarriage since the date of widowhood is material.

14.12. Contributions

In the present example the contribution does not vary with the marital status of the member and ceases at age 65. The differences in mortality up to age 65 according to marital status are not likely to be sufficient to produce important differences in the value of the contribution payable until age 65, and it would probably be satisfactory to value the contributions for all members together by means of factors $\dfrac{\sum\limits_{t=0}^{64-x} D_{x+t+\frac{1}{2}}}{D_x}$ calculated from a life table based upon all members' mortality rates, which would lie between the rates appropriate to married and unmarried members. If allowance is made for the withdrawal element in the calculation of the liabilities, similar allowance should be made in the valuation of contributions by using a table subject to the decrements of death and withdrawal.

14.13. Example B

A widows' scheme is run in conjunction with a staff pension fund for males, who are entitled to a pension on retirement at age 65 or on earlier ill-health retirement.

The widow's benefit consists of a pension of £4 per annum for each year of service of the husband up to the date of retirement on pension or the date of death in service. This benefit is only available for widows where marriage took place before the husband's retirement and ceases on the remarriage of the widow.

A monthly contribution is payable by the members during active service at a certain rate (c) whilst unmarried and at double that rate whilst married. An equivalent sum is paid by the employer.

On withdrawal unmarried from the service or on death or retirement as an unmarried person there is payable a benefit equal to one-half of the total contributions paid by the member without interest.

As the widow's benefit depends upon the period of service of the member and as marriages contracted after retirement do not rank under this widows' scheme, it is clearly necessary to differentiate between males in active service and after retirement.

Tables required:

(i) A service table for males involving decrements of withdrawal, death in service, retirement on ill-health and age retirement at 65. This table will be in exactly the same form as that used in the valuation of the member's own pension, but for the reasons discussed in §7.7 the rates may not be identical. Differentiation may be necessary between bachelors and married members.

(ii) Marriage rates of bachelors and remarriage rates of widowers.

(iii) A life table appropriate to wives of members.

(iv) Mortality rates of widows.

(v) Remarriage rates of widows.

(vi) A table of average age differences at marriage—ignoring for this purpose any marriages contracted after retirement.

(vii) Mortality rates of members after retirement on ill-health pension—these would be select in form.

(viii) Mortality rates of retired members who reach age 65 in service.

14.14. Present wives of existing married members

Consider a member now aged x with a wife aged y, the member having joined the service at age $(x-n)$.

The widow's benefit arising on the *death of the member in service* in respect of the n years of service rendered to date is $4n$ per annum, and this would be valued by the factor

$$
{}^{m}B_{xy}^{d} = \frac{\sum\limits_{t=0}^{64-x} d_{x+t} \cdot D_{y+t+\frac{1}{2}} \, \bar{a}'_{y+t+\frac{1}{2}}}{l_x D_y} = \frac{\sum C_{x+t:\,y+t}^{d(wa)}}{l_x D_y},
$$

where D_y is based upon table (iii), $\bar{a}'_y$ is calculated from tables (iv) and (v), and d_{x+t} and l_x are derived from table (i).

In respect of future years of service the widow's benefit of £4 for each year of service accruing on death in service would be valued by the factor

$$
{}^{m}(IB)_{xy}^{d} = \{ \tfrac{1}{2} C_{xy}^{d(wa)} + 1\tfrac{1}{2} C_{x+1:\,y+1}^{d(wa)} + \ldots + (64\tfrac{1}{2} - x)\, C_{64:\,y+64-x}^{d(wa)} \} / l_x D_y
$$

$$
= \frac{\sum\limits_{t=0}^{64-x} (M_{x+t:\,y+t}^{d(wa)} - \tfrac{1}{2} C_{x+t:\,y+t}^{d(wa)})}{l_x D_y}.
$$

The benefit £$4n$ already accrued in respect of past service would also give rise to a liability on the *member's death after his retirement*, and this would be valued by a factor

$$
{}^{mr}B_{xy}^{d} = \frac{\sum\limits_{t=0}^{64-x} r_{x+t} D_{y+t+\frac{1}{2}} \, \bar{a}'_{x+t+\frac{1}{2}\,|\,y+t+\frac{1}{2}} + r_{65} D_{y+65-x} \, \bar{a}'_{65\,|\,y+65-x}}{l_x D_y}
$$

$$
= \frac{\sum\limits_{t=0}^{65-x} {}^{r}C_{x+t:\,y+t}^{d(wa)}}{l_x D_y} = \frac{{}^{r}M_{xy}^{d(wa)}}{l_x D_y} \quad \text{say.}
$$

The liability on the member's death after his retirement of £4 in respect of each year of future service between age x and age 65 would be valued by the factor

$$
{}^{mr}(IB)_{xy}^{d} = \frac{\sum\limits_{t=0}^{64-x} ({}^{r}M_{x+t:\,y+t}^{d(wa)} - \tfrac{1}{2}{}^{r}C_{x+t:\,y+t}^{d(wa)})}{l_x D_y}.
$$

As already described in connexion with Example A these sets of factors would be calculated for a few specimen age differences $(x - y)$ and then applied to the existing married membership suitably grouped in a way corresponding to those age differences, so as to reduce the volume of the work.

$\bar{a}'_{x|y}$ is a reversionary annuity to a widow after the death of a pensioner who has just retired at age x. In the calculation of the reversionary annuity the values of the annuity to the widow would, of course, make allowance for cessation on remarriage, as described in § 14.6, and as regards the male life heavy rates of mortality appropriate to an ill-health pensioner would be used, except of course for the value corresponding to retirement at age 65.

For convenience the factors $^mB^d$ and $^{mr}B^d$ could be calculated together, and similar action is possible for $^m(IB)^d$ and $^{mr}(IB)^d$. Again it should be noted that if membership commences at a fixed age, or if the range of entry ages is sufficiently narrow to justify the assumption of an average entry age x_0, the two factors $^mB^d$ and $^m(IB)^d$ could be amalgamated thus:

$$\frac{\sum\limits_{t=0}^{64-x} (x-x_0+t+\tfrac{1}{2})\, C^{d(wa)}_{x+t:y+t}}{l_x D_y}$$

(which form lends itself directly to commutation column work), and similarly the factors $^{mr}B^d$ and $^{mr}(IB)^d$ could be calculated together in the form

$$\frac{\sum\limits_{t=0}^{64-x} (x-x_0+t+\tfrac{1}{2})\,^rC^{d(wa)}_{x+t:y+t}+(65-x_0)\,^rC^{d(wa)}_{65:y+65-x}}{l_x D_y}.$$

14.15. Future first wives of unmarried men

For the purpose of valuing the liability arising in respect of such wives a marriage and service table extending to age 65 is required with columns $(bl)_x$, $(bm)_x$ and $(bg)_x$ representing the relative numbers of bachelors respectively in service at age x, marrying at age x last birthday and ceasing to remain in service from all causes at age x last birthday (the same benefit is payable on the death, withdrawal or retirement of a bachelor in Example B, so that all decrements apart from marriages may be considered together).

The factor required to value the benefit in respect of each year of service already rendered by the bachelor aged x at the valuation date is

$$^m_bB^d_x = \frac{\sum\limits_{t=0}^{64-x} v^{x+t+\frac{1}{2}}\,(bm)_{x+t}\,\{^mB^d_{[x+t+\frac{1}{2}]:y+t+\frac{1}{2}}+{}^{mr}B^d_{[x+t+\frac{1}{2}]:y+t+\frac{1}{2}}\}}{v^x (bl)_x},$$

where the $B_{[x]:y}$ functions would be calculated from the values $^mB^d_{xy}$ and $^{mr}B^d_{xy}$ already calculated by reference to the age-distribution of wives of members marrying at age $(x+t+\frac{1}{2})$, as explained in § 14.8 above. It should be noted that the weighted average age y_1, such that $^mB^d_{x:y_1}=^mB^d_{[x]:y}$, is not necessarily equal to the weighted average age y_2 given by the equation $^{mr}B^d_{x:y_2}=^{mr}B^d_{[x]:y}$, since the incidence of the liability is quite different in the two functions.

As regards the benefits accruing in respect of years of service rendered after the valuation date, the appropriate valuation function* is

$$^m_b(IB)^d_x$$

$$=\frac{\displaystyle\sum_{t=0}^{64-x} v^{x+t+\frac{1}{2}}(bm)_{x+t}\left\{(t+\frac{1}{2})(^mB^d+^{mr}B^d)+^m(IB)^d+^{mr}(IB)^d\right\}_{[x+t+\frac{1}{2}]:y+t+\frac{1}{2}}}{v^x(bl)_x}$$

$$=\frac{\displaystyle\sum_{t=0}^{64-x}\left\{\sum_{n=t}^{64-x} v^{x+n+\frac{1}{2}}(bm)_{x+n}(^mB^d+^{mr}B^d)_{[x+n+\frac{1}{2}]:y+n+\frac{1}{2}}\right.}{v^x(bl)_x}$$
$$\frac{\left.+v^{x+t+\frac{1}{2}}(bm)_{x+t}(^m(IB)^d+^{mr}(IB)^d-\frac{1}{2}{}^mB^d-\frac{1}{2}{}^{mr}B^d)_{[x+t+\frac{1}{2}]:y+t+\frac{1}{2}}\right\}}{v^x(bl)_x}.$$

Precisely the same formulae would apply to widowers in respect of future wives, although as the liability in this case is likely to be relatively small the assumption of an average entry age, with a consequent simplification of the factor work, would generally be justified.

14.16. Future wives of present married men

The valuation functions appropriate to second wives of present married members would be built up in similar fashion from the two factors $^m_bB^d_x$ and $^m_b(IB)^d_x$ in conjunction with a service and widower-hood table for married members, corresponding to the table used in the valuation of first wives of married members but with the added decrement of widowerhood based upon average ages of wives of married members alive at age x.

---

* The second expression for $^m_b(IB)^d_x$ has been given, as this form lends itself more readily to commutation column work; alternative forms of certain factors are also given for the same reason subsequently.

14.17. Further marriages

These would be dealt with as indicated in § 14.10. As remarriages after retirement do not rank for the purpose of this scheme the liability in any case would be relatively very small and might be covered by a small additional reserve.

14.18. Benefits to widows of members who have already retired and to incumbent beneficiaries

The benefit would be a known amount in each case, and an individual valuation by reversionary or immediate annuity factors could be made. If there were a sufficient number of reversionary annuities to value some grouping might be effected according to the age differences of husbands and wives on lines similar to those indicated for the reversionary valuation of the benefit to married men (see § 14.7).

14.19. Contributions

These vary with marital status. The basic rate (c) payable whilst unmarried could be valued for all members as in Example A, whilst the further contribution (c) payable only by married members could be valued as follows:

(i) *During present marriages of married members.* The appropriate factor is

$$\bar{a}^m_{xy} = \sum_{t=0}^{64-x} \frac{D_{x+t+\frac{1}{2}:y+t+\frac{1}{2}}}{D_{xy}},$$

where $D_{xy} = l_x D_y$, l_x being based upon the service table for married men and D_y on the life table for wives. This temporary joint annuity factor would not vary very materially with the varying age differences of the husband and wife, and it would probably be quite satisfactory to calculate two sets of factors only corresponding to $y = x - 2$ and $y = x - 8$ say, which would be applied to married members where the age difference $x - y$ was not more than 5 years and over 5 years respectively.

(ii) *During future married status of present bachelors and widowers.* The factor is of the form

$$_b\bar{a}^m_x = \frac{\sum_{t=0}^{64-x} v^{x+t+\frac{1}{2}} (bm)_{x+t} \bar{a}^m_{[x+t+\frac{1}{2}]:y+t+\frac{1}{2}}}{v^x (bl)_x},$$

where $\bar{a}^m_{[x+t+\frac{1}{2}]:\,y+t+\frac{1}{2}}$ would correspond to the weighted average value of $\bar{a}^m_{x+t+\frac{1}{2}:\,y+t+\frac{1}{2}}$ for members marrying at age $x+t+\frac{1}{2}$. In this case any error involved in replacing $\bar{a}^m_{[x+t+\frac{1}{2}]:\,y+t+\frac{1}{2}}$ by $\bar{a}^m_{x+t+\frac{1}{2}:\,y+t+\frac{1}{2}}$ corresponding to the mean value of $y+t+\frac{1}{2}$ is likely to be very small indeed, particularly if only two sets of values of $\bar{a}^m_{xy}$ have been calculated.

Different factors should strictly be calculated for bachelors and widowers, having regard to the markedly different rates of marriage and remarriage.

It may be decided to ignore more remote marriages in the valuation of the contribution, as the probability of a second marriage occurring before age 65 is likely to be very small, and the term during which the extra contribution would be payable would be relatively short. Some overall estimate based on broad averages should be sufficient in a case where the value of this further contribution was regarded as material.

14.20. Benefit to unmarried members on cessation of membership

The value of this is relatively small, and a valuation by the reversionary method would not normally be justified. The formulae by the alternative collective method are given in the next chapter. For the sake of completeness, however, the reversionary factors are given here.

(a) *Present unmarried members.* A benefit equal to one-half of the total past contributions would be payable on cessation of membership before marriage, and would be valued by means of the factor

$$^b A_x = \frac{\sum\limits_{t=0}^{64-x} v^{x+t+\frac{1}{2}}(bg)_{x+t} + v^{65}(bg)_{65}}{v^x (bl)_x} = \frac{\sum\limits_{t=0}^{65-x} {}^b C^g_{x+t}}{^b D_x}$$

$$= \frac{^b M^g_x}{^b D_x},$$

where $(bg)_x$ represents all unmarried exits from the service at age x last birthday out of $(bl)_x$ bachelors.

The corresponding further benefit arising in respect of future contributions would be valued by the factor

$$^b(IA)_x = \frac{\frac{1}{2}{}^bC_x^g + 1\frac{1}{2}{}^bC_{x+1}^g + 2\frac{1}{2}{}^bC_{x+2}^g + \dots \text{ etc.}}{{}^bD_x}.$$

$$= \frac{\sum\limits_{t=0}^{64-x} \left({}^bM_{x+t}^g - \frac{1}{2}{}^bC_{x+t}^g\right)}{{}^bD_x}.$$

This factor would be multiplied into one-half of the total yearly contributions payable by unmarried members aged x at the valuation date.

(b) *Present married members.* A benefit equal to one-half of the total past contributions would be payable on cessation of membership during widowerhood but before age 65 and would be valued by the factor

$$\frac{\sum\limits_{t=0}^{64-x} D_{x+t+\frac{1}{2}}\, d_{y+t}\, {}^bA_{x+t+\frac{1}{2}}}{D_x l_y}.$$

It would be sufficient in practice to assume an average age difference for present married couples, or alternatively to use a service and widowerhood table.

The corresponding further benefit arising in respect of future contributions, with due allowance for the reduction of the rate of contribution by 50 % after widowerhood, would be valued by the factor

$$\frac{\sum\limits_{t=0}^{64-x} D_{x+t+\frac{1}{2}}\, d_{y+t}\left\{(t+\frac{1}{2})\, {}^bA_{x+t+\frac{1}{2}} + \frac{1}{2}\, {}^b(IA)_{x+t+\frac{1}{2}}\right\}}{D_x l_y}$$

$$= \frac{\sum\limits_{t=0}^{64-x} \left\{ \sum\limits_{n=t}^{64-x} D_{x+n+\frac{1}{2}}\, d_{y+n}\, {}^bA_{x+n+\frac{1}{2}} + \frac{1}{2} D_{x+t+\frac{1}{2}}\, d_{y+t}\left({}^b(IA)_{x+t-\frac{1}{2}} - {}^bA_{x+t+\frac{1}{2}}\right)\right\}}{D_x l_y}.$$

This factor would be multiplied into one-half of the total yearly contributions payable by married members aged x at the valuation date. ^bA and $^b(IA)$ should strictly be the factors appropriate to widowers, as the factors calculated for bachelors would be somewhat too large.

The liability in respect of cessations after a further period of marriage before age 65 would be so small that it would be sufficient to make an overall estimate of the reserve required.

14.21. Example C

The general arrangements are the same as in Example B (see § 14.13) except that the benefit is calculated as a percentage (k) of the total salary received by the member in service, whilst the contribution payable is a fixed percentage (e) of salary whilst unmarried and double that rate whilst married.

Tables similar to those in Example B would be required.

If the relative salary scale at age x last birthday is s_x the actual rate of salary at age x nearest is S_x and the total past salary $(TPS)_x$, the valuation factors would be very similar to those already evolved in the previous example, except that s_x would have to be incorporated in the numerator and denominator at the appropriate stages.

Present wives of existing married members. $^{m}B_{xy}^{d}$ and $^{mr}B_{xy}^{d}$ would be as before (see § 14.14), but would now be applied to $\cdot 01k\,(TPS)_x$ instead of to $4n$.

$^{m}(IB)_{xy}^{d}$ would be replaced by

$$^{sm}(IB)_{xy}^{d} = \frac{\sum\limits_{t=0}^{64-x} s_{x+t}\left(M_{x+t:\,y+t}^{d(wa)} - \tfrac{1}{2}C_{x+t:\,y+t}^{d(wa)}\right)}{s_{x-\frac{1}{2}}\,l_x D_y}$$

and would be applied to $\cdot 01kS_x$. Similarly, $^{mr}(IB)_{xy}^{d}$ would be replaced by $^{smr}(IB)_{xy}^{d}$, incorporating the salary scale function.

The assumption of an average entry age referred to in § 14.14 above effected a considerable simplification. If a similar simplification were required here it would be necessary to assume that the past salary careers of members had progressed in ratio to the salary scale from a fixed entry age to their present levels at all attained ages. Such an assumption would, however, rarely be possible if only on account of the marked changes in salary levels which have occurred in past years.

14.22. Future first wives of unmarried men

The factor $^{m}_{b}B_{x}^{d}$ would be as before (see § 14.15) but would now be applied to $\cdot 01k\,(TPS)_x$ instead of $4n$.

The factor ${}^{m}_{b}(IB)^{d}_{x}$ would be replaced by

$${}^{sm}_{b}(IB)^{d}_{x} = \frac{\sum\limits_{t=0}^{64-x} v^{x+t+\frac{1}{2}}(bm)_{x+t}\left\{\left(\sum\limits_{n=0}^{t-1} s_{x+n}+\frac{1}{2}s_{x+t}\right)({}^{m}B^{d}+{}^{mr}B^{d})_{[x+t+\frac{1}{2}]:\,y+t+\frac{1}{2}} + s_{x+t}\left({}^{sm}(IB)^{d}+{}^{smr}(IB)^{d}\right)_{[x+t+\frac{1}{2}]:\,y+t+\frac{1}{2}}\right\}}{s_{x-\frac{1}{2}}v^{x}(bl)_{x}},$$

which would be applied to $\cdot 01kS_{x}$.

For convenience of calculation the expression

$$\sum\limits_{n=0}^{t-1} s_{x+n}+\tfrac{1}{2}s_{x+t}$$

could be put into the form $\sigma_{x}-\sigma_{x+t+\frac{1}{2}}$,

where $$\sigma_{x}=\sum\limits_{n=0}^{64-x} s_{x+n}$$

and $$\sigma_{x+t+\frac{1}{2}}=\tfrac{1}{2}(\sigma_{x+t}+\sigma_{x+t+1}).$$

14.23. Contributions

In the factors required for the valuation of the basic contribution for all members and the additional contribution for married members during the state of marriage to existing wives s_{x+t} would be introduced into the numerator and associated with $D_{x+t+\frac{1}{2}}$ and $D_{x+t+\frac{1}{2}:\,y+t-\frac{1}{2}}$ whilst $s_{x-\frac{1}{2}}$ would appear in the denominator associated with D_{x} and D_{xy} (see §14.19).

As regards the additional contribution payable during the future married status of present unmarried members, the revised factor for married members with the salary scale function would be used, whilst $s_{x+t}(bm)_{x+t}$ and $s_{x-\frac{1}{2}}(bl)_{x}$ would appear in place of $(bm)_{x+t}$ and $(bl)_{x}$ respectively.

Similar adjustments would be made in the factors for valuing the benefit on the death, withdrawal or retirement of an unmarried member.

14.24. Example D

As for Example C, except that the widow's benefit is expressed as a fixed percentage (say $k\%$) for each year of service of the member's average salary during the last 5 years of service.

The factors for the valuation would be similar to those in Example B subject to the introduction in the numerator of $z_{x+t+\frac{1}{2}}$ or z_{65} in the first-stage summations and $s_{x-\frac{1}{2}}$ in the denominator, where

$$z_x = \tfrac{1}{5}(s_{x-5} + \ldots + s_{x-2} + s_{x-1}).$$

Thus, for example, the factor $^mB^d_{xy}$ (see § 14.14) would be replaced by

$$^{zm}B^d_{xy} = \frac{\sum\limits_{t=0}^{64-x} d_{x+t} D_{y+t+\frac{1}{2}} \bar{a}'_{y+t+\frac{1}{2}} z_{x+t+\frac{1}{2}}}{s_{x-\frac{1}{2}} l_x D_y},$$

and this would be applied to $\cdot 01 kn S_x$, where n is the number of years of service rendered by the member to the valuation date.

Similarly, $^m_b(IB)^d_x$ (see § 14.15) would be replaced by

$$^{zm}_b(IB)^d_x = \frac{\sum\limits_{t=0}^{64-x} v^{x+t+\frac{1}{2}} (bm)_{x+t} s_{x+t} \left\{ (t+\tfrac{1}{2})(^{zm}B^d + {}^{zmr}B^d)_{[x+t+\frac{1}{2}]:\, y+t+\frac{1}{2}} \right.}{s_{x-\frac{1}{2}} v^x (bl)_x}$$

$$\left. + (^{zm}(IB)^d + {}^{zmr}(IB)^d)_{[x+t+\frac{1}{2}]:\, y+t+\frac{1}{2}} \right\}$$

$$= \frac{\sum\limits_{t=0}^{64-x} \left\{ \sum\limits_{n=t}^{64-x} v^{x+n+\frac{1}{2}} (bm)_{x+n} s_{x+n} (^{zm}B^d + {}^{zmr}B^d)_{[x+n+\frac{1}{2}]:\, y+n+\frac{1}{2}} \right.}{^{sb}D_x}$$

$$+ v^{x+t+\frac{1}{2}} (bm)_{x+t} s_{x+t} \left[(^{zm}(IB)^d + {}^{zmr}(IB)^d)_{[x+t+\frac{1}{2}]:\, y+t+\frac{1}{2}} \right.$$

$$\left. \left. - \tfrac{1}{2}(^{zm}B^d + {}^{zmr}B^d)_{[x+t+\frac{1}{2}]:\, y+t+\frac{1}{2}} \right] \right\}$$

where the $B_{[x]y}$ and $(IB)_{[x]y}$ factors themselves include the salary-scale function z in the numerator and s in the denominator as indicated above.

14.25. Age-disparity adjustments

Frequently widows' schemes include arrangements for reducing the benefit in any case where the widow of the member is more than α years younger than the husband. The object of such an adjustment is to protect the fund against undue risks caused by a member marrying a person much younger than himself. Variations in the age difference of husbands and wives clearly involve corresponding variations in the value of the benefits being provided, and an adjustment such as that referred to would to some extent limit such variations and preserve a reasonable balance between individual members. It would not, of course, adjust the relative positions of, say, a member who failed to marry and one who married soon after commencing membership.

The adjustment may be made in one or other of the following ways:

(a) A fixed percentage reduction depending only on the age difference.

(b) A fixed percentage reduction which would depend upon the age of the husband at date of marriage as well as the age difference.

(c) A percentage reduction which would depend upon the ages of the husband and wife at the date of death of the husband.

If B_{xy} is the total value of widows' benefits arising in respect of a member aged x now married to a wife aged y and C_{xy} is the total value of the future contributions payable by the member, the percentage adjustment (r_t) where the age difference is t years may be calculated under method (a) from the equation

$$(1 - \cdot 01 r_t) B_{\bar{x}:\,\bar{x}-t} - C_{\bar{x}:\,\bar{x}-t} = B_{\bar{x}:\,y_0} - C_{\bar{x}:\,y_0},$$

where $\bar{x}$ is an average age at marriage, and $y_0 = \bar{x} - \alpha$ if age differences up to α years are permitted without adjustment.

Under method (b) the same equation, replacing $\bar{x}$ by the actual age x of the member at marriage should be used. It may be noted that, for a given age difference, the weighted average of the factors r_t in this method will be the factor r_t under method (a).

Under method (c) the adjustment should be obtained from the equation

$$(1 - \cdot 01 r_t) \bar{a}'_y = \bar{a}'_{y_0}, \text{ where } y = x - t.$$

Again, the weighted averages of these factors from the age at marriage (of the member) onwards will represent the factors under method (b).

In practice it may be found that the adjustment has been fixed somewhat arbitrarily or on some basis which does not coincide with the valuation basis, and the revision of the scale of adjustments may need to be considered. Where the adjustment is adequate on the valuation basis it may be considered satisfactory to proceed on the basis of treating all existing and prospective wives more than α years younger than the husband as being exactly α years younger and valuing the benefit without adjustment by means of factors constructed in such a way that all age differences of more than α years had been replaced by α. A similar modification of the age differences should be made in the contribution factors.

As the factor r_t (method (b)) will usually increase with age at marriage, the results obtained by valuing the full benefits on the basis of the modified age disparity will tend to underestimate the liabilities whether method (a) or method (b) is employed, and therefore will be only approximately correct.

If the adjustment is seriously out of line with the valuation basis and no action is possible to rectify the position as regards existing members, the valuation factors should be constructed by replacing $\bar{a}'_y$ by $(1 - \cdot 01 r_t) \bar{a}'_y$ and applying the modified factors to the normal benefit. This adjustment must of course be made to individual values of $\bar{a}'_y$ by reference to the actual age difference t before the calculation of any weighted average values of the widow's annuity for incorporation in the factors.

It should be noted that method (c) is open to some objection in that the amount of the widow's benefit is not finally known until the member dies and moreover, if as is usually the case the wife is younger than the member, the prospective widow's pension decreases as the member grows older.

Occasionally the adjustment for age disparity takes the form of an additional contribution. In such a case the valuation should proceed on normal lines bringing into account the full range of age differences of husbands and wives and taking credit for the value of the additional contributions at present payable by certain married members and for the value of additional contributions arising on a proportion of future marriages.

14.26. Marriage fines

Some schemes provide for the payment of 'fines' on the marriage of members and the amount of the fine may vary with the age difference so as to cover part at least of the additional liability due to any abnormal age difference. If $F_{x+t+\frac{1}{2}}$ is the average amount of such payment on the marriage of a bachelor at age $x + t$ last birthday (allowing for the age distribution of wives if the sum payable varies with the age of the wife), the value of prospective fines by bachelors would be determined by means of factors

$$\frac{\sum_{t=0} v^{x+t+\frac{1}{2}} (bm)_{x+t} F_{x+t+\frac{1}{2}}}{v^x (bl)_x}.$$

Fines payable on second marriages could be valued by reversionary factors built up in chain fashion as for ordinary contributions, but in practice an overall estimate may be sufficient if the value of this further asset is relatively small.

CHAPTER 15

VALUATION OF WIDOWS' FUNDS: COLLECTIVE METHOD

15.1. As an alternative to the reversionary method for the valuation of a widows' fund which was the subject of the preceding chapter it may be possible to employ a collective method of valuation. As will have been observed, under the reversionary method the progress of an individual member as regards his marital status is traced in the future for the purpose of valuing the prospective benefits and contributions. Under the collective method, on the other hand, the marital status of the individual does not enter explicitly into the valuation methods, but instead an average proportion married at a particular age for all members combined is introduced. In order to illustrate this alternative method the collective valuation formulae will now be derived for the four specimen cases considered in the preceding chapter.

15.2. Example A (see § 14.6)

Tables required:

(i) A life table appropriate to male members irrespective of marital status.

(ii) A table showing the proportions married $h^d_{x+\frac{1}{2}}$ among members dying at age x last birthday.

(iii) Mortality rates of widows.

(iv) Remarriage rates of widows.

As in the reversionary method, a withdrawal rate may have to be allowed for in table (i), whilst from tables (iii) and (iv) values of $\bar{a}'_y$ (the annuity payable to a widow and ceasing on remarriage) would be calculated.

The average value per member now aged x of a widow's annuity of 1 is given by the formula

$$\frac{\sum\limits_{t=0}^{\infty} v^{x+t+\frac{1}{2}} d_{x+t} h^d_{x+t+\frac{1}{2}} \bar{a}''_{y+t+\frac{1}{2}}}{D_x},$$

where D_x, d_{x+t} are based upon table (i) and $\bar{a}''_{y+t+\frac{1}{2}}$ is the weighted average value of the widow's annuity, ceasing on remarriage, for widows of members dying at age $x + t$ last birthday.

It should be noted that in deriving the proportion of members married at date of death (h^d), all marriages, whether first or subsequent marriages, would be brought into account, so that the above formula should enable the liabilities in respect of all future widows left by existing members to be valued together.

15.3. In practice the experience of the fund, unless it is very large, will not be sufficient over a fairly recent period to enable a satisfactory series h_x^d to be derived. In view of this an alternative formula is generally used, viz.

$$\frac{\sum_{t=0}^{\infty} D_{x+t+\frac{1}{2}} h_{x+t+\frac{1}{2}} m'_{x+t} \bar{a}''_{y+t+\frac{1}{2}}}{D_x},$$

where $h_{x+t+\frac{1}{2}}$ is the proportion married among members *alive* at age $x + t$ last birthday and m'_{x+t} is the central mortality rate applicable to married men; h_x would be derived from a considerably larger body of data than h_x^d. As a further alternative, if reliable rates of mortality for married members alone are not available, m'_{x+t} may be replaced by m_{x+t}, the central death rate for all males combined, and since $D_{x+t+\frac{1}{2}} . m_{x+t} = v^{x+t+\frac{1}{2}} d_{x+t}$ the formula then reduces to

$$\frac{\sum_{t=0}^{\infty} v^{x+t+\frac{1}{2}} d_{x+t} h_{x+t+\frac{1}{2}} \bar{a}''_{y+t+\frac{1}{2}}}{D_x},$$

which is the same as that given in § 15.2, except that h now replaces h^d. This last formula would generally over-estimate the liability to a small extent, since the mortality experience of married members is usually somewhat lighter than that for bachelors and hence also lighter than the experience for all males combined.

Again, owing to paucity of data the weighted average value of an annuity to the widow of a member dying at age $x + t + \frac{1}{2}$, viz. $\bar{a}''_{y+t+\frac{1}{2}}$, may be replaced in practice by the weighted annuity derived from the statistics of wives of husbands who are alive at age $x + t$ last birthday. If the age of the wife corresponding to the weighted average values $\bar{a}''_{y+t+\frac{1}{2}}$ is $(y + t + \frac{1}{2})^d$ or $(y + t + \frac{1}{2})^l$, according as the experience relates to members dying or alive respectively, $(y+t+\frac{1}{2})^d$ will generally exceed $(y+t+\frac{1}{2})^l$. The excess may be fairly large at certain ages over 50, but will eventually tend to zero at the higher ages. Hence if the average annuity value in the formula is derived from the more voluminous data relating to living married members, the liability would be over-estimated somewhat, and some adjustment to the annuity value may be desirable on this account.

This conclusion may be arrived at from general reasoning if consideration is directed to the probable trend of three tables showing the average difference between the ages of husbands and wives, in each case according to the age of husband:

(a) at date of marriage,

(b) at a valuation date, of all husbands then alive,

(c) at death of a husband.

Assuming sufficiently extensive data, the differences shown by the three tables will be identical at the earliest age at which marriage of members takes place. As the age of husband advances, however, the differences will diverge, and will be greatest in table (a), intermediate in table (b) and least in table (c).

The bachelor who marries young usually marries a wife whose age does not differ to any marked extent from his own, but the bachelor who avoids matrimony until he reaches an advanced age has, so to speak, a much wider range of choice, and the marriage of an elderly bachelor to a comparatively young wife is not an occurrence of such striking singularity as the converse case of a young bachelor marrying an elderly wife. Thus the differences shown by table (a) may be expected to increase continuously and at the end to be fairly large. The difference shown by table (b) at a particular age relates to husbands who have married at all previous ages and have survived with their wives. Those of them who married at young ages will have wives of about the same age as themselves, and those recently married will have younger wives, but the average difference in age will be less than that shown in table (a) as applying to members who marry at that age. Again, since marriage is to some extent a selective force, members who have recently married are less likely to die than members who have been married for some time, and since deaths will therefore be largely composed of the latter, the difference shown by table (c) at a particular age will, again, be less than that in table (b) at the same age. Tables (b) and (c) will obviously tend to become the same as new marriages become unimportant and the effect of selection wears off.

One or other of the factors described above would be applied to the total number of members aged x at the valuation date, irrespective of marital status, in order to arrive at the total prospective liability for all widows' benefits arising on the death of such members. It will be noted that the series $h^d_{x+t+\frac{1}{2}}$ or $h_{x+t+\frac{1}{2}}$, as the case may be, relates only to the attained age and would be derived from the statistics of the fund and graduated before incorporation in the factors. If the factors incorporating $h_{x+t+\frac{1}{2}}$, derived from the statistics relating to living members, are used this implies the assumptions (i) that the proportion married among the survivors of members now aged x would be the same at age $x+t+\frac{1}{2}$ as the proportion married among members now aged $x+t+\frac{1}{2}$, and (ii) that this relationship would hold good irrespective of the present age x and of the particular composition of those members as regards marital status.

15.4. It is not an essential feature of the method that the same series h should be applied to the whole membership at the valuation date; if thought desirable two or more sets of h could be used and corresponding sets of valuation factors calculated in order to value different sections of the membership, although some difficulty might be experienced in deciding on appropriate series of h.

It may be noted that a group of members at a particular age at the valuation date among whom the proportion married is higher than normal would tend to produce a higher proportion of married members among the deaths than normal. This effect would be reduced, however, with the passage of time by reason of the fact that the proportion of potential married members (i.e. the unmarried) is subnormal in the group.

Now in the process of graduation of h the actual proportions married among those dying (or, as an approximation thereto, among those existing) at particular ages will be lost sight of. The application of the graduated proportions married to the whole membership thus involves the further assumption that any variations in the proportions dying due to variations of the actual proportions among the membership existing at the valuation date from the graduated proportions will be such that any errors in the estimates on this account will largely cancel out. Clearly there will be no certainty in this, and to reduce the degree of uncertainty it has been suggested that the liability for members aged x should be adjusted by the factor h'_x/h_x, where h'_x is the actual proportion married out of the members valued at age x (nearest) and h_x is the corresponding proportion assumed in the factors. This is equivalent to assuming for members now aged x that the proportion married among the survivors of such members at some future age $x+t$ will be $h_{x+t}(h'_x/h_x)$. Such an adjustment may give reasonable results where h'_x/h_x does not differ appreciably from unity. If h'_x is considerably in excess of h_x for a group of members at a particular age, however, the adjustment may lead to the absurd result that the proportion assumed married at some future age $x+t$ exceeds 100 %.

An alternative method of adjustment which avoids the difficulty just noted is to construct two sets of factors (i) on the normal basis including the normal series h_x and (ii) on a special basis replacing h_x by 1 throughout at all ages. If the liabilities for members aged x calculated on these two bases are L_1 and L_2 (L_1 being of course the unadjusted liability), the adjusted liability may be taken as

$$L_1 + \frac{(h'_x - h_x)(L_2 - L_1)}{1 - h_x}.$$

The adjustment, which would be in the same form whether h'_x is greater or less than h_x, is in effect based on the assumption that the liability would change from L_1 to L_2 in the same proportion as h'_x changes from h_x to 1.

15.5. Value of contributions

These would be valued by the factor

$$\frac{\sum_{t=0}^{64-x} D_{x+t+\frac{1}{2}}}{D_x},$$

since in Example A the contribution ceases at age 65 and does not vary with marital status.

15.6. Example B (see §14.13)

In this example the benefit varies with the period of service up to retirement of the member, and hence, as in the reversionary method, it is necessary to treat separately the periods before and after retirement.

Tables required:

(i) A service table applicable to male lives, irrespective of marital status, with decrements of withdrawal, death in service, retirement on ill-health pension and age retirement at age 65.

(ii) A table of proportions married, either $h^d_{x+t+\frac{1}{2}}$ or $h_{x+t+\frac{1}{2}}$, extending to age $64\frac{1}{2}$.

(iii) Mortality rates of members on pension appropriate to married members only (since bachelors would cease to be interested in the fund after retirement), and distinguishing between ill-health pensioners and those who retire at age 65.

(iv) Mortality rates of widows.

(v) Remarriage rates of widows.

15.7. Value of widows' benefits to members in service at the valuation date

(*a*) *Benefits arising on the death of members in service.*

(i) The benefit accrued in respect of *service to date* of a member aged x who entered service at age $(x-n)$ is $\pounds 4n$, and for all members now aged x the total accrued benefit is $\pounds 4\Sigma n$. If the mortality rates appropriate to all members are used and the proportions married are derived from the data relating to the living as in the second formula given in §15.3, this benefit would be valued by the formula

$$\frac{\sum_{t=0}^{64-x} v^{x+t+\frac{1}{2}} d_{x+t} h_{x+t+\frac{1}{2}} \bar{a}''_{y+t+\frac{1}{2}}}{D_x} = \frac{\sum C^{d(wa)}_{x+t}}{D_x}$$

$$= \frac{M^{d(wa)}_x}{D_x}, \text{ say.}$$

D_x and d_x would be based upon the service table (i).

(ii) In respect of *future years of service* the benefit to be valued for n_x members aged x for each year of future service is $£4n_x$, and the appropriate factor is

$$\frac{\sum_{t=0}^{64-x} (M_{x+t}^{d(wa)} - \tfrac{1}{2}C_{x+t}^{d(wa)})}{D_x}.$$

(b) *Benefits arising after the retirement of members.*

(i) In respect of *service to date* the accrued benefit is $£4\Sigma n$, and the appropriate valuation factor is

$$\frac{\sum_{t=0}^{64-x} v^{x+t+\frac{1}{2}} r_{x+t} h_{x+t+\frac{1}{2}} \bar{a}''_{x+t+\frac{1}{2} \mid y+t+\frac{1}{2}} + v^{65} r_{65} h_{65} \bar{a}''_{65 \mid y+65-x}}{D_x} = \frac{\sum_{t=0}^{65-x} {}^r C_{x+t}^{d(wa)}}{D_x}$$

$$= \frac{{}^r M_x^{d(wa)}}{D_x}, \quad \text{say.}$$

(ii) In respect of the benefit accruing on *future years of service* the factor required is

$$\frac{\sum_{t=0}^{64-x} ({}^r M_{x+t}^{d(wa)} - \tfrac{1}{2}{}^r C_{x+t}^{d(wa)})}{D_x}.$$

In the above factors, $\bar{a}''_{x+t+\frac{1}{2} \mid y+t+\frac{1}{2}}$ is the average value of a reversionary annuity to the wife of a married member who retires on ill-health at age $x+t+\frac{1}{2}$, allowing of course for the widow's annuity to cease on remarriage. As in the case of $\bar{a}''_{y+t+\frac{1}{2}}$ this average value would be calculated from the experience of the living if the data as regards ill-health retirements were not sufficient to give satisfactory values. ($\bar{a}''_{65 \mid y+65-x}$ is the corresponding value for members retiring at age 65.)

It should be noted that it has been assumed in the above factors that the rates of retirement for married and unmarried members are the same; if the experience justified a differentiation, r_{x+t} would have to be replaced by $l_{x+t}(rq)'_{x+t}$, where $(rq)'_{x+t}$ is the central rate of retirement of married members at age $x+t$.

(c) *Benefits to widows of members who have already retired and to incumbent beneficiaries.*

These would be valued as indicated in § 14.18 under the reversionary method.

15.8. Contributions

Allowing for the fact that the contribution of an unmarried member is at rate c whilst the contribution of a married member is double that rate, the factor required is

$$\frac{\sum\limits_{t=0}^{64-x} D_{x+t+\frac{1}{2}}(1+h_{x+t+\frac{1}{2}})}{D_x},$$

and this would be multiplied by cn_x to obtain the value of the future contributions payable by n_x members aged x at the valuation date. In this formula $h_{x+t+\frac{1}{2}}$ should, of course, be derived from the 'live' experience and not from deaths.

15.9. Benefit to unmarried members on cessation of membership

If $g_x = d_x + r_x + w_x$ from the service table (i), the value of a benefit of 1 on exit from the scheme is

$$\frac{\sum\limits_{t=0}^{64-x} v^{x+t+\frac{1}{2}}g_{x+t}(1-h_{x+t+\frac{1}{2}})+v^{65}g_{65}(1-h_{65})}{D_x} = \frac{\sum\limits_{t=0}^{65-x} C_{x+t}^{g(1-h)}}{D_x}$$

$$= \frac{M_x^{g(1-h)}}{D_x}, \quad \text{say.}$$

On the assumption that unmarried members ceasing membership will have paid contributions throughout at rate c, the value of that part of the benefit which has accrued in respect of contributions paid to date is $\frac{1}{2}c(\Sigma n) M_x^{g(1-h)}/D_x$, whilst the value of the corresponding benefit arising in respect of future contributions is

$$\frac{\frac{1}{2}cn_x \sum\limits_{t=0}^{64-x} (M_{x+t}^{g(1-h)} - \frac{1}{2}C_{x+t}^{g(1-h)})}{D_x}.$$

To the extent to which some of the seceding members are widowers who will have paid contributions during part of their membership at rate $2c$ these formulae will understate the liability. A correction could be applied by incorporating a further item $(1+\theta_{x+t+\frac{1}{2}})$ in the construction of the factors, where $\theta_{x+t+\frac{1}{2}}$ represents the ratio of the average additional contributions paid as a married member to the basic contributions paid at rate c, the average being obtained by reference to the benefits actually payable to seceding unmarried members and not from the corresponding data for all existing members including those married. In practice, as the value of this benefit is in any case relatively small, an adjustment made by reference to the over-all average value of θ may be considered sufficient.

15.10. Example C (see § 14.21)

The formulae for this example will be constructed in similar fashion to those for the previous example, except that it will now be necessary to incorporate in them the salary scale function s_x.

(*a*) *Benefit on death and retirement in respect of salary accrued to date.* The factors required are in exactly the same form as in Example B, but they will now be applied to $\cdot o1k\,(TPS)_x$, where k is the fixed percentage used in the calculation of the amount of the widow's benefit and $(TPS)_x$ is the total past salaries of members aged x at the valuation date.

(*b*) *Benefits in respect of future salaries.* Per unit of present salary the value of the benefit associated with future salaries which will arise on the *death of the member* in service is given by the formula

$$\frac{\cdot o1k \sum_{t=0}^{64-x} s_{x+t}\left(M_{x+t}^{d(wa)} - \tfrac{1}{2}C_{x+t}^{d(wa)}\right)}{s_{x-\frac{1}{2}}\cdot D_x,},$$

whilst the corresponding value in respect of *members who retire* on pension is

$$\frac{\cdot o1k \sum_{t=0}^{64-x} s_{x+t}\left(^rM_{x+t}^{d(wa)} - \tfrac{1}{2}{}^rC_{x+t}^{d(wa)}\right)}{s_{x-\frac{1}{2}}\cdot D_x}.$$

(*c*) *Benefits to widows of retired members.* These would be valued directly by reversionary annuities since the amount of the benefit would be known in each case.

(*d*) *Value of contributions.* The valuation of future contributions per unit of present salary would be made by means of the factor

$$\frac{\sum_{t=0}^{64-x} s_{x+t}D_{x+t+\frac{1}{2}}\left(1+h_{x+t+\frac{1}{2}}\right)}{s_{x-\frac{1}{2}}\cdot D_x}.$$

(e) *Value of benefit on cessation of membership*. The value of the benefit associated with the past contributions would be made by the same factor as in the previous example, viz. $M_x^{g(1-h)}/D_x$, this factor being applied to $\cdot 005c\,(TPS)_x$, where c is the contribution rate per cent of salary payable as an unmarried person.

In respect of future contributions the value per unit of present salary is

$$\frac{\cdot 005c \sum_{t=0}^{64-x} s_{x+t}\left(M_{x+t}^{g(1-h)} - \tfrac{1}{2}C_{x+t}^{g(1-h)}\right)}{s_{x-\frac{1}{2}}.D_x}.$$

As before, a correction could be applied by incorporating $(1+\theta)$ in $C^{g(1-h)}$ from which M functions are calculated.

15.11. Example D (see § 14.24)

The formulae for the value of the contribution and the benefit on secession would be in exactly the same form as in Example C.

The factors for the valuation of the widow's benefit would be similar to those derived for Example B (see § 15.7), subject to the C_{x+t} function in the numerator being replaced by $z_{x+t+\frac{1}{2}}C_{x+t}$ before summation to form the M functions, and the replacement of D_x by $s_{x-\frac{1}{2}}.D_x$ in the denominator. Thus the factor for the benefit arising after retirement in respect of future years of service would be

$$\frac{\sum_{t=0}^{64-x}\left\{{}^{zr}M_{x+t}^{d(wa)} - \tfrac{1}{2}{}^{zr}C_{x+t}^{d(wa)}\right\}}{s_{x-\frac{1}{2}}.D_x,},$$

where

$${}^{zr}C_x^{d(wa)} = z_{x+\frac{1}{2}}{}^{r}C_x^{d(wa)}$$

and

$${}^{zr}M_x^{d(wa)} = \sum_{t=0}^{64-x}{}^{zr}C_{x+t}^{d(wa)} + z_{65}{}^{r}C_{65}^{d(wa)}.$$

This factor would be applied to $\cdot 01k\Sigma S_x$, the summation extending over the current salaries of all members aged x nearest at the valuation date.

15.12. Age-disparity adjustments

These would be dealt with in the valuation in the same manner as already described for the reversionary method of valuation by appropriate adjustments to the annuity values $\bar{a}_y''$ or $\bar{a}_{x|y}''$. The age-disparity adjustments would be directly allowed for in the *individual* values in the calculation of the averages before the final graduated series of values is obtained for incorporation in the factors.

The calculation of a suitable scale of age-disparity adjustments cannot be made by collective method formulae, since attention must be directed for this purpose to the individual age differences of married couples; one or other of the formulae indicated in the previous chapter, or some analogous formula would have to be employed.

15.13. Marriage fines

These would be valued under the collective method by a factor of the form $\Sigma D_{x+t+\frac{1}{2}} f_{x+t+\frac{1}{2}} / D_x$, where $f_{x+t+\frac{1}{2}}$ is the average payment per member (married and unmarried together) receivable at age $x+t+\frac{1}{2}$. As this item is generally of relatively small importance it would normally be sufficient to obtain f direct from the recent experience of the fund.

CHAPTER 16

VALUATION OF ORPHANS' BENEFITS

16.1. In many widows' benefit schemes orphans' benefits are also included in the arrangements; a scheme providing for orphans' benefits alone is comparatively rare.

The various kinds of benefit normally provided have already been mentioned in §4.2. The method of valuation may be governed by the method adopted for the valuation of the widows' benefits although this is not essential; it may, in fact, be decided to value the widows' benefits by a reversionary method and the orphans' benefits by a collective method. As the liability in respect of orphans' benefits is usually a relatively small part of the total liability, less refined methods of valuation than those employed for the widows' benefits would often be adopted in practice. Thus as the liability would only be affected to a small extent by the mortality of children, this would generally be ignored with a consequent slight over-estimate of the liability. In the formulae given in this chapter this procedure will be followed.

16.2. If the benefit consists of an annuity of the same amount to each child of a deceased member payable up to a fixed age a reversionary valuation could be carried out, dealing separately with (a) existing children and (b) children to be born in future to present members, whether as issue of existing marriages or as issue of future marriages. As regards (a) the valuation factor would be similar to those set out for existing married members and their wives in § 14.14; in essence the factor is a reversionary annuity but, as the mortality of children is being ignored and the orphan's benefit ceases at a relatively early age, the calculation of the factor would be much easier than in the case of the widow's benefit.

In the simplest case where the benefit is the same whether the member has retired or not the appropriate factor per unit of benefit is

$$\frac{\sum_{t=0}^{k-c-1} d_{x+t} v^{x+t+\frac{1}{2}} \bar{a}_{\overline{k-c-t-\frac{1}{2}|}}}{D_x} = a'_{x|c} \text{ say,}$$

where x is the age of the father, c the age of the child, k the age of the child at which the benefit terminates and d_{x+t}, D_x would be taken from a table applicable to married and widowed members combined.

This factor would generally vary fairly rapidly with a variation in c and relatively slowly with a variation in x, and accordingly any grouping made with the object of reducing the volume of the calculations should be done primarily by reference to the parent's age.

16.3. For the valuation of the benefit to future children in a fund where the valuation of the widow's benefit is being carried out on a reversionary basis, a number of alternative methods of procedure are possible involving in varying degrees both the collective and reversionary methods.

If reliable issue rates are available in the form of rates applicable to 'any male' (say i_x = central issue rate) the factor per unit of child's benefit would be

$$\frac{\sum_{t=0}^{\infty} v^{x+t+\frac{1}{2}} l_{x+t+\frac{1}{2}} i_{x+t} a'_{x+t+\frac{1}{2}|0}}{D_x},$$

where $a'_{x|0}$ is the same as $a'_{x|c}$ for existing children calculated, however, for $c = 0$ and l_{x+t} and D_x would be taken from a table applicable to all members.

It will be noted that this factor gives the average liability for any existing male aged x whether married or unmarried. Hence if the issue rates are derived from a population other than that of the fund itself, any divergence between the two bodies of data in the proportions married at the important ages up to about 50 may give rise to a serious error, unless the issue rates are appropriately adjusted before incorporation in the factors. Quite apart from this it may be thought desirable to adjust the rates in order to allow for trends in the general level of issue rates.

If the issue rates are those applicable to married men only the 'any male' issue rates could be obtained from them by multiplying by proportions married before use in the factors. Alternatively, it would be possible to use married men's issue rates in conjunction with a married men's service table with the added decrement of widowerhood in order to value the liability in respect of future children of present marriages. It would also be necessary to value the liability arising in respect of the issue of future marriages of unmarried members and of subsequent marriages of other members. Theoretically this could be done by valuing an assurance on marriage by the use of a bachelor's mortality and marriage table and building up factors in precisely the same manner as already explained for widows' benefits valued by the reversionary method. In practice approximate methods would be employed at some stage of the work, depending upon the circumstances of the case, and in particular the relative importance of this further liability.

16.4. When, as is often the case, the number of children per family eligible for the orphan's benefit at any one time is limited, it would be necessary to reduce the value of $a'_{x|c}$ in the factors. The exact form of the correction would necessarily be very complex if formulae of the type described in § 16.3 are employed, and approximate methods would almost certainly have to be used. Thus the extent of the adjustment to the value of the benefit vesting on the death of a member at age x last birthday could be estimated for a few specimen ages by calculating for the membership existing at the valuation date, on the assumption that death occurs immediately, the total value of the children's benefits at risk for all existing children of such members (*a*) with no limit to the number of eligible children and (*b*) with the limit operating in each family. The ratio of the aggregate value with allowance for the limit to the corresponding value without allowance for the limit could then be graduated and incorporated in the factors. This correction could be applied in constructing the factors for valuing the benefits in respect of existing children as well as in the factors appropriate to future children.

A similar method of adjustment could be employed where the orphans' benefit is not at the same rate for each child.

16.5. When the rate of orphans' benefit can be readily related to the rate of widows' benefit it would be possible to value the two benefits together, including for this purpose both existing and future children in the one calculation. It would be necessary to calculate for specimen ages of the member the ratio (say r) of the average value of the 'family annuity' at risk in respect of existing children of married members to the corresponding average value of the widow's benefit at risk, taking for this purpose an average age difference of husbands and wives. The annuity to the widow a'_y included in the various reversionary annuity factors would then be replaced by $a'_y(1+r)$—after making such adjustment to r as may be considered desirable to allow for future trends—and the combined value of the orphans' and widows' benefits would thus be obtained. In order to avoid the necessity of valuing separately the orphans' benefits arising on the death of widowers, allowance could be made for such benefits by including the children of widowers in the family annuities entering into the calculation of r.

Even when there is no direct relationship between the rates of orphans' and widows' benefits it may still be possible to obtain a sufficiently accurate estimate of the additional liability due to the orphans' benefits by means of the method outlined in this paragraph.

16.6. When the main widows' benefit is being valued by the collective method, the orphans' benefit would also be valued by that method. In certain circumstances the two benefits could be valued together as indicated in § 16.5, the method there outlined being equally applicable in a collective valuation.

If it is not possible to value the two benefits together or if a separate value of the orphans' liability is required a factor of the form

$$\frac{\sum_{t=0}^{\infty} v^{x+t+\frac{1}{2}} d_{x+t} h_{x+t+\frac{1}{2}} (Oa)_{x+t+\frac{1}{2}}}{D_x}$$

would be constructed and applied to all males aged x. In this factor $(Oa)_{x+t+\frac{1}{2}}$ is the value of the 'average family annuity' for children's benefits at risk for married men (including widowers) aged $x+t$ last birthday, and $h_{x+t+\frac{1}{2}}$ is the proportion of married and widowed members to all members at age $x+t$ last birthday. The 'average family annuity' would be calculated by the formula

$$(Oa)_x = \frac{c_0 \bar{a}_{\overline{k-\frac{1}{2}}|} + c_1 \bar{a}_{\overline{k-1\frac{1}{2}}|} + c_2 \bar{a}_{\overline{k-2\frac{1}{2}}|} + \text{etc.}}{n_x},$$

where $c_t =$ the number of children aged t last birthday of living members aged x; $n_x =$ the total number of married and widowed members aged x; and $k =$ age at which the orphan's benefit ceases.

If the number of children who may receive a benefit is limited to a maximum of, say, 3, then only the youngest 3 children in each family would be included in this calculation. $(Oa)_x$ would be graduated before incorporation in the factors.

If it is considered desirable to distinguish between married members and widowers, in view of the fact that widowers would on the average tend to leave smaller families than married members of the same age, the factor would be modified to the form

$$\frac{\sum_{t=0}^{\infty} v^{x+t+\frac{1}{2}} d_{x+t} \{h_{x+t+\frac{1}{2}} (Oa)_{x+t+\frac{1}{2}} + h'_{x+t+\frac{1}{2}} (Oa)'_{x+t+\frac{1}{2}}\}}{D_x}.$$

d_{x+t} and D_x would be taken from a table applicable to all members, whilst unaccented functions within the bracket relate to married men and accented functions relate to widowers, the 'average family annuity' in this formula being calculated as an average benefit per married member or widowed member as the case may be. In practice it may not be possible to obtain reliable values of $(Oa)'_{x+t+\frac{1}{2}}$ or even of $h'_{x+t+\frac{1}{2}}$.

When the benefit is more complex, e.g. when it depends on salary or length of service, the formula would have to be suitably extended on lines similar to those already explained fully in Chapter 15. It would then be desirable to calculate $(Oa)_x$ as the average family annuity per unit of salary or year of service, as the case may be, rather than as an average total benefit. If the average total benefit is used (which would be analogous to valuing on the basis of emerging costs) the results obtained might be unsatisfactory if the level of salaries or the average age at entry has altered. Even in the unlikely event of the level of salaries having been reasonably stable over a number of years, it would still be desirable to base the estimate of liability upon salary forecasts from present salaries by means of factors incorporating the salary scale in order that the liability should be consistent with the value of the future contributions which would also be based upon salary forecasts.

CHAPTER 17

RATE OF INTEREST: GUARANTEE OF SOLVENCY: INCOME TAX: INVESTMENTS

RATE OF INTEREST

17.1. In earlier chapters dealing with the basis for the valuation of a fund and the calculation of rates of contribution a number of general considerations have been discussed affecting the rate of interest to be employed. It is now proposed to deal with these points in greater detail.

17.2. Existing funds

In determining the rate of interest to be employed in the valuation of an existing fund, the various considerations which have to be taken into account may be enumerated as follows:

(*a*) The trustees' investment powers, and the way in which those powers have been exercised in the past. Generally their skill in investment will clearly affect the yield obtainable.

(*b*) The present portfolio of investments should be examined with special reference to the nature of the securities and the period outstanding until the various redemption dates. The present interest yield (j) of the book value of the fund should be calculated, with allowance, of course, for amortization.

(*c*) The effective long-term rate of interest (i) which the fund may expect to earn upon the investment of new monies and upon the reinvestment of securities which fall in for redemption assuming that the existing investment policy remains unchanged. Sometimes the actuary may deem it wise to advise some change in the investment policy in order to obtain more suitable securities for the fund, and in such cases he should reserve his estimate of i until the changes have been made.

(*d*) The amounts of money which will fall to be invested at various times in future at the rate of interest i. These will be governed largely by the rate of growth of the fund and the redemption dates of existing securities.

17.3. It may be objected that it is impossible to determine i with any degree of certainty and that, accordingly, this should not be one of the factors to be considered. Even if i is not determined explicitly, however, the adoption of a particular valuation rate of interest is equivalent to making an assumption as to the value of i. Hence, as a preliminary, it is desirable to examine the position of the particular fund to ensure that the assumption made is reasonable. It will be useful at this point to consider theoretically the relationship of the rate of interest to be employed in the valuation to the two rates i and j.

Consider first the case of a fund where the current yield j is greater than i. Clearly, as a result of reinvestments and, if the fund is growing, of new investments, the average yield may be expected to fall towards i if this long-term rate remains steady. Obviously a valuation of the liabilities based upon rate j would be over-optimistic and inconsistent with the long-term investment prospects as measured by i. In these circumstances there are two principal alternative methods which could be adopted.

One method would be to treat the fund as though it were closed to new entrants and use a rate of interest $i + r$ intermediate between i and j and based on the average yield likely to be secured over the future lifetime of existing members. At subsequent valuations it would be necessary for the valuation rate to be successively reduced as the proportion of the fund invested at rate i increases (using excess interest earnings over the current valuation rate to meet the cost of the reductions), until eventually, in the absence of any other variations, the valuation rate would be reduced to i. This course would be tantamount to taking credit for future excess interest above rate i and using it for the benefit of existing members.

In practice, having regard to the peculiar uncertainties in the forecast of the rate of interest, it would be regarded as unrealistic to vary the valuation rate by finely shaded differences. At the least the rate would be varied by $\frac{1}{8}\%$ at a time, more probably by $\frac{1}{4}\%$. Alterations of even $\frac{1}{8}\%$, however, would result in somewhat abrupt

changes in the value of the liability and valuation strains are therefore bound to occur on this account, even though there may be no
change in the general financial conditions in which the fund is
operating.

17.4. Coupled with this difficulty in the valuation of the
liabilities is the concurrent one of the value to be placed on the
existing assets. The assets may appear in the balance sheet of
the fund at values which bear no direct relation with present market
prices, and, in the circumstances where j exceeds i, market values
would usually exceed book values in the aggregate. A writing up
of the assets would automatically reduce j and require a recon-
sideration of the valuation rate of interest. Again book values
which are frequently at cost prices, adjusted possibly for amortization, may be quite out of relationship with the value of the assets
as measured in terms of rate i.

17.5. The converse situation where j is less than i creates
similar problems. Frequently it may be found in such cases that
the increase in the market rate of interest has led to depreciation
in the value of the portfolio of securities. The problem can then in
part be dealt with by writing down the securities, so increasing the
current yield towards that obtainable upon new investments.

In the case of a recently established fund the yield may be low
on account of the relatively large proportion of the fund uninvested.
This proportion, however, should diminish rapidly as the fund
grows and the existence of a temporarily low yield should not be
given too much weight in determining the valuation rate of interest.

If in the actuary's opinion i is a reasonable rate to assume as a
measure of the long-term prospects of the fund he must expect the
average yield on the fund to increase gradually from j towards i, so
that it would be reasonable to employ a valuation rate of interest
(say $i-r$) intermediate between j and i. In such a case successive
valuations would show valuation strains due to interest losses until
the earned rate exceeded $i-r$, unless the valuation rate were
gradually increased towards i as the earned rate itself increased.

17.6. An alternative method which would avoid the difficulties
discussed in earlier sections would be to fix the valuation rate at i in

all cases, whether j is greater or less than i, and at the same time to revalue the assets on a basis consistent with rate i. Thus in the case of a first-class security the difference (positive or negative) between the value of that security at rate i and the book value would be brought in as an item of credit or debit. An adjustment need not of course be made to the individual book values, the difference for the investments as a whole being brought into the valuation balance-sheet as a special item, after reserving whatever sum may be deemed to be required or desirable as a margin for contingencies on the investments. Under this method the valuation of the liabilities and of the assets is made explicitly in terms of rate i, the necessary adjustment in the value of the assets being a calculated figure.

17.7. New entrants

Before a final decision is taken on the valuation rate of interest consideration should be given to the position of future entrants to the scheme. It will have been seen that, in determining whether the scale of contributions for new entrants is adequate, the criterion should be rate i, and not rate $(i+r)$. If, therefore, on the basis of rate i new entrants are likely to cause a strain, the actuary should recommend the adoption of a new contribution scale based on rate i. In most cases there is power to change the rate of contribution or the benefits, but even where there is no specific power to take action the actuary should press strongly for such a change, for clearly a scheme cannot continue indefinitely to receive new entrants at inadequate rates. To the extent to which there is a surplus, action to remedy this situation might be deferred temporarily.

17.8. New funds

From some points of view the determination of the rate of interest upon which the contribution scale for a new fund shall be calculated is of even more importance than the determination of the rate to be employed in the valuation of an existing fund as discussed in the preceding sections. To a certain extent it is possible to correct the latter rate at successive valuations, but if the former proves to be too optimistic and differs substantially from the rate which subsequent experience shows the fund capable of earning, there may be no alternative to a radical reconstruction of the financial basis of the pension scheme concerned. For these reasons it is important that the greatest care should be exercised in deciding upon the rate of interest for a new fund, but in other respects the problem is free from many of the complications arising in an existing fund, since the actuary will only be concerned with the yield likely to be obtained upon the type of security in which the trustees intend to invest the monies at their disposal. If the trustees of the fund are inexperienced in investment matters they may be tempted to sacrifice income for security of capital by investing only in gilt-edged securities, and in these circumstances the actuary could offer useful advice regarding other classes of security suitable for this type of investment or, alternatively, he could suggest that the trustees should seek the aid of experts in the field of investments suitable for pension funds.

GUARANTEE OF SOLVENCY

17.9. In the case of a scheme where a definite scale of pensions is laid down, the purpose of funding is, of course, to make provision for the liability as it accrues with years of service. It is sometimes felt that temporary fluctuations in the interest earnings on the funds may involve an element of uncertainty which may be detrimental to the scheme as a whole, and the suggestion has therefore been made that the difficulty may be avoided if the employer is prepared to guarantee a rate of interest upon the invested funds. With such a guarantee it would be possible to value the scheme at the guaranteed rate at successive valuations, thus avoiding valuation strains due to variations in the valuation rate of interest.

The granting of such a guarantee introduces certain difficulties if, as is sometimes the case, the guaranteed rate is at a fairly high level and substantially above that which would otherwise be secured. The following objections may be mentioned:

(*a*) The guarantee will represent an addition to the employer's contribution to the fund, and he will thus be called upon to bear a substantially higher proportion of the total cost than is indicated in the subdivision of the ordinary contributions. The extent of this extra burden falling upon the employer is unlikely to be appreciated by the members.

(b) From the employer's point of view, one important purpose of the fund is to prevent an uneven impact upon profits in consequence of variations in the requirements for pensions. The payment required under an interest guarantee, however, will be inconsiderable in the early years of the scheme when the fund is small but may eventually rise to a large figure when the scheme reaches its ultimate position. In other words, the guarantee of a relatively high rate of interest will tend to defer for many years an appreciable part of the liability, which may be contrary to the general intention underlying the funding of the scheme, namely, the liquidation of the employer's liability for pensions concurrently with its growth.

(c) From the employees' point of view, the security afforded by the fund is weakened, since the solvency of the fund will be dependent upon the fulfilment of the guarantee by the employer. Consequently, if, for example, the firm were to go out of business, it would be necessary for the fund to be reconstituted on the basis of the rate of interest which can actually be earned, or for accrued benefits to be secured through an insurance company or the Post Office on their terms. This would quite clearly involve a reduction in the accrued pension benefits for active members of the staff and possibly a reduction in the pensions actually payable to incumbent beneficiaries.

In the event of the interest guarantee being at a rate approximating to the long-term average interest prospects the interest actually earned in the fund may upon occasion exceed the rate guaranteed. When this occurs, it may be desirable to set up an interest reserve account in which such excess interest would be accumulated as a reserve to be drawn upon to meet future deficiencies in interest earnings before calling upon the employer to implement his guarantee. Whatever course may be decided upon in regard to this point, it is important that specific provision should be made in the terms of the guarantee incorporated in the trust deed.

17.10. As has already been indicated an employer sometimes offers a guarantee of the solvency of a fund. In such a case, the employer can be called upon to make additional contributions if a deficiency is shown by a valuation, and these may take the form either of a lump-sum payment or of a series of deficiency payments. A guarantee of this type, however, should be treated as an emergency precaution against unforeseeable fluctuations in the experience of the fund and, apart from such fluctuations, the general financial arrangements and the valuation of the fund should be carried through as though the guarantee did not exist.

INCOME TAX*

17.11. Pension funds were accorded special treatment as regards income tax by sect. 32 of the Finance Act, 1921, and similar treatment was extended to widows' and orphans' funds by sec. 19 of the Finance Act, 1930. Largely owing to the wide discretionary powers of approval granted to the Commissioners of Inland Revenue there has since developed some complexity in the practical application of this and subsequent income tax legislation affecting such funds. Moreover, the present position has been reached by piecemeal legislation over a number of years, and it is by no means completely consistent. In addition, it may be noted that the conditions which the Commissioners attach to approval have been varied from time to time, so that an existing approved fund may include certain provisions which would render a new fund incapable of approval at the present time. The essential basis upon which both the statutory enactments and the Inland Revenue practice are in general based is, however, relatively straightforward and may be expressed in a few general principles, as indicated in the following paragraphs.

* The Income Tax Act 1952, which became law whilst this book was in the hands of the printers, repealed and re-enacted all the Income Tax legislation referred to in this Chapter. The new Act is a pure consolidation Act, which, it is understood, does not amend the law in any respect. A table indicating the sections of the new Act which correspond to the sections of earlier Acts referred to in this chapter and in Appendix I is given in Appendix III.

17.12. Income tax (F.A. 1921, sect. 32 and F.A. 1930, sect. 19)

The essential principle underlying the whole of this body of income tax law is to relieve from the operation of income tax funds which are set aside to provide for future benefits which will themselves in due course become liable to income tax. The general principle holds good whether tax actually becomes payable upon the benefits or whether they escape tax through the operation of the normal personal reliefs granted upon individual incomes. This relief depends upon the approval of the Commissioners of Inland Revenue, and where such approval has been secured the following benefits arise:

(*a*) Employer's contributions:

Ordinary annual—may be deducted as an expense in determining income tax liability.

Other than ordinary annual (e.g. special contributions to meet a deficiency arising at the inception of the fund or otherwise)—may be deducted as an expense in determining income tax liability, but the Inland Revenue may spread the relief over a period (usually about 10 years) in the case of a single payment or payments spread over a very short period.

(*b*) Employees' contributions:

Ordinary annual—may be deducted from income as an expense and thus secure relief of tax at the highest rate applicable to the individual.

Other than ordinary annual—no allowance granted.

(*c*) Interest income of the fund—entirely exempt from income tax. N.B. Any payment by an employer under the terms of an interest guarantee is treated as an employer's ordinary annual contribution.

(*d*) It may be noted also that pensions when received are treated as earned income (Income Tax Act, 1918, sect. 14 (3)).

17.13. Conditions of approval under 1921 Finance Act

An essential condition of approval under the 1921 Act is that the fund shall have for its 'sole purpose' the provision of annuities for persons employed in the trade or undertaking either on retirement at a specified age or earlier ill-health retirement or for the widows, children or dependants of employees at death. It would, however, obviously be impracticable to refuse to permit payments upon the occasion of the death or withdrawal of an employee and, in order to provide for such cases, power is given to the Commissioners of Inland Revenue to approve funds where provision for such payments is made or where the provision of annuities is permitted in other circumstances than those mentioned above, e.g. on voluntary retirement before the specified age.

The statute contains a number of other conditions for approval, including a requirement that the employer must be a contributor to the fund. The section of the Act and the Statutory Rules and Orders (no. 1699 of 1921) which contain administrative rules are printed as an appendix to this volume and should be carefully studied, particularly the terms of subsection 3 of the Finance Act, 1921, sect. 32. It will be noted that condition (*b*) is drawn so narrowly that a fund will very rarely satisfy it. Consequently, the majority of funds are approved under the terms of the proviso to the subsection. This has enabled the Commissioners to attach to approval a series of conditions which must be satisfied by any fund seeking approval.

In certain cases where some of the benefits provided fall outside those permitted to an approved fund, but the fund is otherwise one which could secure approval, the Commissioners have power to grant partial approval. An example of such a case would be a fund in which not more than about 25% in value of the benefit on retirement took the form of a lump-sum payment. In the case of partial approval it is necessary for the members' contributions and interest income to be apportioned, and those applicable to the 'non-approved' benefit would not secure relief from income tax.

Normally, the approved proportion of the member's contribution is fixed at the outset of the scheme, but the approved proportion of the fund in respect of which the interest income is allowed tax-free would be assessed and varied if necessary on the occasion of the periodic valuations of the fund.

The Commissioners of Inland Revenue do not permit under an approved scheme a cash benefit on withdrawal in excess of the member's own total contributions plus interest. As an alternative to a cash payment on withdrawal it would be permissible to grant a deferred annuity based upon the full actuarial reserve, provided the age at which the annuity vests is not more than 10 years below the normal pension age under the scheme. On death in service a benefit up to the full actuarial reserve is permitted, but any benefit in excess of this would prevent full approval being granted. In practice, the Commissioners may treat a fund as being fully approved for all tax purposes if the non-approved proportion of the benefits is relatively insignificant.

17.14. Income tax (F.A. 1947, sects. 19–23)

The conditions of approval imposed by the Commissioners of Inland Revenue under the 1921 Act have been very largely aimed at preventing the privileges attaching to pension funds being used to secure an excessive income tax advantage. Thus limitations are now placed upon the maximum pension on retirement, the maximum proportion of pension to final salary, dates of retirement, etc., while the inclusion of provisions permitting relatively large capital sum benefits or the commutation of the pension benefit and the payment of a capital sum in lieu thereof would normally preclude even partial approval. It will be seen that one of the objects of the rules is to limit or prevent the payment out of tax-free funds of substantial benefits which escape income tax or surtax, or which owing to the incidence of the payments only attract tax at much reduced rates. The steeply progressive rates of tax now in operation, however, make any scheme which enables the taxpayer to reduce his liability to surtax so attractive that the statutory powers which have so far been described have been found to be inadequate for the purpose of preventing abuse. Accordingly, under sects. 19–23 of the Finance Act, 1947, a new principle is introduced whereby any sum paid by a 'body corporate' for the provision of retirement benefits for an employee is deemed to be income of the employee assessable currently under Schedule E, unless the scheme or arrangement under which the payment is made has been approved for the purposes of this Act by the Commissioners. It will be observed that approval under these sections cannot apply to unincorporated employers, e.g. private individuals or partnerships. A similar ruling applies even in a case where the retirement benefit is not specifically provided for through a scheme or by a contract with a third person; in this case the payments which would have been required to provide the benefit are brought into account. Approval under the 1947 Act is automatically given to any scheme approved under the Finance Act, 1921 and, generally speaking, any other scheme will be approved which is *bona fide* for the provision of reasonable pensions. The intention and main effect of the 1947 Act is to ensure that it shall no longer be possible to provide, e.g. for large pensions to be paid to directors or highly paid employees who had served only a few years with the employer concerned under conditions whereby the employer escapes tax upon the contributions whilst the employee's liability for income tax and surtax is reduced.

17.15. Income tax (Income Tax Act, 1918, sect. 32)

Attention is drawn to one particular exception to the general principle set out in § 17.12. By the terms of the Finance Act, 1921, sect. 32, any payments in respect of which relief can be given under sect. 32 of the Income Tax Act, 1918, are excluded from the operation of the later Act. Effectively, this means that any scheme of pensions which is operated through an insurance company in such a form that the usual life assurance premium relief can be secured by the employee will be subject to the 1918 Act and not to the 1921 Act. Thus, funds which operate by means of endowment assurances with annuity options or by deferred annuities secure relief of tax to the members at rates similar to those applicable to life assurance premiums. It should be noted that although the 1918 Act excludes from relief ordinary deferred annuities effected by individuals after 22 June 1916, there is a proviso which specifically grants relief upon premiums upon deferred annuities effected in connexion with a *bona fide* pension scheme or widows' and orphans' scheme. So far as the employer's contributions to a scheme established under the 1918 Act are concerned, it should be noted that, whilst ordinary annual contributions are allowed to be deducted as an expense from taxable profits, no allowance can be obtained upon payments other than ordinary annual contributions. Although the tax relief under the 1918 Act is more limited than under the 1921 Act, the benefits under the 1918 Act scheme are less subject to tax than those provided by the 1921 Act schemes.

On the other hand, it is possible for a scheme operated through a Life Assurance Company to be brought within the scope of the 1921 Act. This is done by establishing the scheme under a trust deed similar in type to that required for a private scheme and, in effect, reassuring its liabilities with a Life Assurance Company. In practice, it is found that the advantage may lie with the 1918 or the 1921 Act, according to the circumstances of each individual case, the 1918 Act having frequently in the past proved more advantageous where the employee's earnings were low and such as only to attract income tax at the lowest rate. In consequence, however, of the higher general level of incomes and the higher rates of tax now operating, it is now unusual for a scheme under the 1918 Act to be more advantageous, and the majority of new life office schemes are written under the 1921 Act.

INVESTMENTS

17.16. Principles of investment

It is not proposed to deal in detail with the nature of the securities in which the trustees would be expected to invest the funds under their control, seeing that, in the main, the general principles of investment of this type of fund are similar to those applicable to other funds with which the actuary is familiar. There are, however, certain special considerations which arise in connexion with a pension or widows' and orphans' fund which should be noted. The problem of investment is essentially similar for both widows' and orphans' and for pension funds, and the remarks which follow are, therefore, applicable to both.

17.17. Powers of investment

The investment powers of the trustees are normally laid down in the trust deed. On some occasions in the past there has been a tendency to restrict the field of investment available to a fund, particularly where the investment experience of the trustees has not been wide. It is considered desirable, however, that the powers should be drafted widely so that the funds may be invested in suitable securities outside, for example, the trustee class. It has been found that a restrictive investment clause, however appropriate it may have been to the circumstances at the time when it was drafted, may have unexpected repercussions to the detriment studied, particularly the terms of subsection 3 of the Finance Act, of the fund in the changed circumstances which may arise many years later. Further, skilled professional advice upon the investment of funds of this type is available, so that inexperience on the part of the trustees need not constitute a danger to the finances of the fund.

17.18. Distribution of investments

The spread of the investment portfolio over the various types of security is a matter of great importance, and the actuary should give the maximum guidance possible to the trustees of the fund with which he is associated. In so doing, he should have clearly before him the special features of this type of fund, viz. the long-term nature of the liabilities and the fact that there is no liability to income tax. The first point will, of course, influence the selection of securities according to maturity date, the considerations in this respect being similar to those applicable to a life assurance fund. The freedom from liability to income tax enables the fund to secure an advantage by the selection, for example, of high-yielding securities purchased at a premium. By this means, a higher redemption yield would be secured, since the fund would be in a position to write off the premium out of gross interest, whereas an ordinary investor would have to write it off out of net interest.

CHAPTER 18

THE INAUGURATION OF A FUND

18.1. The establishment of a new fund may well be described as 'making bricks without straw'. The actuary engaged in the valuation of an existing fund has before him the past history of that fund for use as a guide in determining the bases to be used. In the case of a new fund, however, suitable records of the past experience of the employees concerned are usually non-existent, whilst even if they are available they must be accepted with caution. As has already been indicated, almost all the decremental rates which govern the contribution rates are likely to be affected in greater or less degree by the introduction of a scheme of pensions. The only course, therefore, is to adopt the experience of an existing fund or funds whose members appear likely, in the judgement of the actuary, to have a similar experience to that which will be shown by the members of the proposed fund. In this connexion the actuary will have to consider the classes of members to be covered by the scheme (e.g. males or females, clerical, administrative or weekly paid staff), the general conditions and nature of the employment, and possibly also the geographical distribution of the staff.

18.2. In view of these difficulties, it will be helpful first to recapitulate the matters already discussed which will call for decision, and then to deal with other points which will arise.

The first step to be taken is, of course, to discuss with the employer the type of scheme which is required and to prepare a preliminary draft to serve as a basis of discussion. Before the scheme is finally adopted it is desirable that it should be discussed with representatives of the employees concerned, especially as a condition of approval under the Finance Act, 1921, is the 'recognition' of the fund by the employees. Before doing so, however, it is obviously necessary to settle with the employer the broad outlines of the scheme in relation to his staffing policy and to the paramount question of cost.

18.3. Existing staff

When the general outline of the scheme has been determined so far as new employees and the future service of existing employees are concerned, the next and very important question to be dealt with is the benefits to be given to the existing staff and the contributions which they will be required to pay. If the existing employees are treated as new entrants at their attained ages, and pensions depend on duration of membership of the fund, the pensions of the older existing employees, based on the normal scale applicable to new entrants at young ages, would be very small. Their contributions, moreover (if they were to be required to pay, say, one-half of the total required), would be impracticably heavy. Special treatment, therefore, involving additional cost to the employer must be accorded to these employees, if the scheme is to fulfil from the outset its purpose as a superannuation scheme.

If a graduated scale of contributions is adopted, with the general intention that in the normal case the total shall be shared equally by the employer and employee, the scale may rise to such an extent that the contributions payable by employees entering over a certain age may be too heavy to impose in practice. In such cases, the employer must decide what is the maximum rate which the employees can reasonably be required to pay, and must undertake the balance of the liability himself, or, alternatively, provide modified benefits. These special considerations will apply both to existing employees and to future entrants (if any) at the ages concerned.

18.4. In order to provide adequate pensions for the existing elderly staff, it is in most cases essential for the employer to make special grants, and the amount which the employer is able and willing to provide for the purpose naturally determines the extent to which special concessions can be made. A plan which is in common use in funds where the normal contributions are shared equally by the employer and the employee is to give pension rights to the employees in respect of all service rendered before the establishment of the fund at one-half of the normal rate. The cost of this is borne wholly by the employer, but the capital liability need not be met immediately in full. Provided that care is taken to ensure that the fund has enough cash resources in hand in the first few years to meet the benefit payments as they emerge, any initial capital liability undertaken by the employer may be spread over a period of years. The idea underlying the grant of back-service rights at half the normal rate is that the resulting pensions represent roughly the amounts which would have been provided by the employer's contributions alone if the fund had been in existence throughout the entire service of the employees affected.

18.5. The cost of the concession referred to in the previous section may be more than the employer can shoulder, and some more limited scheme may be necessary. The best use will have to be made of the money available, and instead of giving back-service rights to all at a still further reduced rate, it may be decided to grant rights only to the more elderly. Thus, if past-service rights at half-rate were granted in respect of service rendered since the age of (say) 35 or 40, the cost would be reduced and the money would be used for the benefit of those most in need of it. The younger employees in the group will have the prospect of serving for another 20 or 25 years, and it is not so important to give them back-service rights as it is in the case of employees nearing the retiring age when the fund starts.

18.6. Actuarial report

When a preliminary decision has been reached upon the proposed scheme of pensions and the terms to be offered to existing employees, the actuary should submit a report setting out in detail both the proposals and the estimated cost thereof to the employer and to the employees on the assumption that all the eligible employees will join the scheme. For this purpose it will be necessary to determine

(*a*) the scale of contributions to be paid by new entrants;

(*b*) the corresponding scale to be paid by existing employees (which may not be identical with (*a*)); and

(*c*) the contributions to be paid by the employer in respect of the employees' past and future service.

It may be found that the scheme tentatively decided upon is impracticable on the score of cost, and therefore a variety of experimental calculations may be necessary before a scheme is evolved which meets the requirements satisfactorily.

18.7. Before a start can be made with the calculations, full particulars of the staff in the grades to be covered by the scheme (including, possibly, movements over the preceding five years) must be supplied to the actuary. For this purpose a card similar to that illustrated on pp. 70 and 71 could be employed. If the pensions are to be based on earnings, it will be necessary for particulars of earnings to be inserted in the card, and if these can be completed for, say, the previous 5 years this information may be of considerable assistance in determining the salary scale unless there have been changes in the general level of salaries during this period. The salary scale will be developed on the lines described in Chapter 13, and it should be possible to construct a scale suitable for use from the actual data, since the introduction of a pension scheme is unlikely to influence salary levels materially.

The experience in regard to the various decremental rates may be extracted by the methods described in earlier chapters, but as indicated in § 18.1 the results are unlikely to be of great value except as a guide in the selection of suitable rates derived from the experience of a similar but well-established scheme.

The rate of interest to be assumed for the purpose of the calculations should be determined having regard to the long term investment prospects (see Chapter 17).

18.8. The necessary basic monetary functions will then be calculated by the use of formulae developed according to the principles and methods already described in earlier chapters. The next step will be to calculate, for specimen entry ages, the rates of contribution to be paid by new entrants, by equating the values of benefits and contributions. If the scheme of pensions depends upon salaries, the contribution rate would probably be expressed as a percentage of the salary receivable from time to time, whilst, if the pension scale is not related directly to salaries, the contribution could be expressed in terms of units of pension to be secured.

18.9. Rates of contribution

As an illustration of the manner in which the rate of contribution may be found to vary with age at entry, specimen contribution rates have been calculated on the basis of the hypothetical tables, with interest at 3 %, which appear in the *Actuarial Tables for Examination Purposes*,

(*a*) assuming a salary scale of the 'officer' type

    (i) when the pension scale for each year of service is $1\frac{1}{2}$% of 'final average salary'; and

    (ii) when the pension scale is $1\frac{1}{2}$% of total salary throughout service (i.e. $1\frac{1}{2}$% of average salary throughout service for each year of service); and

(*b*) assuming a level salary scale

    when the pension scale is $1\frac{1}{2}$% of total salary throughout service (i.e. $1\frac{1}{2}$% of average salary throughout service for each year of service).

In each case the contribution is assumed to be shared equally between the member and the employer, and the benefit payable on death or withdrawal in service is an amount equal to the total contributions paid by the member, without interest.

The results under headings (*a*)(i) and (*a*)(ii) may be taken as appropriate to a scheme where the membership is confined to male clerical and administrative staff, whilst the results under heading (*b*) may be taken as representing approximately the contributions required in a scheme for male weekly paid staff where the salary scale is likely to be almost level, except at the younger ages.

It should be emphasized that the rates shown in Table 18.1 have been calculated merely for the purpose of illustration and should not be regarded as suitable for an actual scheme.

It may be deduced from this table that, other things being equal:

(*a*) the contribution increases more slowly with the age at entry in a scheme where the salary scale has a steep gradient than in the case of a scheme with a relatively flat salary scale;

(*b*) in the case of a 'final average' salary scheme, the percentage rate of contribution required may be almost a constant percentage of salary for the main entry ages up to 40 if the salary scale is of the 'officer' type, with a steep gradient;

(c) the contribution rate is lower for an 'average throughout' salary scheme than for a 'final average' salary scheme providing the same scale of benefits;

(d) the percentage contribution required at a particular age at entry for a given scale of benefit is greater when the gradient of the salary scale is steeper (compare (a)(i) and (a)(ii) with (b)).

TABLE 18.1

Age at entry	Specimen total rates of contribution expressed as percentage of salary		
	(a)(i) Pensions on final average salary basis	(a)(ii) Pensions on average salary throughout service basis	(b) Pensions on level salary throughout service
20	11·4	8·2	7·2
30	11·3	9·4	8·9
40	12·0	10·9	10·7
50	13·3	12·8	12·8

18.10. Income tax

The income tax advantages that can be secured by pension, widows' and orphans' funds have already been outlined (see Chapter 17), and are such that almost without exception new funds are so constituted as to qualify for these reliefs by securing full or partial approval under sect. 32 of the Finance Act, 1921. In the discussions with the employer referred to in the foregoing paragraphs, it will, therefore, be necessary to have continuously in mind the requirements for approval in order to ensure that the proposed scheme complies with them.

18.11. Legal status

The creation of a definite legal status is not only a *sine qua non* for the approval of a fund for income tax purposes, but is also obviously desirable for the protection of the interests of members generally and to give them a legal right to their pensions.

The principal methods by which this has been achieved are as follows:

(a) by registration as a Friendly Society under the Friendly Societies Act, 1896: this is, however, not generally appropriate since the maximum pension which could be paid would be £104 per annum;

(b) by promotion of a special Act of Parliament: this was the course adopted, for example, by a number of railway company funds, but is not nowadays commonly followed;

(c) by virtue of a general Act of Parliament, as in the case of Local Authority Funds: such an Act would normally lay down the framework within which each fund permitted by the Act must operate;

(d) by the execution of a deed setting up a trust fund under the control of trustees: this, the most commonly adopted method, is further considered below.

The function of such a trust deed is twofold, viz. the creation of the trust fund and of a legal body (the trustees) to operate it, and the definition of the objects and scope of the trustees' operations, including the financial provisions of the scheme. This division of functions is normally effected by relegating to a schedule annexed to the trust deed the rules and regulations setting out the details of the scheme which can in case of need be varied without requiring a new deed. Whilst the drafting of the deed and rules is, of course, a matter for the employer's legal advisers, the actuary should be closely associated with this work, and should satisfy himself that the final document interprets accurately the proposed scheme on which his reports and estimates have been based. The deed should also specify, *inter alia*:

(a) the investment powers of the trustees;

(b) the requirement of a periodic valuation of the scheme (normally quinquennial) and the action to be taken in regard to any deficiency or disposable surplus; and

(c) the circumstances in which the fund may be wound up and the principles then to be followed in apportioning the available funds.

Under the provisions of the Truck Act, 1831, an employer is prohibited from making any deductions from wages except for certain specified purposes for which the written consent of the employee is required. Further, the Shop Clubs Act, 1902, debars an employer from making it a condition of service that an employee shall join some society unless it is a registered friendly society. The latter Act is in practice disregarded in the case of pension funds, but a written agreement by the employee to submit to deductions from his pay of contributions to the scheme has been held to be in compliance with the Truck Act, and the rules should provide for such an undertaking to be obtained. On the inauguration of a scheme, existing staff cannot be compelled to join, but future staff can be brought into the scheme automatically by including the requirement to join the scheme in the terms of appointment.

18.12. Superannuation and other Trust Funds (Validation) Act, 1927

The period for which moneys can be tied up in a trust is normally restricted by the rule of law against perpetuities, under which the duration of the trust must be limited to the lifetime of some persons living when the trust was created and 21 years thereafter. Many superannuation trust deeds in existence at the time of the passing of the Finance Act, 1921, did not contain any such limitation, and when in due course applications for approval under sect. 32 of that Act were made doubts arose as to the validity of such deeds. A test case* was taken to the courts, and it was held that the trust was illegal and consequently void *ab initio*. In these circumstances the Commissioners of Inland Revenue found themselves unable to approve any fund unless there was a provision limiting its duration.† In the long run, however, a clause of this nature would require a succession of trusts which might be attended by some injustice to the beneficiaries of the fund. In order to secure the maximum benefit from a superannuation fund it should be permanent.

The position was accordingly examined by a Departmental Committee‡ which, after considering various alternatives, recom-

---

* Telegraph Construction and Maintenance Co. Ltd., see *J.I.A.* vol. LVI, p. 211.
† See specimen clause in Appendix II.
‡ Report of the Departmental Committee on the effect of the Rule of Law against Perpetuities in its application to certain Superannuation Funds and Funds with analogous purposes (Cmd. 2918), see *J.I.A.* vol. LVIII, p. 318.

mended that a special Act should be passed to enable superannuation funds to be relieved from the operation of the perpetuity rule. The outcome was the passing of the Superannuation and other Trust Funds (Validation) Act, 1927 (see Appendix I), under which superannuation funds and certain other types of fund may be exempted from the ordinary law regarding perpetuities. In order to obtain this privilege, certain conditions set out in the Act have to be complied with, and the trusts have to be registered with the Chief Registrar of Friendly Societies, but as a special class, under the Act of 1927, and not as Friendly Societies.

Registration under the Act of 1927 is not obligatory, nor is it essential for the purpose of obtaining the income tax concessions, although it facilitates matters in that respect. A fund which is not registered under the Act of 1927 is still subject to the perpetuity rule. It may, however, obtain approval for income tax purposes, but in that event the limitation clause has to be incorporated in the deed in order to secure its 'approval', while the fund is subject to the attendant disadvantages of periodic reconstruction.

(*Note*. In Scots Law there is nothing corresponding to the 'rule of law against perpetuities'.)

CHAPTER 19

ANALYSIS OF SURPLUS

19.1. As will be realized from the earlier chapters the valuation of a pension fund or of a widows' and orphans' fund may be quite complex and may involve a considerable amount of numerical calculation in the computation of the valuation factors and in the valuation of the various benefits by means of those factors. Hence it is extremely desirable to apply to the work some check which, as far as possible, should be independent of the ordinary valuation calculations; the more complex the scheme the more desirable it is that an independent check should be made. An analysis of the results of the valuation, in which the main sources of profit and loss since the previous valuation are segregated, provides such a check. It would hardly be overstating the position to say that the actuary should not be satisfied with his valuation until he has reconciled the results with those shown at a previous valuation by an analysis of profit and loss, assuming, of course, that full details of the previous valuation and of the experience in each year of the intervaluation period are available.

The degree of accuracy or detail attempted in the analysis would naturally depend on the extent to which the actuary may feel the need for confirmation of his valuation work. Theoretically, it would be possible to trace with complete accuracy the whole of the surplus or deficiency shown at the valuation by an analysis of the financial effect of all the various decremental rates, the salary scale and the rate of interest, but this would entail even greater labour than the ordinary valuation. In practice, therefore, the analysis would be made by approximate methods sufficient to afford a sound overall check on the valuation work.

19.2. In view of the number of factors entering into the valuation and of their interaction, it is possible to make the analysis in a number of ways. One method of procedure for a pension scheme is considered in some detail later in this chapter, but the actuary will normally devise his own methods having regard, *inter alia*, to:

(i) the relative financial importance he anticipates will attach to the various items of profit and loss;

(ii) the method by which the experience as regards the mortality and other decremental rates and salary progression has been investigated as a preliminary to the valuation; and

(iii) the methods adopted in the valuation itself.

The various headings under which profit or loss* may occur in a pension fund such as that considered in Chapter 10 may be enumerated as follows:

(*a*) changes in the valuation basis;

(*b*) alterations in benefit and contribution arrangements;

(*c*) interest earnings;

(*d*) mortality during active service;

(*e*) withdrawals;

(*f*) retirements;

(*g*) salaries;

(*h*) pensioners' mortality;

(*i*) admission of new members;

(*j*) realization of negative values;

(*k*) capital profits or losses on investments; and

(*l*) special income or expenditure.

19.3. The order in which the various items of profit are estimated would depend to some extent on the anticipation of their relative financial importance. If there have been any important changes in basis as compared with the previous valuation, probably the first stage in the analysis of surplus would be to estimate the effect of any such changes by reworking, either in full or by approximate methods, the present valuation on the old basis or, alternatively, by performing the previous valuation on the new basis. If the present valuation is reworked, the subsequent analysis should be based upon the various decremental and other rates

---

* In the present chapter reference is generally made for the sake of simplicity only to profit, but it should be understood that this is intended to cover the case where the item appears as a negative quantity, i.e. as a loss. Similarly the term 'surplus' should be understood generally in this chapter to include the negative case. viz. deficiency.

entering into the old basis of valuation; if the previous valuation is recalculated, the new valuation basis would be employed throughout the subsequent analysis. If the new valuation basis reflects reasonably closely the actual experience of the intervaluation period the latter method of analysing the surplus would reveal little in the way of 'experience' profits. Normally the former method is to be preferred as being more informative. The first stage in the valuation work would have been to compare the actual experience during the intervaluation period with that expected according to the last valuation basis. If as a result of the comparison it was decided to change the basis an analysis of surplus by reference to the old basis would show the financial effect of the variations between the actual and expected results which led the actuary to alter the basis. The difference between the results of valuations on the old and the new bases at the end of the period represents the capital value of the corresponding profits and losses which would have emerged in the future if the old basis had been retained and if the future experience conformed with the new basis.

The next step would be to estimate the effect of any alteration in the financial basis, e.g. in the benefit and contribution arrangements, which may have occurred during the intervaluation period; such an estimate may well have been made at the time the alteration was effected.

19.4. Interest

The interest profit would be calculated directly from the revenue accounts of the fund as follows:

If A = amount of fund at beginning of the first year of the quinquennium,

$\quad B$ = amount of fund at end of the first year of the quinquennium,

$\quad I$ = actual interest income in the year, less income tax (if any),

$\quad i$ = valuation rate of interest,

the interest profit as at the end of the year

$$= \left(I - \frac{A+B-I}{2} i \right),$$

which would be accumulated at rate i to the valuation date. Similar calculations would be made for each year of the inter-valuation period.

In addition, each of the other items contributing to the total profit should be increased by interest at the valuation rate i from the middle of the year in which the profit arose to the end of the period. In practice, it would generally be sufficient to add $2\frac{1}{2}$ years' compound interest for a quinquennial period, on the assumption that the profit has emerged evenly over the period, although in a particular case (e.g. salary experience loss due to a sudden change in salary levels) a more accurate adjustment for interest may be desirable.

Interest for the period at the valuation rate i should also be added to the surplus carried forward unappropriated from the previous valuation.

19.5. Pensioners' mortality

The profit arising from pensioners' mortality is the difference between the actual and expected release of reserves on death. The expected release per member exposed to risk at age x last birthday is the product of the average reserve per member at that age (less the average benefit, if any, payable on death) and the force of mortality at age $x+\frac{1}{2}$. As an approximation, the total expected release may be taken as the product of

(a) the mean of the total valuation reserves, less the total amount of death benefit 'at risk' at age x last birthday at the beginning and end of the valuation period (say 5 years) and

(b) $5\mu_{x+\frac{1}{2}}$,

aggregated for all ages.

The actual release of reserves would be calculated directly from the individual cases of pensioners dying (with a suitable grouping if the numbers are sufficient to justify this).

19.6. Mortality and withdrawal of active members

The profit under each of these headings would be calculated in a manner similar to that indicated in the previous paragraph.

Alternatively, the profit from the mortality experience at age x, for example, may be taken as the product of

(a) actual less expected deaths at age x, and

(b) the average release of reserves per death at age x, the release of reserves being, of course, the active staff member's reserve minus the benefit payable on death, e.g. a 'return' of contributions with interest thereon.

The average release of reserves could be taken as the mean of the appropriate figures for members aged x at the beginning and at the end of the valuation period. If the actual deaths are not a representative sample of the membership at risk, as may well be the case in a fund where the range of salaries or entry ages is relatively wide, it would be more satisfactory to calculate separately the actual release from the particulars of the deaths which have occurred.

As a further approximation, the expected release may be calculated by working on quinary groups if the rates are small or do not vary rapidly, as would be the case for the mortality rates over the greater part of the range of ages of active members.

19.7. Ill-health retirement of active members

The profit due to the ill-health retirement experience would be calculated in a similar manner, it being noted, however, that in this case there would normally be a strain on retirement equal to the difference between (a) the initial reserve required to be set up for a member on transfer to the pension roll as an ill-health pensioner and (b) the normal reserve held in respect of the member whilst on the active staff.

19.8. Age retirement

The profit on the age retirement experience, assuming that such retirement may occur at more than one age, would be estimated as the difference between the expected and actual strain. The expected strain for a particular retirement age may be taken as the expected number of retirements at such age multiplied by the average reserve per member immediately after retirement at that age less the corresponding average reserve immediately before retirement. Similarly, the actual strain arising from each new pensioner is the actual reserve required to be provided immediately after retirement less the reserve accumulated immediately before retirement. It would, of course, be necessary to calculate the various reserves before retirement by reference to the appropriate 'select' factors if, as may well be the case with optional retirement ages, the valuation has been made in select form (see § 7.5). It may be found possible to employ approximate methods similar to those indicated in § 19.6.

If there is a fixed normal retirement age and members invariably retire at that age, no profit or loss would arise under this heading. It may be found, however, that some members defer retirement beyond the normal age, and if this is the case, there may, on this account, be an important contribution towards profit unless the pension ultimately payable is adjusted to allow for the period of deferment. These cases would probably have to be considered individually. The profit arising from this source from a member who was due to retire at age 65 with a pension of P per annum but who actually retired at age $(65 + t)$ with a pension of P' is

$$(P'' - P') \, \bar{a}_{65+t},$$

where P'' is the pension which could have been allowed in place of the original pension P after allowing for benefit of survivorship and any additional contributions paid after age 65.

19.9. Salary experience

The principal profit due to the salary experience to be calculated as a separate item may be taken as the difference between

(i) the reserves which would have been required at the end of the period had the salary scale forecasts proved to be correct, and

(ii) the actual reserves held based upon the actual salaries reached at the end of the period.

From this profit should be deducted the corresponding loss on contributions paid due to the divergence of the actual salary experience from the forecast.

It may be remarked that, in calculating the profits arising from death, withdrawal and retirement the reserves at the date of exit have been calculated by reference to the actual attained salaries at that date, either directly or by approximation. Hence, there is a further item of profit or loss due to the salary experience equal to the difference between the aggregate reserves at date of exit on the bases of expected salaries and of actual salaries respectively.

If the present members at age x are subdivided into (i) those who were members at the previous valuation date and (ii) new entrants, then, for the first group the expected salaries attained at the present valuation date, and received during the period are respectively

$$\frac{S_{x-5}s_{x-\frac{1}{2}}}{s_{x-5\frac{1}{2}}} \quad \text{and} \quad \frac{S_{x-5}\sum\limits_{x-5}^{x-1}s_t}{s_{x-5\frac{1}{2}}},$$

where S_{x-5} is the aggregate annual rate of salary current at the previous valuation date and s_x is the relative salary scale as described in previous chapters. For the second group, the expected salaries attained and received, assuming that entry occurred on the average half way through the quinquennium, may be taken approximately as

$$\frac{S'_{x-2\frac{1}{2}}s_{x-\frac{1}{2}}}{s_{x-3}}, \quad \text{and} \quad \frac{S'_{x-2\frac{1}{2}}(\frac{1}{2}s_{x-3}+s_{x-2}+s_{x-1})}{s_{x-3}},$$

where $S'_{x-2\frac{1}{2}}$ is the aggregate of the commencing salaries of such new entrants.

A comparison of the actual and expected salaries (probably for quinary age groups) will readily enable an estimate to be made of the release of reserves at the valuation date and the corresponding loss on contributions. Thus if the scale of pensions is 1% of total salary and the joint contribution rate payable is $2k\%$ of salary, of which $k\%$ is returnable on death or withdrawal before retirement on pension, the release of reserves in respect of salary received to the valuation date would be

·01 (expected salary during quinquennium less corresponding actual salary)
$$\times \frac{M_x^{ra}+kM_x^d+kM_x^w}{D_x}.$$

The release of reserves in respect of future salary similarly would be

·01 (expected salary attained at end of quinquennium less corresponding actual salary)
$$\times \frac{{}^s\overline{R}_x^{ra}+k^s\overline{R}_x^d+k^s\overline{R}_x^w-2k^s\overline{N}_x}{D_x}.$$

The various factors above are those described in detail in Chapters 10 and 12.

19.10. The analysis of surplus described in this chapter may be summarized as follows. It will be noted that this skeleton summary has been drawn up on the assumptions that the tracing of the various 'experience' items has been made by reference to the old valuation basis (see § 19.3) and that the valuation period is 5 years:

		£
1. Surplus brought forward from last valuation		....
add interest for 5 years at rate *i* (valuation rate)		....
		———
		....
2. Interest earnings on the funds in excess of the valuation rate		....
3. Intervaluation profits and losses	£	
Mortality during service	....	
Withdrawals	....	
Retirements	....	
Pensioners' mortality	....	
Admission of new members	....	
Realization of negative values (see § 19·11)	....	
	———	
Total	....	
Interest for 2½ years at rate *i*	....	
	———	....
4. Alterations in benefit and contribution arrangements (with interest)		....
5. Capital profits or losses on investments (with interest)		....
6. Special income or expenditure (with interest)		....
7. Strain from increased salaries		....
8. Untraced profits/losses		———
9. Surplus/Deficiency on old basis		....
10. Effect of change of basis		———
11. Surplus/Deficiency on new basis, as shown by the Valuation Balance Sheet		═══

19.11. Realization of negative values and profit on new entrants

Normally, if negative values arise on a valuation they would be excluded, although the particular circumstances in which the scheme operates may justify some relaxation of this normal practice. If negative values are excluded, there will be a profit equal to the contributions received in respect of 'negative value' members so long as the reserve is negative. If negative values are not fully excluded, only a proportion of the contributions for 'negative value' members would give rise to a profit. There would also be a capital profit realized on new entrants equal to the negative value not excluded. There may, of course, on the other hand, be losses sustained in respect of new entrants equal to the initial reserves at entry if these are positive.

19.12. The profit and loss analysis of a widows' benefit scheme would proceed on lines similar to those outlined in preceding sections for a pension scheme. The methods used would, of course, be related to the method employed in the valuation, i.e. a collective or reversionary method or a combination of both. Thus if the valuation has been made on collective lines, it would be necessary to estimate the financial effect of variations from the valuation assumptions of the proportions married and average age differences of husbands and wives among emerging new claims for widows' benefits. On the other hand, if a reversionary method of valuation has been employed, the financial effect of the experience as regards rates of marriage, widowhood and remarriage corresponding to the various changes of marital status entering into the valuation will have to be examined.

19.13. Finally, it may be reiterated that in a pension or widows' scheme there are usually so many interacting forces that a complete and accurate tracing of all the items of profit and loss would prove to be very difficult and probably quite impracticable. The preliminary statistical investigation of the experience should give an indication of the main items requiring estimation, and the extent to which further investigations would be pursued would depend largely upon the amount of the profit or loss then remaining untraced.

CHAPTER 20

EMERGING COSTS

20.1. Up to this stage the normal method of valuation has been dealt with by which future benefits or contributions are discounted at interest and reduced to present values. Occasionally, however, the information required may be not the present values, but the estimated periodical cash expenditure and receipts of a scheme over a series of years in the future, usually referred to as 'emerging cost' estimates.

In the case of a fund closed to new entrants it is clear that if all future emerging payments are discounted at interest to the present time the result should reproduce exactly the normal actuarial valuation of such payments, provided that the bases adopted in the two sets of calculations are the same. The basis adopted in the normal actuarial valuation may, however, make allowance for future trends in the various rates by the use of forecast rates intended to represent the average expected future experience. In this event the emerging cost figures should, theoretically, be based upon rates which are assumed to change gradually in the future if complete consistency is desired. The employment of the forecast rates used in the valuation would, of course, give too much weight to the expected future trends in the emerging cost figures in the early years.

Where the fund is not closed to new entrants emerging cost figures will include a growing proportion arising in respect of future entrants, and on this account these forecasts would not be equivalent to the calculations made in a normal valuation, under which allowance for new entrants is only made in very special circumstances.

20.2. The general method of procedure is to calculate, on the basis of the various probabilities involved in the estimates, the income and outgo in successive years in the future in respect of each group of members now aged x. The figures for the total membership for any particular year in the future would then be obtained by aggregating the results obtained for each separate age x. As the calculations are necessarily more extensive than those made for the normal valuation it is usual for a certain amount of grouping to be made, either by reference to the attained ages of members or by reference to future years, or both. If emerging cost figures are calculated for quinquennial dates in the future, figures for intermediate years, if required, would be obtained by interpolation.

Where the fund is not closed to new entrants assumptions must be made as regards the numbers of new entrants and their ages and salaries at entry, and these assumptions will depend to some extent upon the rate of 'turn-over' of the existing staff as measured by the rates of decrement assumed. It may be decided that the flow of new entrants assumed should be such that the total staff would remain approximately constant both as regards numbers and salaries; or, alternatively, it may be required to assume for the purpose of the emerging cost calculations that the staff would gradually change over a period of years to a new level of membership and salaries.

20.3. Ultimate position

The problem involving the easiest type of calculation is to find the estimated income and expenditure of the fund when it has reached a stationary condition. This is, of course, a theoretical question as it depends for its solution on the assumptions that

(i) after a certain time the various decrement rates as well as the rate of interest and the average actual salaries payable age by age will not alter;

(ii) the contributions in respect of new entrants are exactly sufficient to provide the benefits, after due allowance has been made for any expenses chargeable to the fund; and

(iii) there is no surplus or deficiency carried forward in the fund before the ultimate state is reached.

As an example of the calculations which would be required to determine the ultimate position, the pension scheme outlined in § 9.2 will be taken as a basis.

20.4. Active staff

If there is a fixed entry age x_0, say, the number of members in service age by age will be proportionate to the numbers shown by the service table compiled on the basis of the ultimate decrement rates. Now the total population represented by the service table is $\sum\limits_{x=x_0}^{64} L_x$, where $\qquad L_x = \tfrac{1}{2}(l_x + l_{x+1})$.

If the total number of staff in the stationary condition is T, all estimates based upon the numbers of the service table will have to be multiplied by the factor

$$\alpha = T \left/ \sum_{x=x_0}^{64} L_x. \right.$$

In consequence of assumption (i) of §20.3, s_x, the salary scale, may be taken in these calculations as representing not only the relative scale but also the average actual salary per annum receivable by members between age x and age $x+1$. The total annual payroll of the staff T will thus be $\alpha \sum\limits_{x=x_0}^{64} L_x s_x$, and from this the annual contribution income can be obtained directly when the contribution payable is expressed as a fixed percentage of salary.

The ultimate annual payments in respect of deaths and withdrawals of members in active service can be obtained in a similar manner. Thus the payment made on death at age x last birthday under the scheme is equal to the member's own contributions at rate $c\%$ of salary together with interest thereon of $j(2\tfrac{1}{2})\%$ per annum, or (ignoring any interest on the contributions paid in the year of death)

$$\cdot \text{o1}c\{s_{x_0}(1+j)^{x-x_0} + s_{x_0+1}(1+j)^{x-x_0-1} + \dots$$
$$+ s_{x-1}(1+j) + \tfrac{1}{2}s_x\} = f_x, \quad \text{say.}$$

To facilitate the formation of commutation columns, f_x may be rewritten in the form

$$\cdot \text{o1}c(1+j)^x(s_{x_0}v^{x_0} + s_{x_0+1}v^{x_0+1} + \dots + s_{x-1}v^{x-1} + \tfrac{1}{2}s_x v^x).$$

The total annual payment in respect of this benefit is thus

$$\alpha \sum_{x=x_0}^{64} d_x f_x.$$

20.5. Pensioners

The ultimate population of pensioners generated by r_x retirements at age x last birthday is $r_x \overset{\circ}{e}'_{x+\frac{1}{2}}$, where $\overset{\circ}{e}'_{x+\frac{1}{2}}$ is the complete expectation of life calculated by reference to the appropriate pensioners' mortality and modified to allow for the fact that the pension payable under the scheme would in any event be continued for a minimum period of 5 years. Thus

$$\overset{\circ}{e}'_{x+\frac{1}{2}} = 5 + {}_5p_{x+\frac{1}{2}}\,\overset{\circ}{e}_{x+5\frac{1}{2}},$$

where $\overset{\circ}{e}_{x+5\frac{1}{2}}$ is the complete expectation of life at age $x + 5\frac{1}{2}$.

TABLE 20.1

Age	No. of retire- ments	Annual pension $\dfrac{(x-x_0)}{60}z_{x+\frac{1}{2}}$	New pension roll each year $(2)\times(3)$	$\overset{\circ}{e}'_{x+\frac{1}{2}}$	Ultimate	
					Total no. of pensioners $(2)\times(5)$	Total annual pension roll $(4)\times(5)$
x	r_x					
(1)	(2)	(3)	(4)	(5)	(6)	(7)
Totals		—		—		

The ultimate annual amount of pension on the scale of $\frac{1}{60}$ths of final average salary payable in respect of members who have retired at age x last birthday, having entered at age x_0 is

$$P_x = \frac{\alpha(x-x_0)}{60}z_{x+\frac{1}{2}}r_x\overset{\circ}{e}'_{x+\frac{1}{2}},$$

assuming that complete years only are allowed to rank for pension purposes, and the total annual pension payments would be obtained by summation of P_x over all possible retirement ages. It should be

noted that as final retirement under the scheme takes place at age
65 exact

$$P_{65} = \frac{\alpha(65 - x_0)}{60} z_{65} r_{65} \mathring{e}'_{65},$$

where $r_{65} = l_{65}$ from the service table.

Again, if there is a maximum pension of $\frac{40}{60}$ths, $(x - x_0)$ in P_x
would be replaced by 40 in any case when $(x - x_0) > 40$.

A suitable arrangement of the working sheet for pensioners is
given in Table 20.1.

20.6. If entry to the scheme is not confined to a single age it may
be sufficient for the purpose of the emerging cost estimates to
assume an average entry age. If this is not practicable, it would be
necessary as a first step to determine the proportions of the new
members who enter at the various ages. The calculations would then
proceed on the lines indicated in §§ 20.3–20.5. In the first place the
numbers shown by the service table would be used, the staff and
pensioners corresponding to each entry age (or group of entry ages)
being treated separately throughout. The results would then be
aggregated in the appropriate proportions having regard to the age
distribution of members at entry, and the aggregate figures would
then be scaled up or down so as to provide results for a total staff
of T. Alternatively, for pensioners' estimates, it might be possible
to work from a single service table, which would be modified, however, so as to incorporate rates of entry as well as the usual decrements. These rates of entry would have to be such as to produce the
desired proportions of entrants at the various permissible entry ages.

20.7. Size of fund

In the ultimate position the annual expenditure on benefits and
expenses is exactly equal to the annual income by way of contributions and interest at the assumed valuation rate on the accumulated
fund. From this equation the accumulated fund (F) in the stationary
condition is obtained directly as

$$F = \frac{\text{total annual expenditure} - \text{total annual contribution income}}{i},$$

where i is, of course, the rate of interest which it is assumed the
fund will earn and on which the contribution rate is calculated.

20.8. Intermediate stages

To trace the intermediate progress of the fund from year to year, or at quinquennial intervals, is a much more laborious process. In the case of the stationary fund, the calculations proceeded directly by reference to the service table numbers. In the present case, however, it is necessary to proceed by projecting forward the actual distribution of staff and their actual salaries and the existing pensioners at the commencing date by means of the various probabilities shown by the service table and the pensioners' mortality rates. As an illustration of the methods which may be employed the procedure indicated above will now be considered in some detail for the specimen scheme outlined in §9.2. In this connexion it must always be borne in mind that (*a*) it is essential that the programme of work must be most carefully organized if it is to be kept within manageable limits, (*b*) when adopting a system of grouping care is required in choosing the groups so as to give the best result. It may be thought advisable to work out some of the groups in detail for the first 5 years as a check on the results obtained by the use of group values.

20.9. Out of n_x members existing at age x (nearest) at the commencement, the numbers retiring on pension in the first, second, ... tth years will be

$$\frac{n_x r_x}{l_x}, \quad \frac{n_x r_{x+1}}{l_x}, \quad ..., \quad \frac{n_x r_{x+t-1}}{l_x},$$

where l_x, r_x are taken from the service table appropriate to the fund.

Similarly, the numbers of survivors of such pensioners arising from the n_x members will be

$$\frac{n_x \cdot r_x \cdot {}_{\frac{1}{2}} p'_{[x+\frac{1}{2}]}}{l_x}$$

at the end of the first year,

$$\frac{n_x \{ r_x \cdot {}_{1\frac{1}{2}} p'_{[x+\frac{1}{2}]} + r_{x+1} \cdot {}_{\frac{1}{2}} p'_{[x+1\frac{1}{2}]} \}}{l_x}$$

at the end of the second year, and so on, where it is assumed that retirements at age x last birthday occur on the average at age $x+\frac{1}{2}$.

Accented functions relate to pensioners and, as indicated in the formulae, the mortality of pensioners is in select form. Allowance would also be made in the pension functions for the 5 year guarantee period.

20.10. All the items required for the emerging cost estimates could be obtained in similar fashion by a direct application of the probabilities obtained by reference to the service table and the mortality of pensioners, and, where appropriate, the salary-scale functions. In practice approximations are introduced in order to reduce the volume of the calculations. For example, estimates may be made at quinquennial points of time, by quinary grouping of the membership and by using compound factors covering probabilities, etc., for 5 year periods.

Thus the number of retirements occurring in the first 5 year period out of members numbering n_{x-2}, n_{x-1}, ..., n_{x+2} respectively at ages $x-2$, $x-1$, ..., $x+2$ at the outset will be

$$\text{(i)} \quad \sum_{t=-2}^{+2} \left\{ \frac{n_{x-2} \cdot r_{x+t}}{l_{x-2}} + \frac{n_{x-1} \cdot r_{x+1+t}}{l_{x-1}} + \dots + \frac{n_{x+2} \cdot r_{x+4+t}}{l_{x+2}} \right\}.$$

If n_x is assumed to be proportionate to l_x in the age-range $x-2$ to $x+2$, the expression (i) may be replaced by

$$\text{(ii)} \quad k \sum_{t=-2}^{+2} \left\{ r_{x+t} + r_{x+1+t} + \dots + r_{x+4+t} \right\},$$

where

$$k = \frac{n_{x-2}}{l_{x-2}} = \frac{n_{x-1}}{l_{x-1}} = \dots = \frac{[5] n_x}{[5] l_x}.$$

As a further approximation it may be found that $[5]^2 r_{x+2}/[5] l_x$ may be replaced by $[5] r_{x+2}/l_x$ without introducing any serious error, so that expression (i) reduces to

$$\text{(iii)} \quad \frac{[5] n_x [5] r_{x+2}}{l_x}.$$

Alternatively, if the first assumption that n_x is proportionate to l_x cannot reasonably be made, the factor $[5]^2 r_{\bar{x}+2}/[5] l_{\bar{x}}$ appropriate to the weighted average age $\bar{x}$ for the group of members age $(x-2)$ to $(x+2)$ might be used.

Again, if r_{x+2+t}/l_x does not change rapidly with x within a 5-year age-range (as would normally be the case outside the ages in the numerator at which optional or final retirement rates operate), r_{x+t}/l_{x-2} and similar probabilities may be replaced by r_{x+2+t}/l_x. The expression (i) then simplifies to $[5]n_x \cdot [5]r_{x+2}/l_x$, which is the same as expression (iii) above, although it should be noted that the underlying assumptions are different.

In the formulae developed in subsequent paragraphs it will be assumed that the weighted average age $\bar{x}$ does not differ materially from x, or that any error due to such a difference may be ignored for the purpose of the emerging cost calculations. Formulae analogous to expression (ii) will therefore be used.

20.11. The number of new pensions from the same original group of members $n_{x-2}, \ldots, n_{x+2}$ arising in the second 5-year period would be $[5]n_x \cdot [5]^2 r_{x+7}/[5]l_x$.

In the case of the specimen scheme under consideration final retirement occurs at exact age 65, and it will therefore be convenient in the emerging cost calculations to work from age-groups 20–24, 25–29, ..., 60–64.

The age-group 60–64 will give rise to new ill-health pensioners in the first 5 years of

$$\frac{n_{60}(r_{60}+\ldots+r_{64})}{l_{60}} + \frac{n_{61}(r_{61}+\ldots+r_{64})}{l_{61}} + \ldots + \frac{n_{64}r_{64}}{l_{64}},$$

and to new age retirement pensioners in the same period of

$$\frac{n_{60}r_{65}}{l_{60}} + \frac{n_{61}r_{65}}{l_{61}} + \ldots + \frac{n_{64}r_{65}}{l_{64}}.$$

The number of ill-health retirements may be taken as approximately

$$\frac{[5]n_{62}\{r_{60}+2r_{61}+\ldots+5r_{64}\}}{[5]l_{62}},$$

or, alternatively, as

$$\frac{[5]n_{62}[3]r_{63}}{l_{62}},$$

and the number of age retirements as approximately

$$\frac{[5]n_{62}\,5r_{65}}{[5]l_{62}} \quad \text{or} \quad \frac{[5]n_{62}r_{65}}{l_{62}}.$$

Similar formulae will be required for the number of new pensioners arising in the second quinquennium from the present age-group 55–59 and so on, whilst if the scheme involves optional retirement rates, from age 60 say, it would be necessary to give separate consideration to retirements on and after that age, as the survivors of the present age-groups successively reach the optional retiring ages in the future. It may indeed prove just as simple to treat these retirement ages individually for each present age of the members, the pensioners being recombined in quinary age-groups for the purpose of further forecasting in the status of pensioner.

20.12. The annual amount of pension of those who retire within the first 5 years may be obtained by the formula

$$\frac{(w+2\frac{1}{2})}{60} \frac{[5]S_x[5]^2(r_{x+2}z_{x+2\frac{1}{2}})}{[5](l_x s_{x-\frac{1}{2}})},$$

where S_x is the total current annual rate of salary receivable by members aged x at the commencement date and w is the average number of years qualifying at that date for pension at the $\frac{1}{60}$th rate.

This may be expressed more approximately as

$$\frac{(w+2\frac{1}{2})}{60} \frac{[5]S_x \frac{z_{x+2\frac{1}{2}}}{s_{x-\frac{1}{2}}}[5]^2 r_{x+2}}{[5]l_x}.$$

The new annual pension roll surviving to the end of the first 5 years would be obtained approximately by multiplying by the further factor $_{2\frac{1}{2}}p'_{[x+2\frac{1}{2}]}$.

20.13. Schedules

The work would in practice be performed on schedules. Thus in order to forecast the numbers and salaries of the active staff and the pensions at quinquennial dates, two series of schedules are required:

A, showing the survivors of the active staff together with the numbers retiring and the amount of their pensions, and

B, showing the progress of the pensioners.

The schedule forms given in Tables 20.2 and 20.3 show the manner in which the work would be set out for one quinquennial period. Further columns may be added to deal with contributions payable and the benefits on death and withdrawal, or these items could be calculated on separate schedules.

TABLE 20.2

Schedule A, Active Staff

Retirements, New Pensions and Survivors on Active Staff. Sheet 1 (1950–54)

Age-group $x-2$ to $x+2$ on 1 Jan. 1950	Factors				1 January 1950			Retirements 1950–54				31 December 1954		
					No. of members	Total salaries	Average past duration w (1950)	Proportion of salary as pension at duration $(w+2\frac12)$	No. of new pensions	Pensionable salary of retirements	New annual pensions	No. of members	Total salaries	Average past duration w (1955)
	$\dfrac{[5]^2 r_{x+2}}{[5] l_x}$	$\dfrac{[5]^2 (r_{x+2} z_{x+2\frac12})}{[5](l_x s_{x-\frac12})}$	$\dfrac{[5] l_{x+5}}{[5] l_x}$	$\dfrac{[5](l_{x+5} s_{x+4\frac12})}{[5](l_x s_{x-\frac12})}$					$(6)\times(2)$	$(7)\times(3)$	$(11)\times(9)$	$(6)\times(4)$	$(7)\times(5)$	$(8)+5$
(1)	(2)	(3)	(4)	(5)	(6)	(7)	(8)	(9)	(10)	(11)	(12)	(13)	(14)	(15)

Notes. (a) The figures in columns (6), (7) and (8) relate to the assumed commencing date, say, 1 January 1950.

(b) An adjustment would have to be made at certain age-groups in columns (8), (9) and (15) to allow for the fact that the maximum proportion of pension permitted in any individual case is $\frac{40}{60}$ths.

(c) Columns (10) and (12) are transferred to Schedule B, Sheet 1 (1950–54), columns (6) and (7).

(d) Columns (13), (14) and (15) are transferred to Schedule A, Sheet 2 (1955–59), columns (6)–(8) at ages 5 years older than on 1 January 1950; the youngest age-group is then blank. Column (6), 1 January 1955 must be completed by a number representing the survivors of new entrants in the quinquennium, sufficient to bring the total of the column up to the required strength and column (7) is com-

TABLE 20.3

Schedule B, Pensioners

Number of Pensioners and Annual Pension Roll. Sheet 1 (1950–54)

Age-group $x-2$ to $x+2$ on 1 Jan. 1950	Factors		1 January 1950		New pensions 1950–54 age groups $x-2$ to $x+2$		Survivors to 31 December 1954					
	$_5p'_x$	$_{2\frac12}p'_{(x+2\frac12)}$	No. of pensioners	Annual amount of pensions	No.	Amount	From 1 January 1950		New pensions		Total	
							No.	Amount	No.	Amount	No.	Amount
							$(4)\times(2)$	$(5)\times(2)$	$(6)\times(3)$	$(7)\times(3)$	$(8)+(10)$	$(9)+(11)$
(1)	(2)	(3)	(4)	(5)	(6)	(7)	(8)	(9)	(10)	(11)	(12)	(13)

Notes. (a) The figures in columns (4) and (5) are the numbers and amounts in force on the commencing date, 1 January 1950.
(b) Columns (6) and (7) are taken from columns (10) and (12) of Schedule A, Sheet 1 (1950–54).
(c) Columns (12) and (13) are transferred to Sheet 2 (1955–59), columns (4) and (5) at ages 5 years older than on 1 January 1950.

20.14. Approximate methods of valuation

It is possible to proceed with the valuation of a pension scheme by methods analogous to those described above for emerging costs, by a quinary grouping of members and by working on decrements arising in successive quinquennia. This method of approximation is illustrated in the paper by H. Freeman, in *J.I.A.* vol. LXI, p. 9, to which the student pursuing more advanced studies might refer. Frequently the actuary may be called upon to give approximate estimates of liability or of the cost of proposed changes in a scheme, or he may wish to make a rough over-all check on his detailed calculations. It is not possible to indicate any general method to employ for such calculations. Whilst it is in general useful to bear in mind that, basically, pension schemes are merely aggregations of deferred annuities, the actuary who is familiar with the details of the particular scheme under consideration will necessarily have to evolve his own methods in the light of his general training and experience, the nature of the approximations being, of course, governed by the degree of accuracy required and the type of scheme. In this connexion the considerations mentioned in § 20.10, as governing the permissible degree of approximation in emerging cost calculations, would clearly be equally valid in connexion with approximate methods of valuation.

CHAPTER 21

SUPERANNUATION OF LOCAL GOVERNMENT EMPLOYEES

21.1. The actuarial student is presumably not expected to acquire a detailed knowledge of the superannuation provisions affecting civil servants, the armed forces of the Crown, teachers, police and certain other bodies dealt with mainly by Departments of State. But any qualified actuary may be called upon to advise a local authority with regard to the superannuation of its ordinary staff, and this chapter is therefore limited to a discussion of the superannuation schemes of local authorities.

21.2. Historical development

Prior to 1 April 1939 there was no general compulsion on local authorities to provide retirement benefits for their staffs other than for certain specified types, e.g. teachers and police, imposed by special Acts of Parliament. The Metropolitan Boroughs had general powers to grant retirement benefits on a non-contributory basis under an Act of 1866, but this arrangement was not considered satisfactory and nearly all these boroughs promoted private Acts enabling them to set up funds on a contributory basis. Several of the larger authorities outside London also had private Acts enabling them to establish pension schemes. The benefit and contribution arrangements under such schemes showed considerable variations.

In 1922 the Local Government and other Officers' Superannuation Act was passed under which a standard scheme was prescribed for local authorities. Within the framework laid down by the Act a local authority could adopt at its option a pension scheme for its employees. The procedure was thus greatly simplified in comparison with the elaborate and costly method of promoting a private Act which hitherto had been necessary.

As from 1 April 1939 the Local Government Superannuation Act, 1937, came into operation, under which every local authority was required to make provision for the superannuation of its ordinary administrative, technical and other non-manual staff; the inclusion of manual employees in the new arrangements was still left optional on the authority. Funds established under the Act of 1922 were continued in force but were made subject to the provisions of the Act of 1937 as from 1 April 1939. The 1937 Act also included arrangements whereby an authority with a local Act scheme could change to the new Act scheme or continue with its local scheme, subject to certain modifications.

The Local Government Superannuation Act, 1937, applies to England and Wales, and the summary which follows later in this chapter relates to that Act. There is a separate Act, also of 1937, for Scotland in consequence of certain differences in the local government systems, but the superannuation schemes and the financial and actuarial provisions are the same. The Scottish scheme came into force on 16 May 1939. Where reference is made in the remainder of this chapter to a specific section of the Act for England and Wales a note of the corresponding section of the Scottish Act is given in brackets alongside.

21.3. Metropolitan Boroughs schemes

Broadly, the Metropolitan Boroughs schemes provide pensions at the rate of $\frac{1}{60}$th of 'final average' salary for each year of service, although some provide for staff appointed after a certain date pensions at the rate of $\frac{1}{80}$th together with lump sums at the rate of $\frac{1}{30}$th, the option of converting to these alternative benefits being allowed to employees subject to the older arrangements. The employee contributes a fixed percentage of salary, and the balance of liability falls upon the authority, which has to provide for it by means of a 'primary annual contribution'. This is sometimes expressed in the local Act as a percentage of the total payroll of employees in the scheme, or it may be fixed as an annual charge for a period of years, subject in either case, of course, to review after each quinquennial valuation. The percentage rate payable by the employee was originally fixed at a low level (sometimes as low as 2%), but most authorities have now increased the rate payable by new entrants so that approximately one-half of the liability is met by the employees, the other half being met by the authority.

21.4. The Local Government Superannuation Act, 1937
Sects. 1 and 2 (sects. 1 and 2). Under this Act any local authority not having a 'local Act scheme' is required to provide pensions for its whole-time officers either

(i) by setting up its own fund

or (ii) by means of a combination scheme in conjunction with one or more other authorities

or (iii) by becoming an 'admitted authority' in the scheme maintained by an 'administering authority'.

Schemes set up under the 1922 Act are continued, subject in future to the provisions of the 1937 Act.

Authorities with less than 100 employees on 1 October 1938 were not permitted to set up their own scheme (the corresponding limit was 50 under the 1922 Act, and this limit was retained in the Scottish Act of 1937).

21.5. Sects. 3 and 4 (sects. 3 and 4). The main classes of 'contributory employees' covered by the Act are

(*a*) every whole-time officer (male and female) except that temporary officers need not be admitted until they have been employed for two years (sect. 30 (sect. 25)), and

(*b*) every servant or part-time officer in a class or description which the authority may also decide to include.

Employees are excluded from membership until the attainment of age 18 and employees over age 55 cannot join the scheme unless they have completed or can complete before the age of 65, 10 years of service.

21.6. Sect. 5 (sect. 5). This section enables employees of a statutory undertaker (e.g. a water supply undertaking) to be admitted to a superannuation fund maintained under the 1937 Act under an 'admission agreement' on such terms and conditions as the authority administering the fund may think fit and with the approval of the Minister. The Act then applies in relation to the employer and any employee so admitted as if the employer were a local authority and the employee were a contributory employee.

Any admission agreement made under the corresponding provisions of the 1922 Act continues in force subject possibly to minor adjustments. A voluntary organization employing certified midwives with which an arrangement has been made by the local supervising authority for the purpose of the Midwives Act, 1936, may also be regarded as a statutory undertaker for the purpose of sect. 5 (sect. 5) of the 1937 Act. Under sect. 7 of the Superannuation (Miscellaneous Provisions) Act, 1948 (which applies to Scotland as well as to England and Wales), employees of a body representative of local authorities or of the officers of local authorities may also be admitted on suitable terms to the superannuation fund of a local authority.

The Minister has issued a 'model form of agreement' under which provision is made for the payment by the undertakers of an annual sum, as certified by an actuary appointed by the administering authority, to meet the burden imposed on the superannuation fund (i.e. the initial liability) by reason of the admission of its employees as named in the schedule to the agreement. Any further liabilities arising in respect of such employees and of any other employees subsequently admitted are normally dealt with as in the case of an admitted local authority.

21.7. Sect. 6 (sect. 6). The rate of contribution normally payable by an employee is 6% of pensionable remuneration in the case of officers and 5% in the case of servants. Under the 1922 Act the rate was 5% for both classes (employees over age 55 at entry to the scheme did not contribute), and this rate continues to be payable in the case of employees who entered schemes established under the 1922 Act before 1 April 1939 (Scot. 16 May 1939).

Certain special classes, e.g. transferred poor law employees who were formerly superannuated under other legislation, are entitled to contribute at reduced rates ($2\frac{1}{2}$, 3 or $3\frac{1}{2}$%).

The employing authority is required to pay a contribution equal in the aggregate to the amounts paid by its employees in the scheme. It is also required under sect. 22 (sect. 18) to pay certain additional contributions over a fixed term of years to liquidate any liabilities not covered by the ordinary joint contributions.

An employee whose remuneration is reduced may elect to continue to pay contributions on the basis of his remuneration before such reduction.

The rates of contribution payable by the employees cannot be varied except, of course, by further legislation.

21.8. Sects. 7 and 8 (sects. 7 and 8). Normally an employee is pensionable at age 65. The employing authority may, with the employee's consent, extend his service beyond that age, but no contributions are payable during such period of extended service and the amount of the pension is not affected by the deferment.

An employee is also pensionable

(i) after not less than 10 years of local government service on ceasing employment by reason of permanent ill-health or infirmity of mind or body;

(ii) at any time after age 60 and before the normal pension age on the completion of 40 years of service.

In the case of female nurses, midwives and health visitors the normal pension age is 60 with optional retirement after age 55 subject to the completion of at least 30 years of service (sect. 16 (sect. 16)).

The scale of benefits payable* is $\frac{1}{80}$th of 'average remuneration' for each completed year of contributing service plus $\frac{1}{120}$th of average remuneration for each year of non-contributing service, subject to an overall maximum of $\frac{40}{80}$ths.

---

* The 1937 Act and local Act schemes were extended by Parts III and IV of the National Health Service (Superannuation) Regulations (consolidated and amended by Statutory Instrument No. 497 of 1950) so as to allow the payment of the benefits specified in such regulations, in lieu of the normal benefits, to certain employees engaged in local health or school health services or employees of voluntary organizations. Briefly these regulations provide for a pension benefit of $\frac{1}{80}$th on retirement, and a lump sum of $\frac{3}{80}$th plus a widow's benefit of $\frac{1}{240}$th on death in service or after retirement, in respect of each year of contributing service and at half these rates for each year of non-contributing service. In any case where the employee is unmarried on death in service or on retirement a lump-sum benefit of $\frac{3}{80}$ths ($\frac{3}{160}$ths for non-contributing service) is payable in respect of each year since the date when the scheme last ceased to be 'at risk' for a widow's benefit. The benefits are calculated by reference to the average salary during the last 3 years of service, the pension being payable on ill-health retirement or on retirement after the age of 60, subject in each case to the completion of 10 years' service.

(*Note.* The benefit at the $\frac{1}{60}$th rate is calculated by reference to complete years; any further contributing period of less than 1 year is aggregated with the period of non-contributing service, and the period of non-contributing service as so adjusted is reckoned to the nearest number of years for the purpose of calculating the benefits at the $\frac{1}{120}$th rate.)

'Average remuneration' is defined as the annual average of the pensionable remuneration received during the 5 years immediately preceding retirement or attainment of age 65 (60 in the case of female nurses etc. subject to sect. 16 (sect. 16)) whichever is the earlier.

'Pensionable remuneration' excludes overtime payments and expense allowances but includes the value of any emoluments normally attaching to the post held by the employee.

'Service' includes all local government service whether rendered to the present employer or to any other previous employer. The employing authority may increase the part of the pension payable at the non-contributing rate to a rate not exceeding $\frac{1}{60}$th, but the cost of the additional pension is borne by the authority and not by the superannuation fund. In the case of female nurses, etc. (sect. 16 (sect. 16)), the authority may allow up to $\frac{5}{60}$ths additional pension on retirement at age 60 (subject to the total normal maximum of $\frac{40}{60}$ths), similarly payable outside the superannuation fund.

An employee may increase his non-contributing pension up to the $\frac{1}{60}$th scale by an appropriate additional contribution to the fund under a prescribed scale.

Pensions are payable in instalments at intervals not exceeding three months.

21.9. Sect. 9 (sect. 9). Under this section the Minister is empowered to make rules to enable an employee retiring otherwise than on grounds of ill-health to surrender at his option up to one-third of his pension to secure a reversionary annuity of equivalent value to his spouse. According to the rules issued under this section the reversionary annuity must not exceed in amount the employee's own pension as reduced by the surrender, nor must it be less than one-fourth of such reduced pension. Notice of surrender must be given not less than one month or more than two months before retirement and the employee must then be in a good state of health having regard to his age; notification may be cancelled by the employee up to the time of retirement.

21.10. Sect. 10 (sect. 10). On voluntary resignation or dismissal before becoming entitled to a pension the benefit payable is a sum equal to the employee's own contributions without interest.

On withdrawal due to other causes (except dismissal in consequence of fraud or misconduct) or on death before retirement the benefit payable is a sum equal to the employee's own contributions plus interest at 3 % per annum convertible half-yearly.

On death after retirement on pension the benefit payable is the excess, if any, of the employee's own contributions with interest at 3 % up to the date of his retirement over the pension payments actually made. In calculating this benefit the effect of any surrender of pension under sect. 9 (sect. 9) is ignored.

Any contributions paid by the employee to a former local authority employer and included in a transfer value received on entry to the fund (sect. 29 (sect. 24)) are included in calculating the benefit under sect. 10 (sect. 10).

21.11. Sects. 14–20, 27 and 28 (sects. 5, 14–16 and 23). These sections relate to special categories of employees included in the scheme. The most important is sect. 16 (sect. 16), the main provisions of which have already been mentioned. In consequence of the transfer of functions on the introduction of the National Health Service Act, 1946, the great majority of female nurses have been transferred from the local authorities' funds, and the few who remain, together with the midwives and health visitors, will in future normally be encountered only in funds of county councils and county boroughs, i.e. the Local Health Authorities.

21.12. Sect. 21 (sect. 17). The administering authority is required to invest the superannuation fund in trustee securities, or in lieu of such investment may use the moneys for any purpose for which they have a statutory borrowing power or may lend the moneys to any other employing authority contributing to the fund for similar use. The rate of interest on such loans is required to be equal, as nearly as may be, to the rate which would be payable on a loan raised on mortgage. In practice such internal borrowing from the superannuation fund is done extensively by the local authorities.

It may be noted that it has been indicated semi-officially that the administering authority should regard itself as being in the position of a trustee of the fund in fixing the terms of these loans.

21.13. Sect. 22 (sect. 18). On the introduction of the Act an authority setting up a fund under the Act had to obtain an actuary's certificate of the annual charge payable over a period of not more than 40 years required to make the fund solvent, the charge being apportioned between the authorities entering the fund.

Any authority already maintaining a fund under the 1922 Act had to obtain an actuary's certificate as to the increase in its existing charge required to meet the new liabilities incurred as from 1 April 1939 (Scot. 16 May 1939) as a result of the 1937 Act, unless the fund fell due for valuation not later than 31 March 1940 (Scot. 15 May 1940), in which case the new liabilities were to be certified in the report on that valuation.

Every fund maintained under the 1937 Act must be valued quinquennially and may be valued at any other time, by an actuary, a copy of whose report must be sent to the appropriate Government Department. The administering authority has to make a scheme to deal with any deficiency or disposable surplus disclosed by a valuation, and the scheme must be approved by the Minister.

In accordance with regulations issued under this section the valuation report is required to refer to certain prescribed matters and to include certain statistical data relating to the valuation basis and the membership movements in the intervaluation period. In particular, any new liabilities incurred in respect of each authority in the fund on account of new entrants during this period have to be separately ascertained and made good by an annual charge over a period of not more than 40 years from the valuation date. The result of the valuation is arrived at after taking credit as an asset for the value of these liabilities which have to be separately met and thus balancing a corresponding amount of liability on the other side of the valuation balance sheet. Any deficiency or disposable surplus has to be apportioned among the authorities interested in the fund. In general, a deficiency will have to be met by a further annual charge over a period not exceeding 40 years from the valuation date, whilst a disposable surplus would be used to reduce any existing annual charge in amount or term or both, or to reduce the equivalent contributions payable by the authorities under sect. 6 (sect. 6) of the Act by a level annual sum over a period of not more than 40 years. The authorities are thus responsible for the solvency of the scheme, and the employees cannot be called upon to meet any share of deficiency nor can they benefit from any surplus.

The regulations do not indicate any basis on which the surplus or deficiency should be apportioned, as this must naturally be determined by the actuary having regard to all the circumstances of the case. Certain general principles should, however, be observed in this connexion. Where a number of authorities join together in a scheme they should normally be regarded as pooling their individual risks. It follows, therefore, that any profits or losses arising in the scheme as a result of variations in the experience from the assumptions made in the valuation would normally be treated as general experience profits or losses, and not allocated to the authorities having regard to their individual experiences. Similarly, it might be considered appropriate normally to treat profits or losses arising from the salary experience in the same way, since scales of pay are reasonably standardized throughout the local government service, whilst any increases in pay occurring on promotion would generally arise as a consequence of the movement of membership, or in other words as a result of the general experience. On the assumption that the members employed by any authority represent a fair cross-section of the total membership, it would be reasonable to apportion the deficiency or surplus in proportion to the net liabilities attaching to the employees of the separate authorities, after excluding, however, any liabilities in respect of new entrants which have to be separately charged as mentioned in the previous paragraph. In certain circumstances, e.g. where it is known that a deficiency is attributable solely to salary experience losses, it might be found that more reasonable results would be obtained by excluding from the liabilities used as a basis of apportionment any liabilities in respect of existing pensioners. Even when the assumption referred to above is not reasonable at a particular valuation date, it would probably be fair to make such an assumption over a period of years, and the result brought out by a method of apportionment based on existing net liabilities may well prove to be reasonable in the long run. In other circumstances, e.g. when a deficiency arises as a result of capital losses on the investments, it may be more appropriate to divide the deficiency in proportion to the theoretical shares of the fund, or, as an approximation to this, in proportion to the relative net liabilities less the value of any outstanding annual charges, which may vary in term as well as amount between the various authorities.

In addition to the duty imposed upon the actuary of apportioning surplus or deficiency, he may be called upon to give a subdivision under departments of the figures for an individual authority, and similar action may be called for in connexion with a private fund valuation. In this event the considerations discussed earlier in this section should be borne in mind.

21.14. Sect. 25 (sect. 21). Any scheme made under sect. 28(3) of the Widows', Orphans' and Old Age Contributory Pensions Act, 1936, whereby the provisions of the 1922 Act were modified, was continued under the 1937 Act. Under such a scheme a certain proportion of the weekly wages (usually 10s., 15s. or 20s.) would be excluded for the purpose of calculating the contributions and the corresponding pension benefit in respect of contributing service for a particular class of employees who were insured persons under the 1936 Act. Such a scheme, which was designed with the object of avoiding duplication of state pensions and pensions provided by the local government scheme, normally applied to servants only.

On the introduction of the National Insurance Act, 1946, a new type of modification was adopted. Under the new modified arrangements all new entrants, whether officers or servants, subject to local Act as well as to 1937 Act schemes, after 5 July 1948 (in certain cases a somewhat earlier date applied) have their normal contributions reduced by a fixed weekly amount (1s. 2d. in the case of males and female nurses and 1s. 3d. in the case of other females), the contribution of the employing authority being correspondingly reduced. In respect of each year of service during which the reduction in contribution operates the pension payable as from age 65 in the case of males or 60 in the case of females is correspondingly reduced by £1. 14s. 0d. per annum subject, however, to a maximum total reduction of £67. 15s. 0d. per annum (26s. per week). Employees in the local government service on 1 September 1947 were given the option to continue with their old arrangements or to transfer to the new modified arrangements, but in their case, whilst the contribution reduction was the same as for future entrants, the amount of the reduction in the pension was fixed according to the age at the date of exercising the option. The scale of reduction of pension for each year of service for such existing employees was less than £1. 14s. 0d. except at the youngest ages, the reduction in pension on the prescribed scale being broadly equal in value to the reduction in the joint contributions. Again an employee subject, prior to 1 September 1947, to a modified scheme as described in the previous paragraph could opt to continue with the old arrangements or to transfer to the new modified arrangements; if he elected to transfer, the pension payable in respect of any year of service formerly affected by the old modified scheme would be reduced by the same amount as applied to the future years of his service.

It may be noted that under the old type of modified scheme the pension reduction in consequence of a certain proportion of the wage being excluded operated immediately the employee retired, whereas under the new arrangements the pension reduction would not operate until the employee reached age 65 (males) or 60 (females), even though he may have retired earlier on account of ill-health or at his option on the completion of 40 years of service.

Arrangements similar to one or other of the local government modified schemes may be encountered in other pension schemes.

In the case of a new fund it would in general be satisfactory and
certainly simpler to avoid duplication of pensions by basing the
scheme on the full salary and fixing the scale of pensions at such
a level that, in an average case, the total pension provided by the
scheme and the state scheme combined is of the desired amount.
In such funds, arrangements can be made in cases where retirement
(except on grounds of health) may take place before the age at
which National Insurance pension starts, to pay an increased
pension up to age 65 (60 for women) and a reduced pension thereafter so as to secure an approximately level total income during
retirement.

21.15. Sect. 26 (sect. 22). This section requires the modification
of local Act schemes so as to provide for

(*a*) compulsory inclusion for superannuation of all whole-time
officers, as in the case of 1937 Act schemes (see § 21.6);

(*b*) benefit and contribution arrangements not substantially less
favourable than under the 1937 Act for certain special classes of
employees;

(*c*) reckonability on transfer of prior service with another local
authority on terms substantially similar to those operating in 1937
Act schemes (see § 21.16); and

(*d*) substitution at the option of the local Act authority of the
general provisions of the 1937 Act for those of the local Act.

21.16. Sect. 29 (sect. 24). Under this section a transfer value is
required to be paid when an employee transfers from one local
authority fund to another (including local Act funds), unless there
is a period of more than 12 months between the date of ceasing to
be a member of the first fund and the date of joining the second
fund. On transfer the member's benefits in respect of his former
service are maintained.

A standard scale of transfer values has been prescribed under
this section, and it appears that the amount of the transfer value
represents approximately the past service pension liability only.
In the normal course transfers between local authorities occur fairly
frequently, but as movements take place both to and from a
particular fund, any difference between the valuation reserve and

the amount paid or received on the prescribed basis in an individual case is of relatively small financial importance as compared with the great practical advantage of using a standard table and thus avoiding reference to the actuary in every case when a transfer occurs. It may be noted that any difference between the reserve held in the fund in respect of a member transferring from the fund and the amount of the transfer value paid on the prescribed scale will normally represent a profit, since the total actuarial reserve would include not merely the pension liability in respect of accrued service but also some further reserve in respect of future service. Conversely, the entry of a new member transferring from another fund will generally give rise to an initial strain, and this strain will be increased when, as will frequently be the case, the commencing salary in the new fund is greater than the salary on termination of the former employment on the basis of which the transfer value will be calculated. Whether or not the transfer of a member to or from the fund would give rise to a valuation strain or profit would, of course, depend to some extent upon the actuarial basis of valuation employed for the particular fund in question.

Transfer arrangements have now been extended to cover transfers between the local government service, the civil service and service with public boards responsible for nationalized industries. In so far as this may result in a reduction in the number of ordinary withdrawals where the contributions of the members only were returned, the valuation basis as regards the withdrawal rate may require some revision.

21.17. 'Bulk transfers'

As already observed the use of a standard table of transfer values is of great practical convenience, but these values would not be suitable if large numbers of employees were transferred in a body, a position which arose after the War as a result of the various nationalization schemes. Special arrangements were, therefore, made by regulations under such schemes in place of the normal arrangements under sect. 29 (sect. 24) of the 1937 Act. These arrangements differ according to the manner in which the superannuation costs of the transferred employees were formerly

financed in the local authority's fund, namely, (a) out of the general
rates or (b) out of the revenues of a trading department. Thus for
employees in hospitals (financed out of the rates) who were transferred to the National Health Service as from 5 July 1948 the
amount of the transfer value was to be arrived at in a similar way
to that of the standard transfer values, i.e. by reference to the past
service liability only, but instead of using these standard values the
amount of the transfer value had to be calculated by the actuary on
the same actuarial basis as that used in the valuation of the local
authority's superannuation fund.

For employees in a transferred trading department, e.g. the
electricity department, which had been financed out of its own
revenues and not out of the rates, a more elaborate method was
adopted, as the revenues were, of course, transferred along with
the undertaking on nationalization. The relevant regulations
prescribe that as a first step the full valuation reserves for the
transferred employees had to be calculated, and from this was to be
deducted the capital value of the outstanding instalments of any
equal annual charges which hitherto have been paid out of the
revenues of the transferred undertaking into the superannuation
fund of the local authority (the authority obviously had to be
relieved of these charges as the revenues which had been providing
them were being taken away). Finally, the amount had to be
adjusted in respect of any new surplus or deficiency which had
arisen since the last valuation of the fund preceding the transfer.
As in effect it was thus required to apportion the deficiency or
surplus between the transferring section and the remainder of the
fund, it was normally necessary to make a complete valuation of
the whole fund as at the date of transfer in order to arrive at the
proportion transferable.

Income Tax Act, 1918, Sect. 32
(as amended)

32. (1) Any person

(a) who has made an insurance on his life or the life of his wife, or who has contracted for any deferred annuity on his own life or the life of his wife, with any insurance company legally established in the United Kingdom or in any British Possession, or lawfully carrying on business in the United Kingdom, or with a registered friendly society, or, in the case of a deferred annuity, with the National Debt Commissioners; and

(b) who is under any Act of Parliament or under the terms or conditions of his employment liable to the payment of any sum or to the deduction from his salary or stipend of any sum for the purpose of securing a deferred annuity to his widow or provision for his children after his death;

shall, subject as hereinafter provided, be entitled to have the amount of tax payable by him reduced by a sum representing tax at the appropriate rate on the amount of the premium paid by him for any such insurance or contract or on the amount of the sum paid by him or deducted from his salary or stipend.

For the purposes of this section, the expression 'appropriate rate'* means—

(i) where the total income of the claimant from all sources estimated in accordance with the provisions of the Income Tax Acts does not exceed one thousand pounds, half the standard rate of tax:

(ii) where the total income of the claimant from all sources estimated as aforesaid exceeds one thousand pounds but does not exceed two thousand pounds, three-fourths of the standard rate of tax:

(iii) where the total income of the claimant from all sources estimated as aforesaid exceeds two thousand pounds, the standard rate of tax.

---

* So far as payments which come within sect. 32(1) (a) are concerned, the 'appropriate rate' has been varied from time to time, and the rate of relief is now governed by sect. 29 of Finance Act, 1948.

(2) If any such person is charged to tax under any Schedule and has paid that tax, or has paid or has been charged with tax by deduction or otherwise, he shall, on a claim being made to the special commissioners, and on production to them of the receipt for his payment, and proof of the facts to their satisfaction, be entitled to repayment of tax on the amount thereof at the appropriate rate.

(3) No such allowance—

(a) shall be made in respect of any such amounts beyond one-sixth of the total income of the person from all sources estimated in accordance with the provisions of the Income Tax Acts;

(b) (Repealed);

(c) shall exceed, in respect of any premium or other payment payable on a policy for securing a capital sum on death (whether in conjunction with any other benefit or not), the amount of the tax calculated at the appropriate rate on an amount equal to seven per cent. of the actual capital sum assured, and, in calculating any such capital sum, no account shall be taken of any sum payable on the happening of any other contingency, or of the value of any premiums agreed to be returned, or of any benefit by way of bonus, or otherwise, which is to be or may be received either before or after death, either by the person paying the premium, or by any other person, and which is not the sum actually assured;

(d) shall in any case exceed the amount of the tax calculated at the appropriate rate on one hundred pounds in respect of any premiums or payments to which this section applies and which are payable for securing any other benefits than as last aforesaid;

(e) shall, as regards insurances or contracts for deferred annuities made after the twenty-second day of June, nineteen hundred and sixteen,

(i) (Repealed);

(ii) be given except in respect of premiums or other payments payable on policies for securing a capital sum on death, whether in conjunction with any other benefit or not; or

(iii) be given in respect of premiums or payments payable during the period of deferment in respect of a policy of deferred assurance:

Provided that the two last-mentioned restrictions shall not affect premiums or payments payable on policies or contracts made in connection with any superannuation or bona fide pension scheme for the benefit of the employees of any employer or of persons engaged in any particular trade, profession, vocation or business or for the benefit of the wife or widow of any such employee or person or of his children or other dependants, or on any policy taken out by a teacher in a secondary school pending the establishment of a superannuation or pension scheme for those teachers;

(*f*) (Omitted by 1939 (No. 2), s. 9 (1) (*b*) (ii).)

(4) (Repealed.)

(5) War insurance premiums shall not be taken into account in calculating the aforesaid limits of one-sixth of the total income from all sources, or of seven per cent., or of one hundred pounds.

(6) In this section the expression 'war insurance premiums' means any additional premium or other sum paid in order to extend an existing life insurance policy to risks arising from war or war service abroad, and any part of any premium or other sum paid in respect of a life insurance policy covering those risks, or either of them, which appears to the commissioners to whom the claim for relief is made to be attributable to those risks, or either of them.

(7) Where premiums in respect of any insurance effected with a registered friendly society are made payable for shorter periods than three months, a person who claims relief under this section must, in order to obtain relief, produce to the surveyor a certificate, signed by an officer of the society, specifying the correct amount of premiums paid during the year of assessment.

A person who wilfully gives or produces a false certificate shall forfeit the sum of fifty pounds.

(8) Where a premium is paid by a wife out of her separate income in respect of an insurance on her own life or the life of her husband or a contract for any deferred annuity on her own life or the life of her husband, the same allowance of tax shall be made as if the premium were a premium paid by her husband for an insurance on his own life or for a contract for a deferred annuity on his own life, and this section shall apply accordingly.

(9) Where the tax ultimately payable by any person after deducting the allowance under this section is greater than the amount of tax which would be payable if the total income of that person exceeded one thousand pounds or two thousand pounds, as the case may be, the allowance under this section shall be increased by a sum representing the amount by which tax at one-fourth of the standard rate on the amount of the premiums or payment in respect of which the allowance is made exceeds the amount of the tax at the standard rate on the amount by which the total income falls short of one thousand pounds or two thousand pounds, as the case may be.

Finance Act, 1948, Sect. 29

29. (1) This section applies to premiums payable on policies of insurance or contracts for deferred annuities, being policies or contracts made after the twenty-second day of June, nineteen hundred and sixteen.

(2) For the purposes of section thirty-two of the Income Tax Act, 1918 (which provides a relief for life insurance premiums and other payments at a rate depending in part on the total income of the claimant) the appropriate rate shall, in relation to premiums to which this section applies, be two-fifths of the standard rate of tax, irrespective of the total income of the claimant.

(3) If, in any year of assessment, the total premiums to which this section applies in respect of which relief falls to be granted under the said section thirty-two do not exceed twenty-five pounds, the relief to be granted under the said section thirty-two in respect of those premiums shall, instead of being a deduction of tax at the appropriate rate on the amount of the premiums, be a deduction of tax at the standard rate on ten pounds or on the full amount of the premiums, whichever is the less.

(4) Subject to the provisions of this subsection, the relief to be given under the said section thirty-two in respect of premiums to which this section applies shall, for all the purposes of the Income Tax Acts, be deemed to be a deduction of tax under subsection (1) of section forty of the Finance Act, 1927 (which provides for certain reliefs by way of deduction from tax):

Provided that—

(*a*) any reference in this Part of this Act, or in any of the other provisions of the Income Tax Acts, to an amount tax on which falls to be deducted under the said subsection (1) shall, in relation to a premium to which this section applies on which a deduction falls to be made at two-fifths of the standard rate, be construed as a reference to two-fifths of the amount of that premium; and

(*b*) nothing in this subsection affects the mode in which the appropriate rate of United Kingdom income tax is to be calculated under sub-paragraph (v) of paragraph 2 of Part II of the Fifth Schedule to the Finance Act, 1927, for the purposes of relief for Dominion income tax.

(5) In this section, references to the standard rate of tax are references to the actual standard rate, whether or not that rate exceeds seven shillings in the pound.

(6) The following amendments (being amendments consequential on the preceding provisions of this section) shall be made in the enactments hereinafter mentioned, that is to say—

(a) subsections (2) and (7) of section thirty-two of the Income Tax Act, 1918, and subsection (1) of section nine of the Finance (No. 2) Act, 1940, shall not apply in relation to premiums to which this section applies; and

(b) the references to premiums in subsection (9) of the said section thirty-two and in subsection (2) of the said section nine shall not include references to premiums to which this section applies; and

(c) sub-paragraph (i) of paragraph (e) of subsection (3) of the said section thirty-two shall cease to have effect.

(7) This section shall have effect with respect to the year 1949–50 and all subsequent years of assessment.

Finance Act, 1921, Sect. 32
(as amended by sect. 19 of Finance Act, 1930 and Income Tax (Offices and Employments) Act, 1944)

32. (1) Subject to the provisions of this section and to any regulations made thereunder, exemption from income tax shall be allowed in respect of income derived from investments or deposits of a superannuation fund, and, subject as aforesaid, any sum paid by an employer or employed person by way of contribution towards a superannuation fund shall, in computing profits or gains for the purpose of an assessment to income tax under Case I or Case II of Schedule D or under Schedule E, be allowed to be deducted as an expense incurred in the year in which the sum is paid:

Provided that—

(a) no allowance shall be made under the foregoing provision in respect of any contribution by an employed person which is not an ordinary annual contribution, and, where a contribution by an employer is not an ordinary annual contribution, it shall, for the purpose of the foregoing provision, be treated as the Commissioners may direct, either as an expense incurred in the year in which the sum is paid or as an expense to be spread over such period of years as the Commissioners think proper; and

(b) no allowance shall be made under this section in respect of any payments in respect of which relief can be given under section thirty-two of the Income Tax Act, 1918.

(2) Income tax chargeable in respect of an annuity paid out of a superannuation fund to a person residing in the United Kingdom shall, if the Commissioners so direct, be assessed and charged on the annuitant under Schedule E instead of being deducted and accounted for under Rule 21 of the General Rules.

(3) For the purposes of this section, the expression 'superannuation fund' means, unless the context otherwise requires, a fund which is approved for those purposes, by the Commissioners, and, subject as hereinafter provided, the Commissioners shall not approve any fund unless it is shown to their satisfaction that—

(a) the fund is a fund bona fide established under irrevocable trusts in connection with some trade or undertaking carried on in the United Kingdom by a person residing therein;

[(b) the fund has for its sole purpose the provision of annuities for all or any of the following persons in the events respectively specified, that is to say, for persons employed in the trade or undertaking either on retirement at a specified age, or on becoming incapacitated at some earlier age, or for the widows, children, or dependants of persons who are or have been so employed, on the death of those persons;*]

(c) the employer in the trade or undertaking is a contributor to the fund;

(d) the fund is recognised by the employer and employed persons in the trade or undertaking: Provided that the Commissioners may, if they think fit, and subject to such conditions, if any, as they think proper to attach to the approval, approve a fund, or any part of a fund, as a superannuation fund for the purposes of this section

(i) notwithstanding that the rules of the fund provide for the return in certain contingencies of contributions paid to the fund; or

(ii) if the main purpose of the fund is the provision of such annuities as aforesaid, notwithstanding that such provision is not its sole purpose; or

(iii) notwithstanding that the trade or undertaking in connection with which the fund is established is carried on only partly in the United Kingdom and by a person not residing therein.

(4) The Commissioners may make regulations generally for the purpose of carrying this section into effect and, in particular, without prejudice to the generality of the foregoing provision, may by such regulations—

---

* 1930, sect. 19. *Previously* 'the fund has for its sole purpose the provision of annuities for persons employed in the trade or undertaking either on retirement at a specified age or on becoming incapacitated at some earlier age'.

(*a*) provide for the charging of and accounting for tax in respect of contributions (including interest) repaid to a contributor to a superannuation fund and on lump sums paid in commutation of or in lieu of annuities payable out of a superannuation fund as if any sums so repaid or paid were income of the year in which they are repaid or paid;

(*b*) require the trustees or other persons having the management of a superannuation fund, or an employer whose employees contribute to a superannuation fund, to deliver to the Commissioners such information and particulars as the Commissioners may reasonably require for the purposes of this section;

(*c*) prescribe the manner in which claims for relief under this section are to be made and approved, and in which applications for the approval of a superannuation fund are to be made;

(*d*) provide for the withdrawal of approval in the case of a fund which ceases to satisfy the requirements of this section;

(*e*) provide for determining what contributions to a superannuation fund are to be treated as ordinary annual contributions for the purposes of this section.

(5) Where at the commencement of this Act there is in force any arrangement between the Commissioners and the persons having the management of a superannuation fund by which provision is made for allowing any such deductions for the purpose of income tax as may be allowed for that purpose under this section, the arrangement shall, if the fund is approved as a superannuation fund for the purposes of this section for the year 1921–22, be deemed to have ceased to operate as from the sixth day of April, nineteen hundred and twenty-one, and, if the fund is not so approved, shall cease to operate as from the sixth day of April, nineteen hundred and twenty-two.

(6) In this section the expression 'the Commissioners' means the Commissioners of Inland Revenue.

S.R. and O. 1921, No. 1699

Regulations, dated November 10, 1921, made by the Commissioners of Inland Revenue under Section 32 of the Finance Act, 1921. (As amended by S.R. and O. 1931, No. 638.)

1. Application for the approval of any fund or any part of a fund for any year of assessment shall be made in writing before the end of that year by the trustees of the fund to H.M. Inspector of Taxes for the district in which the office of the fund is situated or the fund is administered and shall be supported by a copy of the instrument under

which the fund is established and two copies of the rules and of the accounts of the fund for the last year for which such accounts have been made up and such other information as the Commissioners may reasonably require.

2. Any alteration in the rules, constitution, objects, or conditions of the fund made at any time after the date of the application for approval shall be notified forthwith to the Inspector. In default of such notification, any approval given shall, unless the Commissioners otherwise determine, be deemed to have been withdrawn at the date from which the alteration had effect.

3. If the facts in regard to any fund or part of a fund shall, in the opinion of the Commissioners, cease to warrant the continuance of their approval under the above-mentioned section then and in such case the Commissioners may withdraw their approval and shall give notice to the trustees of the fund of such withdrawal, and of the date from which such withdrawal is to take effect.

4. If a fund or a part of a fund is approved by the Commissioners the fact shall be communicated to the trustees of the fund in writing and where a fund or part of a fund is approved subject to conditions these conditions shall also be communicated to the trustees of the fund in writing.

5. The expression 'ordinary annual contribution' shall mean an annual contribution of a fixed amount or an annual contribution calculated on some definite basis by reference to the earnings, contributions or numbers of the members of the fund.

6. The amount of the employer's contribution which may be deducted as an expense in the case of a local authority which is assessable to income tax in respect of the profits of a trade shall be such part of the authority's total contribution as is made in respect of the persons employed in such trade, and in the case of any other employer shall not exceed the amount contributed by him in respect of the persons employed by him in the trade in respect of the profits of which he is assessable to United Kingdom Income Tax.

7. Where contributions (including interest on contributions, if any) are repaid to the employer the trustees of the fund shall deduct income tax from the amount so repaid at the rate in force for the year in which the repayment is made and such amount shall be deemed for purposes of income tax, super-tax and corporation profits tax to be income of the recipient for that year; the tax so deducted shall be a debt from the trustees of the fund to the Crown and recoverable as such accordingly and the provision contained in Section 2 of the Act of 54 and 55 Victoria, c. 38, in relation to money in the hands of any person for stamp duty shall apply to the tax so deducted.

8. Where any contributions (including interest on contributions, if any) are repaid to an employed person during his lifetime or where a lump sum is paid in commutation of or in lieu of an annuity, income tax on the amount so repaid or paid shall, except in the case of an employed person whose employment was carried on abroad [and in the case of a person who is the widow, child or dependant of an employed person whose employment was carried on abroad*], be paid by the trustees of the fund who shall make such payment at the rate of [one-fourth†] the standard rate in force for the year in which the repayment or payment is made, and the said tax shall be a debt due from the trustees of the fund to the Crown and recoverable accordingly.

9. Where annuities are paid by a superannuation fund to persons residing out of the United Kingdom,. income tax in respect of such annuities shall be deducted and accounted for by the trustees of the fund under Rule 21 of the General Rules applicable to Schedules A, B, C, D and E of the Income Tax Act, 1918, provided that income tax shall not be required to be deducted and accounted for in the case of a person so resident whose employment was carried on abroad [or who is the widow, child or dependant of an employed person whose employment was carried on abroad‡].

10. The trustees or other persons having the management of a superannuation fund and an employer who contributes to a superannuation fund, shall, when required by notice from the Inspector, within fourteen days from the date of such notice—

(a) furnish to the Inspector a return containing such particulars of contributions made to the fund as the notice may require:

(b) prepare and deliver to the Inspector a return containing—

(i) the name and place of residence of every person in receipt of an annuity from the fund,

(ii) the amount of the annuity payable to each annuitant,

(iii) particulars of every contribution (including interest on contributions, if any) returned to the employer or to employed persons, and

(iv) particulars of sums paid in commutation or in lieu of annuities;

(c) furnish to the Inspector a copy of the accounts of the fund to the last date prior to such notice to which such accounts have been made up together with such other information and particulars as the Commissioners may reasonably require.

---

* Added by Amending Regulations, dated 29 July 1931.
† Amending Regulations, dated 29 July 1931. Previously 'one-third'.
‡ Added by Amending Regulations, dated 29 July 1931.

11. Where an employer deducts from the emoluments paid to an employed person or pays on his behalf any contribution of that employed person to a superannuation fund he shall include particulars of such deduction or payment in any return of wages and salaries which he is required to furnish under Section 105 of the Income Tax Act, 1918, or the regulations made thereunder.

12. A claim for relief in respect of income derived from the investments or deposits of a superannuation fund shall be made and signed by the trustees of the fund and all the provisions of the Income Tax Acts which relate to claims for any allowance or deduction or the proof to be given with respect to those claims shall apply to claims for relief under Section 32 of the Finance Act, 1921, and the proof to be given with respect to those claims. Any tax for which the trustees of the fund are required to account may be set off in the settlement of such claim.

13. If a fund or part of a fund for any reason ceases to be an approved fund the trustees of the fund shall nevertheless remain liable to account for tax on any sum paid—

(*a*) on account of returned contributions (including interest on contributions, if any), and

(*b*) in commutation of or in lieu of annuities, in so far as the sum so paid is in respect of contributions made before the fund, or part of a fund ceased to be an approved fund and the provisions of Regulations 7 and 8 shall apply, with the necessary modifications.

By Order of the Commissioners of Inland Revenue.

R. V. NIND HOPKINS,

10 *November* 1921.   *Secretary.*

Superannuation and other Trust Funds (Validation) Act, 1927

An Act to amend the law relating to perpetuities and accumulations, as respects certain benefit funds and as respects trust funds for the reduction of the National Debt.

[22nd December 1927.]

Provisions as to Benefit Funds

1. The rule of law relating to perpetuities shall not apply and shall be deemed never to have applied to the trusts of any fund registered under this Act (in this Act referred to as a 'registered fund').

2. Subject to the provisions of this Act, any fund established under trusts subject to the laws of Great Britain, in connection with an undertaking or combination of undertakings carried on wholly or partly in Great Britain, being a fund of which the main purpose is either—

(a) the provision of superannuation allowances on retirement to persons employed in the undertaking or combination of undertakings in connection with which the fund is established; or

(b) the provision of pensions during widowhood to the widows of persons who are or have been so employed and of periodical allowances to or in respect of children of such persons; or

(c) the assurance of capital sums on the death of persons who have been so employed,

shall be qualified for registration under this Act if the rules of the fund comply with the requirements set out in the Schedule to this Act.

3. (1) Application for the registration under this Act of any fund may be made in writing addressed to the registrar, signed by the trustees of the fund, and every such application shall specify the address at which communications concerning the fund will be received by the secretary (hereinafter referred to as 'the address of the fund') and shall be accompanied by two copies of the rules of the fund and a list of the names and addresses of the trustees of the fund.

(2) Upon application being made in accordance with the provisions of this Act for the registration of any fund, the registrar shall, if he is satisfied that the fund is qualified for registration, register the fund and the rules thereof, and shall enter in the register the address of the fund and the names and addresses of the trustees.

(3) In the event of any amendment of the rules of a registered fund or of any change in the address of such a fund or in the names or addresses of the trustees thereof, the trustees shall, within twenty-one days after the making of the amendment or change, apply for the registration of the amendment or for the correction of the register in respect of the change, as the case may be, by sending an application in writing addressed to the registrar, signed by the secretary of the fund, and accompanied, in the case of an amendment, by two copies thereof signed by one of the trustees of the fund, and in the case of any such change as aforesaid, by the necessary particulars for correction of the register: no amendment in the rules of a registered fund shall be valid until it has been registered, but, upon application for the registration of any such amendment being made as aforesaid, the registrar shall register the amendment if he is satisfied that the rules as thereby amended would not have disqualified the fund for registration under this Act.

(4) Upon the registration under this Act of any fund or of an amendment of the rules of any registered fund, the registrar shall issue

a certificate of registration, and any document purporting to be a certificate issued under this subsection and to be signed or sealed by the registrar shall be received in evidence and be deemed to be so issued, signed or sealed without further proof unless the contrary is shown, and shall be conclusive evidence of the fact certified.

(5) The registration of a registered fund shall not be cancelled unless and until the fund has been wound up, but within fourteen days after the completion of the winding-up of any such fund the trustees shall send notice thereof in writing to the registrar and upon receiving notice that any registered fund has been wound up, the registrar shall, if he is satisfied that the fund has been wound up and the assets thereof applied in accordance with the provisions of the rules of the fund, cancel the registration of the fund.

(6) Such fees shall be payable in respect of the registration of funds, amendments of rules and changes of name or address, and in respect of the issue of certificates under this Act as may be prescribed by regulations made by the Treasury.

4. (1) If upon an application for the registration under this Act of any fund whereof the rules were made before the commencement of this Act, the registrar is satisfied that the rules of the fund contain provisions which were inserted only for the purpose of avoiding the application to the trusts of the fund of the rule of law relating to perpetuities, he may, at the request of the trustees making the application, amend the rules by deleting those provisions therefrom and may, upon the like request, make any further amendments that are, in his opinion, proper in consequence of their deletion.

(2) Where the rules of any fund are amended by the registrar under this section, the rules shall, when registered, have effect subject to the amendments so made.

5. (1) The trustees of every registered fund shall, once in every year, cause to be prepared a statement of accounts and balance sheet of the fund which shall be audited by an auditor, and shall, at least once in every five years, cause an investigation and report to be made by an actuary as to the financial condition of the fund.

(2) A copy of every statement of accounts, balance sheet and report prepared under this section signed by the auditor or actuary, as the case may be, and by the secretary of the fund, shall be sent to the registrar within twelve months after the close of the period to which it relates.

6. (1) The registrar may require any person being a trustee, or officer of any fund for the registration of which under this Act application has been made, or of any registered fund, to furnish, either by statutory declaration or otherwise, any information or explanation which may be necessary for the proper exercise and performance of the powers and duties of the registrar under this Act.

(2) In the event of any breach of trust being committed by the trustees of a registered fund by reason of their making any unauthorised investment or by reason of their committing a breach of any rule of the fund being a rule required by this Act as a qualification for registration of the fund thereunder, the Chief Registrar, or in Scotland the Assistant Registrar for Scotland, shall have the like remedies in all respects for the breach of trust as if he were a person beneficially interested in the fund.

7. (1) If, in respect of any registered fund, default is made in complying with any of the requirements of this Act relating to accounts and reports, in making application in accordance with the requirements of this Act for the registration of any amendment of the rules or for correction of the register in respect of any change in the address of the fund or in the names and addresses of the trustees, or in sending to the registrar notice of the winding up of the fund, every trustee and the secretary of the fund shall be guilty of an offence under this Act:

Provided that it shall be a good defence to any proceedings against any person in respect of an offence under this subsection to prove that the default occurred without his consent or connivance and was not facilitated by any neglect on his part.

(2) If any person lawfully required under this Act by the registrar to furnish any information or explanation which could with reasonable diligence be furnished by him, makes default in complying with any such requirement within fourteen days after written notice thereof has been delivered to him, he shall be guilty of an offence under this Act.

(3) Any person guilty of an offence under this Act shall be liable on summary conviction to a fine not exceeding five pounds, and, in the case of an offence consisting of a continuing default, to a fine not exceeding five pounds for every week in which the default has been continued.

8. In this Act, unless the context otherwise requires, the following expressions have the meanings hereby respectively assigned to them, that is to say—

'Actuary' and 'Auditor' mean persons having such qualifications as may be prescribed respectively by regulations made by the Chief Registrar and laid before Parliament:

'Chief Registrar' and 'Registrar' have the same meanings as in the Friendly Societies Act, 1896:

'Rules' means in relation to any fund, the instrument creating and regulating the trusts of the fund, and includes every such instrument:

'Trust' for the purpose of any application made or intended to be made for the registration under this Act of any fund or proposed fund, includes any trust which before such registration may be void by reason of the rule of law relating to perpetuities, and for that purpose the expression 'trustee' shall be construed accordingly.

9. (Provisions as to funds for the reduction of the National Debt.)

General

10. The Chief Registrar shall in every year make a general report of his proceedings and of those of the assistant registrars under this Act, and his report shall be laid before Parliament, so, however, that no such report shall contain information as to the accounts or reports of particular registered funds.

11. (1) This Act may be cited as the Superannuation and other Trust Funds (Validation) Act, 1927.

(2) Section nine of this Act shall extend to Northern Ireland, but save as aforesaid this Act shall not extend to Northern Ireland.

SCHEDULE

Requirements as to Rules of Registered Funds

The rules of a fund qualified for registration under this Act must make provision for the following matters, that is to say—

1. The whole of the objects for which the fund is established.
2. The appointment and removal of trustees and of a secretary.
3. The vesting in the trustees of all property belonging to the fund.
4. The investment in the names of the trustees of all capital moneys belonging to the fund and for authorising the investments, if any, in addition to those authorised by law, in which the trustees may invest such moneys; so, however, that the rules of a fund may provide for the deposit of such moneys with a bank, and may also provide for their deposit with the employers of persons employed in the undertaking or combination of undertakings in connection with which the fund is established in the following cases, that is to say—

(a) where the rules so provided before the ninth day of November, nineteen hundred and twenty-seven;

(b) where the deposit of such moneys is authorised subject to the conditions that every employer with whom such moneys are deposited must be a body corporate having during each of the ten years last past before the date of any deposit paid a dividend or interest at a rate of not less than three per cent. on its ordinary shares, and that every such deposit must be secured by a charge on the whole or part of the assets of the undertaking carried on by such employer.

5. The making of contributions to the fund by the employers of persons employed in the undertaking or combination of undertakings in connection with which the fund is established.

6. The contributions payable to the fund, and the rates of benefit payable thereout or the method of calculating the benefits so payable.

7. The conditions on which persons may become and may cease to be respectively contributors to and entitled to benefits from the fund.

8. The circumstances in which the fund may be wound up and the manner in which the assets thereof are in that event to be applied.

9. The method by which the rules may be amended.

10. The preparation of all statements of accounts, balance sheets, and reports required by this Act to be prepared.

11. The supply on demand to every person having any rights in the fund, being a person who is or has been employed in the undertaking or combination of undertakings in connection with which the fund is established, of a copy of the rules of the fund and of all amendments thereof, and of the latest statement of accounts, balance sheet and report prepared in accordance with the requirements of this Act.

APPENDIX II

Specimen Clause Limiting Duration of a Trust

'At the expiration of 20 years from the death of the survivor of all the lineal descendants of His late Majesty King George V now living or on any earlier date on which the Company shall go into liquidation whether voluntary or compulsory otherwise than for the purpose of reconstruction or amalgamation the trusts constituted by these presents shall thereupon determine. Upon the determination of the said trusts the affairs thereof shall be wound up and the fund converted into money and subject to the payment of all costs, charges and expenses which may then be owing, the proceeds of such conversion shall in the first place be applied by the Trustees to the purchase from the Government or some Company or Companies of good repute annuities for the remainder of their lives for those of the beneficiaries who are then already in receipt of pensions out of the fund such annuities to be of amounts equal to the amounts of the pensions which such beneficiaries are then receiving. The balance of the said proceeds then remaining shall be applied by the Trustees to the purchase in like manner of annuities or in making other provision for beneficiaries entitled in anticipation to pension benefits out of the fund, regard being had to their respective prospects of becoming entitled to pensions had the fund continued in existence.'

APPENDIX III

Income Tax Act, 1952

Comparative Table of Reference to Certain Sections of Earlier Acts

Section of earlier Act	Corresponding Section(s) of 1952 Act
I.T.A. 1918, Sect. 14	525
I.T.A. 1918, Sect. 32 F.A. 1948, Sect. 29	219, 225, 226
I.T.A. 1918, Sect. 105	27, 30
F.A. 1921, Sect. 32 F.A. 1930, Sect. 19	379
F.A. 1947, Sect. 19	386
F.A. 1947, Sect. 20	387
F.A. 1947, Sect. 21	388
F.A. 1947, Sect. 22	389
F.A. 1947, Sect. 23	390, 391

INDEX

Printed in the United States
By Bookmasters